THE EFFECTIVE CITY CHURCH

THE
EFFECTIVE
CITY
CHURCH

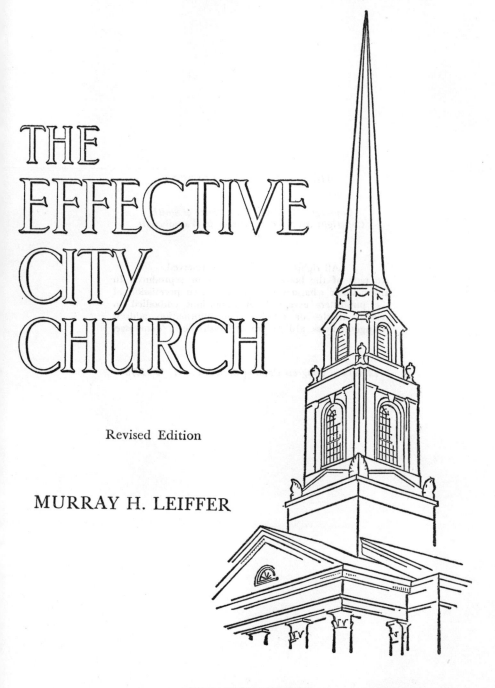

Revised Edition

MURRAY H. LEIFFER

ABINGDON PRESS
NEW YORK ● NASHVILLE

THE EFFECTIVE CITY CHURCH

Nov, 1955

Copyright MCMXLIX by Pierce & Smith
Copyright MCMLV by Pierce & Washabaugh

Library of Congress Catalog Card Number: 55-11070

c
SET UP, PRINTED, AND BOUND BY THE
PARTHENON PRESS, AT NASHVILLE,
TENNESSEE, UNITED STATES OF AMERICA

Foreword

THE future of Protestantism in the United States depends largely on what happens to the church in urban communities, for more and more the cities of America are dominating the entire culture. Yet relatively little attention has been given to the study of the urban church and its problems.

The purpose of this book is to acquaint the reader with the patterns of city growth, the influences of urbanization on people and the church, and methods by which the church may develop its program effectively to reach people in different types of city communities. It is concerned with the interrelations between the community and the church to the end that the Christian message may be more adequately presented and that churches may not only be well placed but also maintain so vital a relation to the community that they will not need to withdraw from it when population changes.

It is hoped that this book will prove useful to students of community life, sociologists, and city planners, as well as pastors, seminary students, and denominational executives. It is designed primarily for leaders, lay and ministerial, in urban churches but should prove of worth to rural people as well, who need to be acquainted with the many effects of urbanization on American life. The techniques described in Part III are applicable in analyzing churches in any type of community, rural or urban. These techniques as well as other aspects of the subject are presented in as brief compass as possible, since it was desired to keep the book at a modest price. For this reason also, the principles of city growth and the influence of the urban environment on people, in Chapters III and IV, are painted with broad strokes to depict the major characteristics. Lack of space prevented inclusion of all the innumerable variants.

This book grew out of twenty-five years of study of urban sociology and church administration. For the material which is here presented I am therefore indebted to hundreds of persons. Former teachers, students, and colleagues in the field, pastors of many churches, denominational executives of city societies, interdenominational leaders—all have made a contribution to my thinking. I wish to express particular appreciation to the men who have been members of my seminars from 1929 to the present, who by their participation, suggestions, and criticisms have helped in developing many of the techniques which are described. It was at the insistence of these persons over many years that this book was written.

MURRAY H. LEIFFER

The new edition of the book grows out of the need for taking into account current United States Census material and other recent data. Tables have been revised and the descriptive text brought up to date.

M. H. L.

Contents

Charts and Tables

CHARTS

TABLES

Part I

THE CITY

AND ITS INFLUENCE

ON RELIGIOUS LIFE

CHAPTER ONE

Cities, Citizens, and Churches

W ELL, that's interesting. We've been living in this community for ten years, and you are the first person from any church to call on us," remarked a pleasant-faced housewife. She was speaking to a young woman conducting a religious canvass in a crowded section of the city.

"No, we don't belong to any church. Well, we used to be members in Missouri. Jim and I were married back there and still have some friends in that church. We've never joined here in the city. . . .

"Oh, yes, we've attended a little community church a few blocks from here, but we didn't like the preacher. Then we went for a couple of Sundays to that big stone church on High Street. We just couldn't stand that. They acted as though they didn't see us. . . .

"Why, Jim and I just take things a bit easy on Sunday. He usually gets a couple of Sunday papers the night before and is buried in them most of the day. We sent the youngsters to a Sunday school around the corner."

Comments like these are heard scores of times in every urban religious canvass. Countless men and women have a vague appreciation of the church — and an undefined nostalgia for the support of the religious fellowship which their parents enjoyed, but they have lost contact with the organized church. "Of course we want our children to learn to be good, so we think there ought to be a Sunday school opened up in our community. . . . No, I'm not sure that we would want to join ourselves." This represents the attitude of thousands of urban parents.

How can the church reach such people? What are the influences of the city that draw them away from their earlier loyalties? Can the program of the church be adapted to meet the needs of the ever-moving, economically and emotionally insecure people of the city? How can the significance of things spiritual be brought home to men and women who are engulfed in a materialistic urban culture? Is it possible to analyze the trends in urban development so that the church can plan wisely?

The urban assumption of competence

Living in the complex physical and social structure which is the modern American city, men have a sense of assurance, confident that they and their fellows are capable persons, clever enough under most circumstances to solve their own problems. The city man is little troubled by the great forces of nature. Weather to him is of minor importance. A serious storm which destroys crops compels the farmer and even the townsman to regard with awe forces which are beyond his control. But the city dweller is merely irritated at having to wear his rubbers and carry an umbrella. His obvious needs are conveniently and efficiently met: water, light, sanitation, the education of his children, and the thousand little aids which make him feel comfortable and competent.

This unquestioning acceptance of material comforts is beginning to characterize the whole of our culture. The securing of a high and then a higher standard of living constitutes the dominant goal for millions of Americans. But it is in the cities that this striving reaches its acme. Here, for many, the parable of the man who built himself larger barns is painfully appropriate.

Yet with all their assurance and apparent adequacy, city dwellers are frequently lonely and uncertain. Secretly they feel the need of guidance, but do not know where to obtain it. Marital tensions, worry over unpaid bills, questions of health, the feeling that the job—and life itself—is a blind alley, occasion a sense of frustration. In spite of surface composure and general appearance of well-being they are, in the long intervals of the night, deeply troubled by the feeling that much of their effort has been a striving after wind. And the smooth sophistication which they have sought for themselves disturbs them deeply when they see it, in even more exaggerated form, in their children.

The urban response to religion

The church by the very nature of its message stands in opposition to some of the basic assumptions of the prevailing materialistic culture and makes demands which are unpopular with many of its own members and are ignored by countless others. Yet these same people, because of their earlier heritage and because of their vague desire for inner security, long for the serenity which they believe accompanies religious living. These are the ones who constitute the overflow on Easter Sunday.

Millions of urban men and women, however, obviously do find in the church a faith and fellowship which enables them to see life in meaningful terms. It assists them in facing courageously their problems of personal and social relations. They have found that the Christian message has bearing on every aspect of living and is itself the supreme solvent for the petty worries and also the deep uncertainties of life and death which assail people whether they live in city apartments or farm homes.

But for the majority, organized religion plays only a minor and usually insignificant role. As a Roman Catholic priest sadly remarked, "Scores of my parishioners come to the church only twice in their lives and are carried both times—for baptism and burial." The fact, as shown by membership statistics, that over half of all the people in American cities feel that the church has no particular function to perform in their lives is itself sufficient evidence that the message of the church has not been presented effectively, with proper emphases and in the right places.

If the church is to reach these people in more than a nominal sense, its responsible leaders, lay and ministerial alike, need to study the city with scientific detachment, but always with religious concern for people. How do cities grow? Can one forecast the changes which will take place in ensuing decades? What does the city do to people? How can churches organize their programs to meet religious needs? These and related problems form the subject matter for this book.

Cities are different

While the Christian message is always the same, the strategy for the church must be made to fit the particular city and community. Cities have personalities. Like people, they vary in age, size, living standards, and even in spiritual development. It is important to recognize some of these differences before considering the general pattern of urban growth.

1. *Size.* Numerous factors mold the life of a city and its churches. One of these is sheer size. The small city, with its surrounding rural area, constitutes a single community. Its social structure is relatively simple, and its citizens are aware of their interdependence. Red Oak is a prosperous Iowa county-seat town of six thousand. Families for miles around share the fun of Saturday shopping in the stores which flank the courthouse square. Some wander over to watch the bingo game sponsored by the American Legion Auxiliary, while others lap ice-cream cones as they stroll along the crowded sidewalks. These people are acquainted with one another. Young matrons, with little apparent concern for their far-ranging progeny, chat with friends of bygone high-school days. Farmers with weathered faces and smooth-shaved city dwellers discuss recent world events, knowing in advance the stock comments of their companions. In a flourishing county-seat town such as Red Oak the church not only serves the spiritual needs of its members but also is a power to be reckoned with in the life of the entire community.

The people of Philadelphia and Memphis speak the same language, read the same magazines, and even laugh at the same jokes as the men and women of Red Oak. But their social worlds are vastly different. The citizens in sprawling, teeming Philadelphia may not know even by sight others living in the same mammoth apartment house with them. And the man whose home is in Frankford or pleasant, suburban Chestnut Hill has no contact with the underprivileged Negroes or Italians of south Philadelphia. Such a metropolis is made up of scores of communities separated from one another by rivers, railroads, and industrial districts. Consequently the people who know well their own streets and alleys may be lost, figuratively and perhaps literally, in another section of the city one mile away.

2. *Population Composition.* The make-up of the population is another reason for the differences between cities. The great flow of immigration from southern and central Europe (1890 to 1914) was to northern industrial America. Germans, Irish, Czechs, Poles, Italians, and Russian Jews settled by the millions in the textile cities of New England and the manufacturing centers and steel mill towns of the middle Atlantic and north central states. Comparatively few of these newcomers found their way into the South, where the Negro, with his traditional subordinate status, furnished a vast reservoir of cheap labor. These differences in population composition are reflected in the pattern of a city's religious life. The Roman Catholic church, in places like Newark, New Orleans with its old French heritage, and San Francisco, embraces from three to four times as many members as all Protestant churches combined. But in contrast it has played an almost insignificant role in representative southern cities such as Winston-Salem, Chattanooga, and Dallas. The Bronx, the northern portion of New York City, presents another contrast: there 60 per cent of the inhabitants are Jews.

3. *Economic Opportunities.* The resources of a city's hinterland (the trade area round about it) help to determine the composition of the population, its cultural life, and the way in which it earns its living. Amarillo, Texas, in the heart of the Panhandle, is a cow town. Altoona, Pennsylvania, is a railroad center at the foot of the big grade in the Alleghenies, dependent for its life on the Pennsylvania Railroad. Gary is a steel town. Dearborn makes automobiles; Charlotte, textiles and cigarettes. And so on.

In heavy-industry cities men outnumber women. Most of the women who are there are the wives of workers; there are few job opportunities to attract single women. But in Washington, D.C., and in state capitals women, attracted by the many white-collar positions, greatly outnumber the men.

So it is that no two cities are alike. Differences in size, rate of growth, and population make-up affect the living standards, attitudes, and habits of the people, and they create different problems in churching, even though the gospel remains the same for all men. Churchmen who would plan for their city's future should give careful thought to these differences and their implications for the church.

CHAPTER TWO

America Goes Urban

IN earlier days cities came into being for various reasons: for protection from the real and imagined dangers of medieval living; for the political advantage of rulers; for educational, religious, and social opportunities; but chiefly for convenience in trading. Here goods were made and sold; here strangers brought products from afar. The process of trading stimulated manufacture, and more and more people found work in the city.

In simplest analysis the city is a gathering place where people come together for commerce and co-operative activity. Man's inventiveness over the centuries has increased both the reasons and the facilities for his meeting with his fellows. The most remarkable social phenomenon of the past hundred years has been the concentration of population in cities.

The location of cities

Throughout the history of man trade and transportation have been closely interdependent. In the United States cities grew up at the confluence of rivers (Pittsburgh, St. Louis), where a river touched the sea (New Orleans, New York), and at the head of navigation of the great rivers (Albany, Minneapolis). Other trading centers developed at transfer points where a highway crossed a river, where lake-borne cargo was transferred to canal barges, at the terminal of a railroad line, at the end of ocean trade routes. The significant fact about these sites is that all of them facilitated the meeting of people and the exchange of goods and services. From the standpoint of both the origins of cities and their further growth the fact that people meet and trade in cities is more important than that they live there. The better the transportation and communication, the larger is the population that can be reached, the wider the hinterland from which raw materials may be gathered, and the broader the market in which urban goods and services can be sold.

The fact of urban growth

For more than two hundred years after the Pilgrims landed, America was essentially rural. The first United States census (1790) showed that only one in twenty of the people lived in the few small urban centers.[1] Although the number living in cities has increased at a faster rate than the total population from then until now, the United States was, up to 1860, still characteristically a rural nation whose exports were primarily agricultural products and whose political orientation was toward the farm rather than toward the city with its industry.

The War Between the States changed all of this. The thousands of manufacturers who were making profits out of war contracts united their forces to push through Congress a high tariff schedule, and, in the words of Charles A. Beard, "at last the economic structure of machine industry towered high above agriculture—a grim monument to the fallen captain, King Cotton." Tariffs, which under the Act of 1857 had averaged 19 per cent, were raised to 47 per cent in the law of 1864. Industry, protected by this tariff and stimulated by the war, began a rapid expansion which, except for periods of depression, has continued at an ever-faster tempo.

Not until that war decade did the cities absorb as much as half of the total population increase. From 1880 to the present approximately three out of every four added to the population have located in urban communities.

CHART I[1]

UNITED STATES POPULATION
URBAN AND RURAL
1790-1950

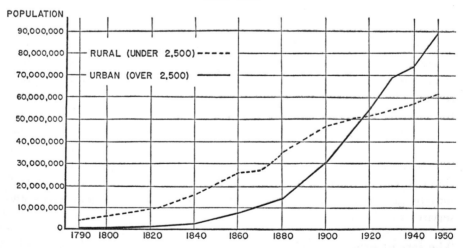

[1] The long-time census definition of "urban" population has been used in making the chart: population which resides in cities and other incorporated areas having 2,500 inhabitants or more.

The above chart indicates the rapid expansion of the urban population in the past hundred years. Approximately two in ten Americans (19.8 per cent) lived in cities in 1860. By 1920, 51.2 per cent were classified as urban. Since then the trend has continued, although at a slower pace, with 56.5 per cent urban in 1940 and 59 per cent in 1950.

The rise of the large city

In the development of the nation not every town has become a city, nor every city a metropolis. While some settlements grew, others proved a disastrous disappointment to their ambitious promoters. For example, as the Union Pacific Railroad stretched west from Omaha, speculators rushed ahead to stake out "cities" at points where they were sure the railroad would establish stations. Eager and gullible would-be merchants bought store and home sites, and the prices of lots soared, only to plummet to the value of farm land when the construction engineers moved past the site to locate a station two miles beyond. The railroad planted stations at intervals of from five to twelve miles. At each of these points a village developed, serving the adjacent countryside.

Years later the advent of the automobile and the improvement of highways made it possible for a farmer to travel past two or three such villages to a larger town where a greater variety of goods and services was available, and he could do this in less time than was formerly required to drive the team to the nearest hamlet. While nearly all of these station-hamlets remain, some smaller now than fifty years ago, every thirty or fifty miles along the route one of them, favored by special advantages, has grown into a prosperous city which has enveloped the trading districts of many small towns.

A similar process has been at work in each section of the country. One or two cities have outstripped the others because of advantages of location, transportation, or perhaps, in earlier stages of growth, an aggressive chamber of commerce. In the densely settled East and North gigantic metropolises have towered over medium-sized cities, just as these in turn have overshadowed smaller towns. In earlier decades businessmen were frequently fearful that the success of other municipalities would jeopardize their own city's economic opportunities. Time has proved this fear to be groundless. Large cities obviously are not injured by the development of secondary urban aggregations within their orbit. As the urban population grows larger, the farmer benefits by an improved and broadened market, and the urban manufacturer and merchant have a more lucrative rural trade opportunity as the farmer becomes more prosperous.

One in every eight of our population now lives in the five cities of over a million inhabitants—New York, Chicago, Los Angeles, Detroit, and Philadelphia. Four out of every ten Americans reside in a city of at least 25,000, and another four live within twenty-five miles of such a city. In other words, more than 80 per cent of our population can drive in less than an hour to a medium-sized or large city to enjoy an evening's entertainment or to shop in the department stores. The influence of urban ideas is therefore practically universal.

The metropolitan area

For several decades a new trend has been in evidence: the rapid suburban development *around* large cities. Recognizing the significance of this expansion, the Bureau of the Census has been experimenting with various classifications in an effort to distinguish between population which is directly related to the large city and that which lies outside its orbit. In the 1930 and 1940 census reports data was presented for "metropolitan districts." In 1950 the concept was slightly revised and the designation changed to "metropolitan area," the county being used as the basic unit. Currently, then, except in New England, the standard metropolitan area is a county or a group of contiguous counties which contains at least one city of 50,000 inhabitants or more. In addition to the county, or counties, containing such a city, or cities, contiguous counties are included if they are essentially metropolitan in character and socially and economically integrated with the central city. The 1950 census has introduced an additional classification, the "urbanized area," which represents the thickly settled core of the standard metropolitan area. Table I distinguishes, in terms of population increase, between central cities and their suburban areas.

Table I

POPULATION INCREASE BY PER CENT
1920-30, 1930-40, AND 1940-50
FOR THE UNITED STATES AND FOR METROPOLITAN DISTRICTS (AREAS)*

POPULATION INCREASE	1920-30	1930-40	1940-50
Total U.S. population	16.1%	7.2%	14.5%
Metropolitan districts (areas)	24.9	9.3	22.0
In central cities	19.4	6.1	13.9
Outside central cities (suburban growth)	39.2	16.9	35.5
Outside metropolitan districts (areas)	10.8	5.4	6.1

* In each column the percentage increase is shown for comparable geographic areas. The 1920-30 figures represent 85 of the 96 metropolitan districts delineated in 1930; the 1930-40 figures, 133 of the 140 metropolitan districts of 1940; the 1940-50 figures, the 168 standard metropolitan areas of 1950.

In each decade the lion's share of the population growth occurred in areas within the metropolitan districts but outside the central cities. It is in these suburban tracts that millions of new homes are being built and young families established. This is one type of community in which the church has a distinctive opportunity.

Factors which make for urban growth

What is it that makes cities grow? Several factors can be distinguished.

1. *The Physical Hinterland Itself.* The topography, climate, rainfall, richness of soil, and subsoil resources all have bearing on productivity and trade, and therefore on the population growth of the city. The hinterland of Des Moines is much less extensive than that of El Paso, and yet the city itself is 60 per cent larger. This is due to the fertility of the Iowa country-side. Were it not for the rich soil and abundant rainfall, Des Moines would be more like Bismarck, the capital of North Dakota, with a tenth the population. Other resources of the hinterland are important. The discovery and exploitation of the near-by oil reserves turned many Oklahoma and Texas cities into booming business and financial centers within a few short years.

2. *The Population of the Surrounding Area.* Fertile farm land permits intensive cultivation and will support more people. Their native intelligence, acquired skills and know-how, and cultural heritage—all combine to shape their living standards and indirectly affect the development of the near-by city. Where there is a tradition of tenancy and little pride in farm ownership and upkeep, the down-at-heels appearance of the countryside will be reflected in unprosperous towns. Conversely, a high rate of farm ownership, an intelligent understanding of agricultural processes and problems, and concern for community well-being are associated with relatively high living standards and a thriving rural-urban trade.

3. *The Actual Productivity of Farms, Forests, and Mines.* The introduction of improved methods of cultivation, the use of better seed, an increase in the yield of grain per acre or milk per cow, mean that the farmer furnishes more goods for sale in the city and in turn has a larger income with which to buy the products of industry. In fact, directly or indirectly every city is built on the surplus output of the nonurban areas which furnish the stuff for our material civilization.

4. *The Ever-increasing Productivity of Industry.* Inventions which at first seem to cause unemployment—such as the Linotype machine, the automatic telephone—end by creating new jobs. One industry attracts another, and together they provide jobs not only for urbanites but also for the thousands of rural young people who invade American cities every year looking for work. The products of industry, automobiles, electric power plants, vast

networks for water supply and sanitation—all essentials for modern city living—stimulate further urban development.[2]

5. *Ease of Transportation and Communication.* Railroads and highways are pipe lines through which the produce of the countryside and the raw materials for manufacture flow into the city. They facilitate the movement of people and the distribution of goods. Impairment of this transportation, as in a railroad strike, would within a few days seriously curtail the food supply and within a week so cut down the flow of coal and other essentials of industry as to threaten the life of a city.

6. *Rural Population Pressure.* Year after year the birth rate of rural-farm areas exceeds their death rate. Were all these people to remain in the communities of their birth, the standard of living of rural America would be steadily lowered. The farmer who is cultivating two hundred acres is unable to keep his grown sons and daughters profitably employed on his land. However, the farm population is no greater now than it was in 1910: the surplus has moved to the city.

7. *The Notion That Farm Life Is Unattractive and Unpleasant.* Undoubtedly it is in many communities where there is little creative leadership or mental stimulation, where housing is bad and income appallingly low. In such places young people with ambition and a desire for adventure feel lonely and repressed. Often the community which is most in need of dynamic leaders is least successful in keeping them. Countless rural teachers and ministers who live in hope of a transfer to the city exert, often unconsciously, a cityward influence on the rural youth who are in their school or church.

8. *The Attractive Power of the City.* This is sometimes referred to as the "urban pull," and it entices many a young man and woman to the adventure of life in the metropolis. The city is its own advertisement. People enjoy its gregariousness, its color, activity, even its noises and smells. Some would rather live in poverty in a city than in relative comfort in a village. Robert Browning expressed it this way:

> Had I but plenty of money, money enough and to spare,
> The house for me, no doubt, were a house in the city square;
> Ah, such a life, such a life, as one leads at the window there!

Or, as another person has remarked, "The country is all right, so long as you don't have to live in it."

9. *Changing Cultural Standards.* Urban patterns of living and ways of

[2] New York and Los Angeles could never have grown to their present size without access to an abundant water supply. New York draws much of its water from a hundred miles away. Los Angeles drilled through mountains and crossed two deserts to secure adequate water for its many needs.

action are now accepted as commonplace throughout America. Even the young person reared on the farm has, through listening to the radio, reading nationally circulated magazines, and attending the movies, become so familiar with urban modes and manners that he feels little hesitation or fright at the prospect of seeking a job or establishing a home in the city. The contrast between the standards of many rural parents and their children or the conflict between the conservative leaders of the small town and some of its less conventional citizens is often a further incentive toward urban migration.

City growth is not a simple phenomenon but the result of countless interweaving forces, many of them economic, others social, and some definitely personal and individual.

Factors which restrict city growth

The rate of urban growth, especially in the large metropolitan centers of the Northeast, is slowing down. Some which appear to be growing are actually merely annexing adjoining towns. In the South and West both large and small cities are attracting population at a rapid pace. They are in the same cycle of expansion which northern and eastern cities enjoyed in earlier decades.

In 1930 the 93 cities which had a population of 100,000 or more had been growing during the preceding decade at a faster pace than the total population of the United States (21.8 compared with 16.1 per cent). During the depression decade from 1930 to 1940 these identical cities as a group experienced a sharp decline in growth and fell below the national average (4.6 compared with 7.2 per cent). In the 1940's, while the acceleration was once more speeded up, it did not attain the pace of the 1920's (15.7 per cent for the 93 identical cities and 14.5 per cent for the United States). The increase for the five largest cities was only 9.4 per cent, while the remaining 88 averaged a 20.5 per cent gain. There are several reasons for this slowing down in the development of the largest American cities.

1. The per capita operating costs of government mount as a city grows. This is the result of increasing complexity, expanded governmental services, and the professionalization of the various tasks of city administration. A park board is developed with a staff of specialists. Public welfare services are broadened. Aldermen who once served without compensation now devote full time to their work and consequently receive a commensurate salary.

Table II gives evidence of the price that must be paid for city growth. The average per capita municipal tax in the cities of over a million inhabitants is twice as high as in the cities of 25,000 to 50,000, while the per capita municipal debt is over three times as high. The same sharp contrasts characterize expenditures for other public services. Tax rates are reflected in rents. And higher rents in turn affect every phase of living costs and necessitate higher wages.

Table II
RELATION OF PER CAPITA MUNICIPAL COSTS
TO SIZE OF CITY: 1953

SIZE OF CITY	1,000,000 & over	250,000- 500,000	50,000- 100,000	25,000- 50,000
Number of cities	5	23	126	249
Per capita municipal tax	$ 88.10	$ 46.58	$ 45.48	$ 41.03
Per capita municipal debt	340.61	129.68	97.77	101.51
Expenditures for:				
employee retirement	8.24	2.41	1.15	0.89
police	12.33	8.39	7.11	6.85
public welfare	12.58	8.71	3.66	2.77

2. Increasing costs of city administration and consequent high taxes constitute an incentive for families of wealth to move beyond the city boundaries—perhaps even across a county or state line—to a desirable suburb with lower tax rates. Here they can still enjoy the economic and cultural advantages of the city, but escape financial responsibility for its complex government. The result is that the per capita costs rise still farther for the citizens who remain. This is a situation which is perplexing many a tax assessor.

3. Industrial establishments, especially those in the large cities, are faced with mounting tax rates and high urban labor costs. Therefore in our keenly competitive economic society when new plants are established, they tend to be located in smaller cities or in suburban towns along the railroad lines, perhaps near enough to draw on the population of the city for workers, but far enough out to secure cheaper land and avoid the higher taxes. The newer factories are commonly being housed in one-story structures which require an extensive acreage but at the same time provide more attractive and comfortable surroundings for employees. The same money wage in a city of 25,000 permits a relatively higher living standard than it does in the metropolis.

4. The efficiency of labor is somewhat impaired as a city grows larger. Workers are scattered over a wide area and may spend an hour or more each day on a crowded, noisy conveyance going to and from work. This

creates a feeling of strain and discontentment which may adversely affect the quality of their work.

5. Urban congestion becomes an increasing irritant as the city grows. The difficulty of securing satisfactory housing, a feeling of being cooped up in a small apartment, looking out on dirty streets, and lack of a suitable place for the children to play cause many people who are at first intrigued by the metropolis to move, when opportunity offers, to a smaller city.

6. The larger the city grows, the more complicated become the movement and control of traffic. Public transportation is often inconvenient and is certainly not popular, while traveling by private automobile is exasperating because of traffic congestion and parking difficulties. The constant effort to improve the efficiency of highways adds to the tax burden and the additional facilities are almost immediately absorbed by a larger volume of traffic. Total dollar volume of sales in the downtown stores of some major cities has failed to rise, in spite of growing population and higher unit price of merchandise, chiefly because people are showing a preference for shopping in the large, new, and more accessible marketing centers.

7. An increasingly important deterrent to growth of the major cities is the grim threat of modern war. Especially since the creation of the atomic and hydrogen bombs, they and their suburbs have become highly vulnerable. Indeed the metropolis constitutes a prime war objective. It is a nerve center within the nation, and its destruction would radiate confusion in all directions. Therefore, the metropolis and its environs are correspondingly less attractive to industry and to the potential city dweller.

While these factors retard the rate of growth of the largest cities, they do not noticeably affect those under 750,000 population. As a matter of fact, the disadvantages of the great city are an indirect stimulus to the growth of suburban and satellite, as well as independent, urban centers. The long-term trend will continue; America will be increasingly urban. However, the major growth will be in the medium-sized and smaller cities, especially in the South and West.

CHAPTER THREE

The Pattern of City Growth

THE cities of America, while they differ noticeably one from another, have nevertheless many fundamental traits in common. It is the recognition of these likenesses, often overlooked, which renders the city intelligible and permits the prediction of its future. Certain basic principles of urban development may be enumerated. These "laws" are not applicable in every detail to any specific city; but unless one has a general knowledge of the way in which cities grow, he will be unable to deal effectively with problems of city churching.

Cities grow on their fringes

Every city, even though it may not be growing rapidly, experiences a continuous changing and shifting of population. As income rises, many who live in the poorer sections seek to move into a better neighborhood. Apartment-house dwellers buy a home in a new subdivision. A steady flow of new residents arrives from other cities and the countryside, many of them locating in the rooming-house district or other "ports of entry."

Cities are like trees; they do their most rapid growing on the circumference.[1] This is true even of the small city. While for a time population density may continue to increase near the center of town, eventually mounting real-estate values and taxes prohibit residential use of the land except for intensive occupancy, as in an apartment house or multistoried hotel. Home owners conclude it is wiser to sell the old house and with the money build a modern residence beyond the area of congestion, where land is less expensive, living is pleasanter, and there is play space for the children. These advantages appeal particularly to young couples rearing families.

Transportation determines the structural pattern of the city

A city is a place that is easy to get to. Roads from every direction lead toward it. The ford in the Rock River, in northern Illinois, was a logical focus for travelers from east to west. This was the only convenient place for

---

[1] Cities such as Boston, which are hemmed in by other municipalities, have no fringe to grow in. Consequently as population moves out, the suburban communities manifest a rapid increase, while the city may actually decline in size.

crossing. It was also a natural water-power site, first for feed mills, later for factories. An early map of the town of Rockford, which grew up on the west bank of the river, shows roads running north and south along each side of the stream and coming in from east and west. The early pattern of roads reaching into the countryside is the skeleton around which the whole system of Rockford streets and highways has developed. There is the same persistence of early trails and wagon roads in the modern maps of Baltimore, New Orleans, Seattle, and practically every other city.

A city on an open plain which is not cut up by a river or precipitate hills would, theoretically, present a star-shaped pattern, with roads radiating in all directions. If the surrounding territory was homogeneous, the traffic along these roads would increase and the urban development proceed at about the same pace in all directions. In actual fact there are always biasing influences which stimulate or retard the growth. One road, along higher land, furnishes better all-weather transportation and gives access to more desirable home sites where the air is fresh and the outlook attractive. Another is in the bottom land near the river and the railroad. Here industries locate, and the houses are poorly constructed and shabby. The section of Kansas City, Missouri, between the bluff and the Missouri River is typical.

Barriers develop as the city grows

Early in its life a city begins to acquire something of a framework based primarily on its topography—rivers, hills, and valleys—and its highway and railroad systems. With the growth of the city the barriers become more marked, as industries multiply, parks and cemeteries are enlarged, and highways are broadened to accommodate increasing traffic. These lines of cleavage divide the city into numerous "natural areas," separating residential districts from each other and affecting population movement.

Heavy through traffic, especially if there are no stop lights, makes it difficult for people to cross the street and trade in the grocery or meat market on the opposite side. The owner of a small food shop in a large city remarked:

The folks in those apartments should mean a lot of trade, but they can't get across the street. I've seen them stand as long as ten minutes on the other side, waiting to get through the traffic. They are afraid to send the children across. . . . I'm getting all the business people on this block to petition for a stop light at our corner.

A stop light or underpass to facilitate safe crossing of a thoroughfare is important for the church as well as for commerce. If there is no such protection, heavy traffic may reduce the area from which a church can draw its membership and, even more significantly, children for its church school.

Specialization occurs in land use and population grouping

Even in a town of five thousand this tendency begins to appear. By that time property facing the town square is used almost exclusively for business purposes. The better new residences are built on higher land to the west, and industries have clustered near the old gristmill between the river and the railroad.

The larger the city, the more marked is the specialization within it. In the metropolis the financial district is easily distinguishable from the department store area. The sorting out process which is continually in operation affects not only commercial establishments and industries, but also the distribution of people in various types of residential communities, racial colonies, apartment-house areas, and the rooming-house district.

Deterioration tends to appear around the central business district

The greater the population and the larger the business volume, the higher will be the land values at the heart of the city. But the effect on the land round about the heart is usually not beneficent. Often people who own this property, which includes many of the oldest residences, move toward the growing edge of the city and rent their former homes to others who either are less fastidious or must live in a low-rent area. Owners feel that there is little point in making repairs or any fundamental improvements in the property unless these will result in a commensurate increase in the rent. They hope that the expanding business will in time reach out and absorb their land, multiplying its value. In the meantime the buildings become run-down, and only people who cannot afford to live elsewhere move in. Consequently this is where immigrants first settled when they came to America and where the larger Negro communities are to be found.

Population moves toward the periphery

People seek to escape from unpleasant surroundings. When a rise in income permits, they think in terms of a more agreeable place to live, and naturally look toward the developing edge of the city where the rent, though higher, is still within reach.

Not all families can afford to buy a new home in a delightful suburb. Many must rest content with a larger apartment or the second floor of a two-flat building. Nevertheless there is a steady and understandable longing to escape from the crowded areas, with their aging buildings and associated ills, into newer, higher-status communities. When they do change their residence, they generally move a half mile or more, playing leapfrog with the families that preceded them ten years earlier. It is the outer territory—served by the familiar highway or transit line which they now use to get to the center of the city—that is first and most carefully combed in their search for a new home.

This outward thrust of population continues beyond the bounds of the city. Here highways and streetcar lines play a less important part than high-speed transportation facilities. Suburban towns are strung along these electric rapid transit lines and railroads, which stretch out like the fingers of a hand. The territory between the fingers is referred to as interstitial, which means literally "set in between."

Status influences the type and distribution of communities

The central business district serves as the focal point for the economic and political life of the city. Innumerable ties bind all other parts of the city to it. The spatial relations of the residential communities to the business center show interesting similarities in most cities.

The city can be envisioned as a number of sectors, each starting at the heart and broadening as it moves out toward the periphery. These sectors have sometimes been likened to cuts of pie. Perhaps a more apt figure is a whorl of leaflets growing out of a central stem. Each leaflet is distinct from the others, and yet it has meaning only in relation to the others, and all of them are held together by the common center. Each sector has at least one major traffic artery like the vein of the leaflet. These arteries serve as a uniting influence through the length of the sector.

As many as six or eight sectors may reach out from the business center, generally separated from one another by railroads and industry, a river, canal, or other barriers which diminish the population movement between adjoining sectors. Some cities are like leaves which have leaflets forming a partial whorl, with sectors covering half of the circle (Cleveland, Miami). Others have sectors radiating in all directions but with some of them less developed than others (Houston, Nashville). No city has perfectly balanced sectors around the whole circle.

Another way of thinking about the distribution of communities with reference to the downtown district is the "concentric circle" or "zonal" pattern. Every large city—and, potentially, smaller ones as well—may be described in terms of zones. The central business district is the first zone. Here are located the major stores, hotels, theaters, and banks. It has a large daytime population, but few people have their homes there. Extending more or less completely around it is the next zone, sometimes called the area of transition or blighted area, where the housing is old and rents are the lowest in the city. Parts of it are occupied by warehouses and factories. Beyond this belt are the humble but comparatively well-kept houses of working men, the "conservation area." Farther out are the better residential districts, and beyond them the uncongested suburban communities. There is a rough, though by no means inevitable, correlation between distance from the center and standard of living: the farther out from the center, the higher the income.

The sectors cut across these zonal bands. One sector may be occupied throughout its length chiefly by a distinctive cultural or racial group—as Polish or Negro. Yet within this sector there is a zonal differentiation; that is, those with lowest income live in the older, less desirable section toward the heart of the city, and the more prosperous farther out in the newer structures with more spacious grounds. Other sectors are used primarily by white American stock, again with an economic differentiation along the sector.

The sector and zonal descriptions cannot be applied with rigidity, for there are many qualifying factors occasioned by each city's distinctive physical setting and economic and cultural life. While each sector tends to represent a continuous flow or succession of the same or similar population groups, having more or less a unity of its own, and each zone has its distinctive economic and physical characteristics, there are usually a number of marooned areas or cultural islands in which live people of a different racial stock, nationality background, or income level, separated socially from the dominant population. In this case the people are always aware that they do constitute an island, with a little neighborhood of their own. This may be an area of relative wealth near the center of the city—perhaps on an eminence, or with a pleasing view of lake or river—surrounded on two or more sides by homes of poverty. Or it may be a low-income neighborhood existing to one side of a high-class suburb, or as in Washington, D.C., a racial group (Negro) living along the alleys in humble quarters back of superior residential property which faces the streets. In spite of the exceptions the concepts of sector and zonal development furnish a framework for understanding urban community life and are helpful in the analysis of church problems.

The time-fare factor affects community growth

The development of the territory toward the fringes of the city is influenced by three interrelated variables: the distance in terms of miles, the time it takes to travel from the home to the place of work (most commonly in or near the center of the city), and the fare or transportation cost. As transportation is speeded up, the suburban development is hastened. Usually people prefer to live farther from the congested areas so long as they can get there quickly, even though somewhat more expensively. Land values rise, and apartment houses are erected along the main bus routes or rapid transit lines. Conversely, areas which are not served by good transportation develop more slowly and, even within the city limits, have a lower land value and a less dense population.

Population movement varies with economic conditions

The outward movement of urban population does not occur at a uniform rate. In a period of depression, or when building materials are unavailable, as during a war, there is little outward thrust. Either people cannot afford to buy or rent a better home, or else new housing is unprocurable. However, when the restricting pressure eases, income mounts, and building materials again are obtainable, a building boom develops and land values rise. Then for a period of time the suburban trend is accelerated.

The type and direction of population movement are predictable

In spite of the many variables involved it is possible, as the telephone and public-service companies have discovered, to predict with reasonable accuracy the direction and rate of population movement and also certain of the characteristics of the people who will fill in particular areas. For example, there is a large Polish settlement in Hamtramck, a separate municipality entirely surrounded by the city of Detroit. Since the principal transit lines from the center of Detroit through Hamtramck are to the north and west, it is predictable that in due course the areas farther to the north will have an increasing population with Polish background; that is, the dominant movement will be along the transportation lines, within the sector. This means that the developing territory will be more congenial to a Roman Catholic than to a Methodist or Presbyterian church; and when one of the latter is founded, it must be permitted a relatively large population on which to draw.

Population movement may be studied in two ways: (1) by observing the flow of a given cultural or national group through a series of communities within a sector, or (2) by noting the succession of population groups which have occupied a given community. Indeed, the history of an urban area can be described in terms of the changes that have taken place in land occupancy. A typical sequence, covering a span of three generations, is as follows:

Land once used for general farming was broken into smaller plots of three to five acres each for intensive truck gardening. These acreages were later bought by a land speculator, who put through streets and staked out large lots, a quarter acre in size. On these, fashionable suburban single-family residences were built. Each home had from eight to twelve rooms, ample for a family and one or two servants. Often a carriage house was placed on the back of the property. Years passed, the older people died, and others moved away. Lots were subdivided and additional houses erected. Newcomers, with lower social status and smaller incomes, began to move in. The property was slowly deteriorating. Single-family residences were transformed into light-housekeeping apartments. Food stores were opened on the ground floor of some of the buildings. Others were taken over by an automobile club, a mortuary parlor, or a school for "beauticians." Some of the more decrepit buildings have now been torn down and a new two-story automobile salesroom and garage erected. The population, which reached a peak density shortly after the houses were subdivided, is declining. Enrollment in the local public school is less than half of what it was twenty years ago. The transformation of the community is complete.

Population changes require institutional adjustments

The community is the soil within which social institutions develop. These agencies usually require a number of years to become firmly rooted; and even if the people who established them move on to another area, they remain behind. An illustration of the process is the kosher [2] delicatessen shop. This type of specialized food store will be found only where there are a number of Jewish families in a community, and will prosper as long as the congenial population remains. With the passage of time the Jews may move away. On the other hand, although business is now declining, the proprietor is loath to sell out because he himself is older and less ready to embark on a new venture. Besides, he probably owns his store and could sell only at a sacrifice. Many of his former neighbors will return for a time to make purchases, since they know him well and like his merchandise. In the end, however, if the community should become dominantly Gentile a kosher store could not survive.

Churches, fraternal organizations, and other social institutions may be similarly affected. They too will weaken and eventually disappear unless they are able to adapt themselves to the newcomers and present a program which will meet their needs. A kosher food store cannot make such adjustments, but a public school, a social settlement, or a Christian church can. *The chief characteristic of the city is mobility, and no institution can remain unaltered by it. It can, however, learn to foresee change and, by planning wisely, adapt its program to meet the new conditions.*

As a rule, religious institutions have not seen this necessity for adaptation to the changing pattern of the local community. One result has been that many a church has gradually become a cultural island surrounded by an indifferent or uncongenial population. Such churches slowly wither away or, as a last resort, merge with others that are equally feeble. If the church is to serve the spiritual needs of men, it must in its planning be as skillful and as farsighted as the public-service company or the county highway commission, moving quickly into developing territories and reorienting its program in older areas as population changes take place.

[2] The term "kosher" is employed by Jews to mean ceremonially pure. A kosher shop handles only those foods which conform to the dietary laws of the orthodox Jews.

CHAPTER FOUR

What the City Does to People

FROM the beginning of recorded history the city has held a fascination for men. They have thought of it as a haven from persecution, a refuge from the loneliness and isolation of the countryside, a place where the lights burned brightly at night and the restraints of the small community were absent. It has been a center of bustling activity, offering romance, comfort, and stimulation.

The city has always drawn to itself the most diverse personalities: the prophet goes there to secure an audience and preach against urban vices; the prostitute flees to it in order to escape the criticism of her townspeople; the genius and the eccentric find companionship there with others like themselves; and thrill-seeking youth look for excitement and adventure. However, the vast majority of city dwellers are neither illustrious saints nor profligate sinners. They are run-of-the-mill men and women seeking to improve their economic status and hoping to give their children more opportunities than they themselves enjoyed in their youth. They, like the others, find in the city diversity and richness of experience in human association which are not easily procurable in the small town or the open country.

The city itself is never inert. Through its countless, varied influences—schools, theaters, newspapers, its churches, politics, rooming houses, its clamor and its beauty—the city is constantly molding the lives of citizens and visitors. Not everyone lives within the same set of urban influences. The economic and social insecurity of the slum, and the early fear of the police—or the "Law," as the patrolman is often called—are unknown to the child who is reared in a more privileged neighborhood. Further, the suggestibility of people varies. The attitudes and behavior of many are shaped by the influences about them. Others, perhaps because of the teaching of the family or the church, resist the dominant thought-ways of the city. Yet there are several aspects of urban life which to a considerable degree affect the thought and actions of most citizens. They can be expressed in the city dweller's own words.

"What a lot of people"

In the city people seem always to be present. If there is a fire or an explosion, or if the police wagon clangs its way down the street, throngs of the curious soon congregate. Along the main business thoroughfare people of all ages are in evidence, and every weekday offers the onlooker the activity, the noise, and color which characterize a Saturday night in a small town. The businessman, lawyer, grocer, plumber have an indefinite supply of clients or customers. Even the urban housewife in her home or apartment, though she may feel somewhat restricted in comparison with her husband, is in frequent contact with tradespeople—the milkman, garbage collector, newsboy, laundryman, meter reader. And when she goes to the local shopping center or downtown, she learns how to meet and deal with bus drivers, fellow shoppers, clerks of all descriptions, ticket sellers, doctors, and policemen.

It is a busy and varied world, which trains adults and youth alike in self-confidence and efficiency in personal relations. It also tends to make them somewhat more callous; a new face is no longer a matter of special interest. The physically handicapped person, who in a small town receives the sympathetic consideration of most whom he meets, is scarcely noticed by the majority of passers-by in the city.

"It's an exciting life"

The open country or village is an intriguing place for certain types of people. For example, an elderly woman dwelling by herself in a mountain cabin has remarked, "I never go to Denver if I can help it. All the interesting things happen up here. In the city they make so much noise they scare away the birds." But for most people the city is filled with possibilities of excitement and thrill. The very clatter of machinery and din of traffic keep them on the alert. Something is always happening—special sales, the high-school football game, the hundredth anniversary of a church or business, a fire, a strike of the clerks in the chain stores, an accident. And the larger the city, the more the activity and the greater the hubbub: rattling streetcars, automobile horns, screeching brakes, riveting machines and pneumatic drills, locomotive whistles, the bang of ash cans and garbage containers, the steady hum of factory machinery, blaring loud-speakers, and an occasional drunken brawl, not to mention the normal sounds of the home, shouting children and "soap opera" on the radio. These noises combine to stimulate people to immediate activity, though often the end result is extreme mental and emotional fatigue.

Many an urbanite values particularly the opportunities for intellectual stimulation and growth. He appreciates the accessibility and rich resources of the library, the public lectures and other programs at the college, the discussions at the local political club, the weekly meeting of the luncheon group. The opera, theater, symphony orchestra, and recitals of distinguished artists, which are seldom available in small communities, bring delight to millions. Even more numerous are the patrons of the movies, who, if they wish, can see a different show every night of the week. As one divorcee remarked, "I hate to be by myself in the evening, so I usually go to the movie four or five times a week."

City people derive great satisfaction from being "where things happen," even though they personally are not involved. They like to feel themselves a part of the scene where important decisions are being made and momentous events are occurring. This is one way of achieving a sense of significance by proxy. Susie Smith from Pleasant Prairie, who works as an assistant junior clerk in the State or Treasury Department in Washington, D. C., shares in the glamour of the nation's capital and delights to write home about what "we are doing."

"Roots are shallow"

America is foot-loose. Four major population shifts can be distinguished: from rural to urban areas; from the metropolitan cities to their suburbs and smaller satellite cities; from East and North to the South, Southwest, and West; and the large-scale movement of Negroes from the South and South Central states to the northern and far western cities. Since World War II more families have been on the move than in any prior period. The extent of this mobility may be judged from a federal census report that between April, 1952, and April, 1953, 30,786,000 persons changed their place of residence, some of them more than once. This is 20.1 per cent of the entire population over one year of age in 1953. Approximately one third of these people moved outside the county to a new home and 5,522,000 moved across state lines.

Young adults move more frequently and over greater distances than do either children or persons past 34 years of age. The highest mobility rate is for those who are 20 to 24 years of age; 40.5 per cent lived in a different dwelling in 1953 than one year earlier. The comparable figure for 18- and 19-year-olds is 28.2 per cent, and for 25 to 29-year-olds, 33.4.

The nonwhite population had a higher mobility rate (27.9 per cent) than whites (19.1 per cent), but their movement was more likely to be within the same county.

Further, population movement has continued to be away from the farms. In spite of the relatively high birth rate of farm families the rural farm population declined by more than seven million between 1940 and 1950, a loss of almost 24 per cent.

The largest population gains were registered by cities between 10,000 and 1,000,000. And these places, understandably, are the ones which showed the highest mobility rate. In urbanized areas with a population of 250,000 to 1,000,000, 25.7 per cent of the population had been on the move in the year 1952-53, while cities of 25,000 to 50,000 outside the urbanized areas registered an even higher rate of restlessness and growth, 27.9 per cent.

People who do not own their homes find it easy to move, the more so when there is a plentiful supply of dwellings with built-in furniture which saves the necessity of buying and moving equipment. When apartments were more readily available, many people deliberately changed their residence every two years, because by that means they would have a freshly decorated home without being troubled by painters and plasterers. The new landlord commonly allowed one month's rent free, which covered the cost of moving.

This frequent change of address has an important bearing on family life and the development of loyalties to community institutions such as the church. Certainly urban Americans do not have the same sense of belonging to a community which their grandfathers did. A change of residence—except in the biennial swapping of apartments—usually means that a family is lifted out of one community and deposited in another. Children change schools and are forced to find another circle of playmates. The husband and wife, if they are to have friends, must discover new ones. If they are loyal church members, they will probably look for a church home of their own denomination. The process can become discouraging. One young housewife, whose husband had been moved by his firm for the third time in five years, remarked:

We have almost come to the conclusion that it is bad luck to join the church. Each time within six months after we have joined, when we are just beginning to get acquainted, Jerry has been transferred to another office of the ——— Oil Company. You know, it is hard to give up your friends, move on where no one knows you and start all over again.

Whether or not urban dwellers change their residence (this is usually called *mobility*) they are constantly on the move. There is the daily travel to and from the job, to the theater, school, shopping center, which may be referred to as *fluidity*. The ever-present automobile and inexpensive public transportation facilitate the formation of friendships on an interest rather than on a community basis. Ease of movement means wider contacts and less dependence on or responsibility to the local community and its institutions. This has significance for organized religion: people can travel three miles across the city to attend a church that they like.

"I'm a stranger here myself"

The villager knows his neighbors by name. He remembers their parents and has watched their children grow up. Their interests, skills, and also their foibles are matters of common knowledge. A semblance of this neighborliness is also found in those sections of a city where the streets are lined with private family residences. The men occasionally are well enough acquainted with neighbors to borrow their lawn mower, and women discuss their children over the back fence or across the hedge. Even here, however, people rarely know by name those who live in the next block.

In the apartment-house district, and to a greater degree the rooming-house area, urban anonymity is seen in its extreme form. People in a large apartment building do not have a speaking acquaintance with fellow tenants and would not recognize them on the street. Indeed, they generally are not eager to become acquainted, and are no more concerned with the personal or family troubles of others who dwell under the same roof than with the worries of the farmers in an adjoining state. The birth of a baby in a village is an event of importance which evokes community interest. In an apartment house it simply involves an additional noise menace.

Apartment-house people have built up a protective shell about themselves. Any minister who has sought to call on them soon learns that many are hesitant to open the door to speak to a stranger, and become suspicious when questions are asked. Ironically enough, this very effort to preserve anonymity results in a sense of loneliness and the feeling that no one really cares.

"There's nobody here to tell you"

A common complaint about rural society is "There is too much gossip." Young people in particular often venture to the city to be free of parental domination and the tongue wagging of neighbors. There the intimate and strict controls of the smaller community are absent, except for certain tightly knit neighborhoods in some residential communities or foreign-language colonies. A young man can go to a large city, establish himself in a rooming house under an assumed name, secure his mail through the general-delivery window at the post office, and be completely on his own. No one, not even the police, need discover his identity. There are no friends or relatives near by to visit or counsel him. His rooming-house keeper conscientiously avoids any appearance of curiosity. The only restrictions placed on him are the conventional laws of the community and such spiritual controls as have been built within him in his earlier life in home, church, and school.

For some sensitive young people this freedom, at first exhilarating, can become a terrifying thing, and they feel themselves lost in the great city. No one knows about them or cares greatly whether they live or die. To a considerable degree this freedom from parental and neighborhood controls has a bearing on the higher divorce rate of the city, on juvenile and adult delinquency, and on mental tension and illness.

"It's that crowd at city hall"

As the city grows larger and as community ties weaken, the voters feel less personally responsible for the welfare of the city. Owners of apartment houses complain that their tenants vote for every bond issue, no matter how extravagant, "because they don't have to pay the taxes." Actually the voting record, particularly in areas of mobility, is poor except when there is a hotly contested local or national election.

In the city the average citizen feels removed from the processes of government. Its structure is unfamiliar to him, and its employees are impersonal functionaries. Consequently he becomes irritated and perhaps resentful toward "the politicians," and develops a feeling of helplessness about changing the situation. So he concludes, "What difference does it make whether I vote or not?" This combined sense of futility and resentment constitutes a threat to efficient city administration and to the democratic way of life. The effect on the city dweller is no less important: he may acquire a cynical indifference toward civic welfare and toward the minor aspects of law observance.

"Family life is different"

City living has produced changes in the family. Many of its former functions have been transferred to other agencies. Its members do not work at a common occupation, as in farming or the running of a general store. Formal education of children, instruction in religion, sharing in recreational activities, are now almost as completely absent from the home as are canning, bread baking, and dressmaking. The family is primarily a consuming and no longer a producing unit. The husband, and frequently the wife, is employed outside the home. (In 1953, 27.8 per cent of married women living with their husbands in urban areas were in the labor force, as compared with 19 per cent in the rural farm areas.) The ties which bind them together are their mutual affections and loyalties, their common interest in the children, and their enjoyment of each other's company, rather than any shared economic activity or feeling of legal or community pressure.

In 1953 the size of the average urban family was 3.4 persons. In contrast, the rural farm families had 4.1 members. More children are born to rural than to urban families, as is quickly seen in Table III.

Table III
NUMBER OF CHILDREN EVER BORN
PER 1,000 WOMEN 15-44 YEARS OLD
IN THE UNITED STATES, APRIL, 1952

Total	1,465	Other urban areas	1,451
Urban	1,285	25,000 or more	1,438
Urbanized areas	1,211	2,500 to 25,000	1,459
3,000,000 or more	1,091		
1,000,000 to 3,000,000	1,110	Rural nonfarm	1,689
250,000 to 1,000,000	1,277	Rural-farm	2,126
Under 250,000	1,400		

Rearing children is a complicated process, particularly in the larger city. A definite economic liability is involved. The wife who has been employed must give up her work for a period of years; income is reduced at the same time that expenses increase. An extra room is needed, at a cost of ten to thirty dollars a month. It is more difficult to rent an apartment because of the objections of landlords. In spite of these handicaps the city birth rate has been rising steadily since 1940—in fact more rapidly than the birth rate in either the rural nonfarm or even the rural-farm areas, according to the estimates of the Bureau of the Census. City dwellers, like men and women everywhere, are hungry for affection, and increasingly feel that one of life's most rewarding experiences has been denied them if they have had no children.

"I don't get any satisfaction from my job"

The typical city man owns neither property nor tools; he has greater freedom to move than the farmer, but less independence. He may earn a better wage, but living costs are higher. He is not his own boss and cannot be sure of his job six months ahead. This economic insecurity often causes nervousness, irritability, and a feeling of inadequacy and frustration. It explains in part the growing strength of the labor movement, and is reflected in the nostalgic desire to "return to the land"—an objective which city dwellers often talk about, but which they would rather contemplate than realize.

Many city workers feel that their job is not vitally related to life. They find little adventure in manufacturing a small gadget or in tending a switchboard. For relief they seek the movie thriller, the race track, the night club, and the detective story. Even war with all its terrors has this advantage for some urbanites: it furnishes excitement and gives them a feeling that their small part has significance in the over-all program. Urban Americans are a worried people, restless and uncertain. Can the church help the city man find purpose and peace?

"Little money, little man; big money, big man"

The growth of urban society has brought increased emphasis on the material aspects of living. Mills and factories, through the ingenuity of inventors and technicians, have steadily increased the output of goods and improved their quality. Cities are naturally connected, in the thinking of people, with the production and display of wealth. Therefore, while rural as well as urban America gives major attention to the satisfying of its material needs, the emphasis on conspicuous consumption and luxurious living is found to the greatest degree in cities. This emphasis is furthered by the ostentatious displays of urban grandeur in the movies and the slick-paper magazines. Housewives sit breathlessly by their radios, listening to the give-away programs, envying the fortunate ones, and hoping that some day they too may win the chance to be "queen for a day" and live in temporary splendor in a New York or Hollywood hotel.

The criterion of success, even among nominally Christian people, is frequently the attainment of the status advantages that go with the possession of wealth. This attitude is exemplified in the bold letters of an advertisement of the American Investors' Union: "What could possibly be of more importance to you than your own financial status?" This general atmosphere no city dweller can escape; and unless he makes a serious effort to combat it, he will find it influencing his standards and those of his children.

"It keeps you on your toes"

City living affects people in a variety of ways. It may demand changes in habit and speed of movement. It introduces new and complex situations which the individual must learn to meet. It will strip him of certain comfortable and perhaps fallacious notions about humans and their behavior and will cause him either to think through to a firmer and more dependable philosophy or to become cynical and distrustful of others. But, like eating of the fruit of the tree of knowledge, living in the city leaves the person never the same again. Once he has experienced the conveniences, the excitement and stimulation, the opportunities for entertainment and self-improvement, and the higher material standards of living of the city, he contemplates returning to his former farm or small-town home like a chick looking at his old shell—he no longer fits into it. For better or for worse, he has been forced out of his rut, his horizons have been stretched apart, he has become a "marginal man." This is true to some extent of all city dwellers, from the onetime sharecropper who has come to the city at the urging of his relatives to the businessman who in all his fifty-five years has never lived more than three miles from his downtown stationery store.

Social imagination and religious insight

Out of the opportunities and new experiences which city living affords may arise a freedom, often not recognized or attained by city people, to think creatively and to gain insight into social situations. This freedom can give zest and purpose to the various aspects of their living. The family, instead of being an institution of convenience or economic necessity, has a chance to become a free association of parents and children bound by affectional ties, mutual understanding, and regard. The job, to an emancipated man or woman, becomes not simply a means of getting money to pay necessary bills and provide for vacations and eventual retirement, but an opportunity for self-expression and a channel for service to the larger welfare.

The sensitive religious man sees the masses of people about him struggling to attain happiness and a sense of security, and recognizes that the methods they are pursuing cannot lead them to the goal of their desire. His interest will not be limited to helping the materially impoverished; in addition and more importantly he will be concerned at the spiritual barrenness which is to be found in every class in the city, concerned for the people who are lonely, unhappy, and insecure and do not know which way to turn to obtain enduring peace of mind.

The cosmopolitan atmosphere of the city, coupled with his religious insights, makes it impossible for him to be narrow or provincial. Instead of becoming either hopeless or cynical at the prejudices and credulity of the urban dweller, he insists on his belief that all men are children of God and therefore both teachable and savable. Consequently the experiences of his urban living confirm him in his loyalty to the Christian Church and in his determination to make it a more effective instrument for transforming the lives of people.

CHAPTER FIVE

Urbanism and the Fortunes
of the Church

LIVING in a city gradually and subtly creates changes in personality, so that when an urbanite visits his rural cousins both he and they are aware of differences in attitudes and manners. In the same way urban institutions are inevitably affected by the peculiar stresses and demands which arise because people live in the mobile, secular environment of a crowded city. As the city grows larger, not only are the school system, the health department, and recreational facilities increased in size because of the larger population, but their officers also must rethink their organization and functioning to meet the new problems which emerge as the city grows in complexity. Similarly it is not enough for the church simply to multiply its local congregations; ministers, laymen, and particularly administrators must be prepared to rethink the functions which the church should perform and methods for making it more effective. Population mobility, urban secularism, and other social forces have a bearing on the fortunes of the church.

Population mobility

When a family changes its residence, it is usually engrossed with its own problems of locating a new house or apartment, signing a lease, and moving furniture. Others are also interested in its change of address: the landlord, the public school, and the church, which is not the least sufferer from urban mobility.

A church located in an attractive residential community where most of the people own their homes is blessed with a relatively stable membership. But in areas of high density and small apartments a minister is confronted with an almost overwhelming task. In such communities pastors who have kept records of membership gains and losses report that they must recruit as high as one fifth of their total membership each year in order to replace the persons who transfer away or simply disappear.

Mobile city people are slow in developing a sense of loyalty to a local church, and are often loath to assume much financial or leadership responsibility within it. Yet it is essential that they be quickly incorporated in the organization and made part of its life, even though they may be in the community for only a year or two. This again calls for skillful planning alike on the part of the minister and the nonmobile lay leaders.

Community specialization and church types

An important characteristic in urban life is the tendency to specialize. One community attracts factory workers and their families; another is occupied largely by white-collar workers. The traits of the community have a significant bearing on the type of church which will be successful in it. An institution with a particular theology—or polity or program—may prosper in one community but win few adherents in another.

With each population shift the character of the community is altered. In every large city there are countless examples of hapless churches which were not aware of and prepared for such change. An area formerly populous is taken over almost entirely by industry, or a new population group moves in, and a once-flourishing church is left stranded. The denomination which complacently continues to maintain its churches as though both they and their communities were static will fail in its mission. In contrast, intelligent, sympathetic understanding of the processes of city life and an alertness to each opportunity for establishing a new church or strengthening an old one will mean that the Christian gospel can not only survive but increasingly influence thought and conduct in the city.

Overcrowding and loneliness

The sense of isolation within the city is, oddly enough, the result of the crowding together of people, sometimes over 100,000 of them residing within a square mile. Few individuals are as lonely as the young man occupying a hall bedroom in a rooming house in a large city. The more people there are around him, the more alone he feels. This sense of isolation exists, though to a less degree, for the members of a family moving into a new apartment. They usually do not avail themselves of the friendly associations which the church can offer. They are not acquainted with anyone who is attending, and are hesitant to take the initiative which is required to enter a strange building and meet, even in a worship service, with a hundred or more persons whom they do not know. It is the feeling of personal insecurity, the fear that they may be rebuffed or ignored, that causes many newcomers to shy away from the church, which could offer them the fellowship they need. In the city the church cannot in good conscience expect the stranger to take all the initiative.

Secularism

Whether secularism is thought of as a neglect of the institutions of religion or is defined as preoccupation with material aspects of life—getting and spending, keeping physically comfortable and in fashion—it is abundantly in evidence in the city. When a man remarks, as did a noted actor, that there are three things he likes about Sunday—"the extra hour in bed, the big Sunday dinner with all the family present, and the spiritual uplift of the philharmonic broadcast"—he lays bare at one and the same time the secular assumptions and the spiritual longings of the urban dweller.

It is important for churchmen to understand the all-pervading influence of secularism in urban life. The young couple who were leaders in their home church in a county-seat town decide to relax when they move to St. Louis or Detroit. No pastor calls on them, and they enjoy a sense of freedom from responsibility. Perhaps they become "cafeteria Christians," tasting a bit of what is offered at the Brick Evangelical Church this Sunday and another week attending the lecture at the Ethical Society. They intend some day to select a church home, but at present the world is too much with them.

There are two important reasons why this attitude is so common among city people. First, church attendance and participation in the program had not become for them, in their earlier religious life, an essential opportunity for self-expression and for the discovery of life values. They had attended because it was the thing to do and they enjoyed the company of other young people. A second reason is the general secularization of urban life, which stresses the accumulation of property, the acquiring of social status, the observance of the conventions, and the enjoyment of leisure. People tend to hide and gloss over their deeper and often mystical longings, lest associates in the business office regard them as sentimentalists.

From the standpoint of the church the prevalence of this attitude presents serious hazards. People who lack both the sense of obligation to the church and the feeling of need for its ministry do not join or, if they are nominal members, seldom attend. In the average city fewer than half of the adults are even nominal members of any religious institution, and only half of these attend as frequently as every other Sunday. The church which may have been a powerful influence in the small town does not, for the majority of city people, enter significantly into their thinking.

To some extent this situation results from poor planning on the part of the city church, and from its failure to seek out the newcomers who are potential members. However, the church where these people had real or nominal associations in their earlier years, whether it was in a small town or a metropolis, must carry some of the responsibility. It had failed to make religion a vital force in their early thinking, and no pattern of loyalty to the church at large was ever developed. Secular attitudes can be changed only slowly, painfully, and in opposition to the dominant trend of the age. Nevertheless, it is a primary task of the church to struggle to effect such change.

Competition from other interests and organizations

The city is so rich in resources and is so highly organized that the church is only one of many agencies calling for a segment of the people's free time. Luncheon clubs, lodges, bridge and bingo clubs, businessmen's bowling leagues, factory baseball teams, local political organizations, the Parent-Teacher Association, lectures, concerts, and the movies—all beckon for attention. If the church is simply a club for friendly association, it must compete with these activities on the basis of the attractiveness of its program and the advantages it can offer.

If, however, the church has a unique message for men concerning the ultimate values of life, it performs an unduplicated and distinctive function in the community. To win the support of men and women in large numbers its contribution to their thinking must be intelligent, socially constructive, and impelling. When it performs this function well, it has a claim to a primary interest and support from serious-minded and emotionally mature people.

Part II

URBAN COMMUNITIES

AND THEIR CHURCHES

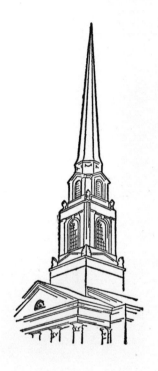

CHAPTER SIX

Cities Within Cities

THE small city, like the village, possesses a certain unity in business life and social organization. It has a single commercial center where nearly all of the stores are located. Churches, lodge halls, movies, the rural electrification office—all are here. Practically everyone in town who is able to walk or ride visits the area several times a week. The city is one community and this is its center. Down by the tracks some families are living in poverty, and on the hill are homes of wealth. Yet the children attend the same high school and participate in the same sports and social functions.

The development of communities

As the city grows larger, from five thousand to fifty thousand inhabitants, pronounced changes take place. More and taller office buildings, bigger department stores, and larger theaters are erected downtown. In outlying sections small "satellite" business centers with grocery and drug stores, barber shops, and beauty parlors develop to meet the needs of local residents. By this time the city has entered a period of growing pains. In older sections there are signs of social disorganization; delinquency is becoming a Problem. While members of the chamber of commerce boast of the larger population and expanding bank clearings, old-timers bemoan the loss of the friendly home-town atmosphere. "Central City isn't what it used to be." It is no longer a unity; competing local community loyalties are beginning to develop. Some of the downtown churches are thinking of relocating, as their memberships scatter.

The larger the city, the more clearly defined are the several residence areas. Indeed, the city is something of a sorting machine which shunts people with distinctive nationality or racial backgrounds into congenial communities and distributes others on the basis of income, consumption standards, or special interests. Each local community may be thought of as an area of selection, drawing to itself people who are similar in background and living standards, and also as an area of characterization, influencing the behavior of those who live within it and affecting their social standing.

An urban community is usually set off from surrounding areas by barriers. The residents within these boundaries identify the area as their own and have, to a degree, a sense of unity among themselves, perhaps calling their community by a particular name, such as Oak Knoll or West Town. The traits which mark it off from its neighbors are most in evidence near its center and frequently disappear completely on its outer fringes, where there is less sense of cohesion. Since most barriers in the city involve noise and dirt, land values for residential purposes decline as one moves from the center of the community toward its edge. When, however, a residential area breaks off sharply because of a prestige barrier, such as a well-kept lake shore or park, prestige and also land values rise.

How communities change

Since the fringe of a community—or the interstitial area between two communities—is commonly less attractive, rents are lower and people with smaller incomes occupy the homes. Often there is considerable mixture of population. Because of their diversity the people may have few ties even with immediate neighbors and do not feel themselves a part of the major community. It tends to be a disorganized area, with a higher-than-average delinquency rate. Since community consciousness and pride are almost absent, it is easier for newcomers with subordinate status to gain entrance. Mexicans and Negroes, who could not rent or buy a home near the heart of the community, can frequently secure a foothold along the less desirable streets bordering railroads or industry.

Most members of these subordinate groups remain indefinitely in the decrepit housing on the edge, by the factories. Even though there are no physical barriers separating the newer from the long-time residents, there is a social barrier (social distance) between them which minimizes contact. However, after a time a vanguard made up of the more aggressive and successful members moves in toward the heart of the community, buying homes as they are put up for sale. In the sight of others of their group and in their own eyes the newly acquired homes are an evidence of improved social standing.

To the older residents, however, the gradual change in population is a sign that the community is deteriorating. The new infiltration creates tension which may even break out in open conflict between gangs of boys. The more financially able and those with younger families are the first to move out into a better and developing part of town. For a period of time the community may consist of two or more subcommunities, living side by side but with different interests and standards. The lines separating such subcommunities tend to run along alleys rather than streets; people feel more united with neighbors across the street than across the alley.

Even after the formerly dominant population group has yielded to the newcomers, some of its members remain behind. Most of these are people whose children have already grown up and moved away, who own their homes and are loath to break the ties which for two or three decades have bound them to the area. Others are the economically unsuccessful who have been unable to move. These become "marooned" in the area, surrounded by a population which has a different heritage. They are remnants of a formerly prevalent culture within the matrix of a new community type. Often their church remains behind with them and serves for them as a symbol of stability in the midst of change.

Determining community characteristics

It is important to city church planners to discover whether population in a community will increase or decline, whether those who will move into the area in later years will be congenial to the Protestant tradition, whether because of low economic status the missionary organizations of the church are justified in giving financial aid. If one is to become sufficiently familiar with his city so that he can plan its churching, he must study not only the city as a whole but also the communities that compose it. What are the characteristics of and trends within these communities? How do the differences between communities affect the responsibility and program of the church?

Untested judgments concerning present community traits and future prospects are commonly inaccurate. More than casual observation is needed if one is to understand the basic traits and problems of the residents. Superficial conclusions can be tested and perhaps corrected by interviewing such people as the principal of the public school, the social case worker, the visiting nurse, the captain at the police station, the postman, storekeepers, old residents. For the thoughtful observer even informal conversations with children will shed light on community life. However, to obtain an accurate and unbiased picture of the city and its communities more complete and objective studies can be made, using the wealth of information which is available from many sources.[1]

Four major community types

Urban communities present an endless variety of patterns, from abysmal poverty to great wealth, from marked social disorganization to wholesome integration and solidity, from extreme mobility to relative permanency. Income, community consciousness, and permanency of residence are but a few of the many possible differentiating criteria. No matter which trait is studied, it will be found that communities are in a continuum from one extreme to the other.

[1] See Appendix A, which describes criteria for characterizing and classifying communities.

However, for purposes of description it is necessary to establish representative types. While recognizing that no two communities in a city are exactly alike, we can group them in a few major classifications. Admittedly these must be somewhat arbitrarily defined. The simplest and most objective criteria, and also the ones most easily applied, are rent, age and physical condition of housing, and crowding. Using these criteria, we may establish three general community types, into one of which any urban residence area will fall. The central business district constitutes a fourth type by itself and has a distinctive physical and functional relation to the rest of the city. The four types which are discussed in detail in following chapters are:

1. *The Downtown Business Section.* Occupied by stores, hotels, and theaters, this is not itself a community, because its population is largely transient and manifests no sense of commonality. However, it has its own characteristics and presents for the church unique problems and opportunities.

2. *Areas of Transition and Underprivilege.* These communities are characterized by much old, deteriorated housing, and are sometimes referred to as blighted areas or slums. Land values and rents are the lowest in the city. Social disorganization and delinquency are conspicuous. These are the areas of immigrant settlements and the major Negro communities.

3. *Stable Communities.* Intermediate between communities in process of decline and those which are registering rapid growth are most of the communities of the city. These range all the way from sections used chiefly by workingmen living in modest, aging, but well-maintained houses, to upper-middle-class areas where many professional persons, proprietors, and other business people live in comfortable private residences. The common elements among all of these communities are that most of the land is built up, the housing generally dates back twenty years or more but is in good condition, there is generally a high proportion of home ownership and little delinquency, and the residents have a sense of belonging.

4. *Areas of Growth.* These communities are usually farther out from the center of the city than those in the preceding classifications, and are characterized by new housing and young families. There is less crowding, and the people are generally in the middle- and upper-income levels. One must add, however, that nearly every city has some suburban slums similar in many respects to the areas of decline.

Within each of the four preceding types there is considerable diversity in population composition and community prospect. Ensuing chapters will describe these major community patterns and their variants, and delineate the opportunities and problems in churching them. Attention will first be directed toward the stable community, since it is the most representative and the most familiar.

CHAPTER SEVEN

The Stable Community

PHOTOGRAPHIC studies of American cities are nearly always concerned with the tall aspiring office buildings and the imposing sky lines of a metropolis. Or with industry, steel mills belching smoke, Bessemer furnaces throwing out shafts of molten light. Or with mammoth factories and bordering railroads. Sometimes they deal with the areas of poverty and vice, and occasionally with new suburban developments. Rarely is attention given to the endless blocks of pleasant but unpretentious houses and small apartment buildings in long-established residential neighborhoods.

Yet it is in communities of the latter type that two thirds of the city dwellers live. These are the stable areas which give coherency and a measure of permanency to city life. Few of the buildings have been erected since the stock market crash of 1929, but nearly all are in good repair and manifest a certain pride in ownership. One has the impression of adequate, durable housing built to sustain wholesome American family life.

Occasionally, particularly in smaller and medium-sized cities, a stable community will be found adjoining the central business district; but usually such areas lie somewhat farther out, beyond the rim of deteriorating, obsolescent homes which constitute the "inner city." [1] They tend to be on high, well-drained land, removed from railroad yards and the major industrial sections—especially if the industry is noisy, smoky, or malodorous. They are also to be distinguished from the burgeoning suburban developments on the outskirts of the city.[2]

Stable communities, where the patterns of individual and community living are in the main settled and dependable, deserve major attention in the study of the city and its institutions. They are geographically extensive, occupying the major portion of the land which is used for residence purposes.[3] More important, the people who dwell there make up the bulk of the population and the main support of the civic structure. Since these

---

[1] See Chap. X.

[2] See Chap. XII.

[3] Approximately 25 per cent of the area of every city is used for streets and alleys. Railroads, industries, lumber yards, parks, and cemeteries occupy a large additional acreage.

areas are unspectacular, they commonly escape not only the photographers but many other analysts of urban life. There the police and the crime reporter have little business, and politics is a less noisy and ostentatious affair.

Physical characteristics of the stable community

The typical stable community, whether it comprises chiefly single-family residences or apartment houses, has certain general characteristics. Some of these are physical, others social.

1. *It is a built-up area.* Ordinarily less than 10 per cent of the building sites stand vacant. Where as many as a third of the lots are unused,[4] the future development of the community remains somewhat in doubt, and householders feel less confidence in the character of their neighborhood. Lots that have stood vacant while the community was growing old become less attractive to people who are contemplating building a new home. They prefer a more recent development which offers the advantages of modernity.

2. *Stable communities are used essentially for residential purposes.* In present-day American cities such areas are usually protected by zoning laws against the infiltration of industry. Where industry creeps in, because of poor zoning laws or relaxing of the ordinance, elements of instability are introduced.

3. *Ordinarily there will be a commercial development somewhere near by,* along the main thoroughfare leading out from downtown. Grocery stores, bakeries, repair shops, gasoline stations form a little nucleus of business to render convenient service for people living on the adjoining streets.

4. *The majority of stable communities in American cities were occupied prior to the beginning of the great depression.* They are neither pristine and ultramodern nor dilapidated. The frame and stucco houses have had numerous coats of paint, and the brick structures have been tuck-pointed once or twice. But the fact of significance is that the buildings are of a permanent type and in good repair. By its very nature a community does not become thoroughly established until some years have passed after the completion of most of the buildings. Temporary housing, which sprang up mushroom-like during and following World War II, cannot furnish the basis for a stable community.

5. *The homes are reasonably comfortable,* equipped with hot and cold running water, electric lights, and sanitary facilities. Most homes and apart-

---

[4] By vacant property is meant salable building lots. For example, the term does not include the additional lot adjoining a single-family residence if this constitutes part of the family establishment and is not for sale. If it is subsequently put on the market, it then becomes vacant property.

ment houses, particularly in the northern United States, are warmed by central heating. Poorly equipped homes are an inducement to mobility.

6. *There has been little doubling up or overcrowding of families* in stable — communities except during the acute housing shortage of the middle 1940's.

The stable community is a pleasant section of the city. However, although it is well cared for, there are some earmarks of change. It is like a person of middle age—mature but not aged. To use an analogy, the metabolism of life balances rather evenly the anabolic or upbuilding and the catabolic or destructive processes. The community is not static, but maintains a relatively even balance, neither booming nor declining.

Social characteristics

Family patterns and life organization in stable areas reflect the balancing of forces which is seen in the physical structure of the community.

1. *These families constitute the bulk of the great middle and upper classes of urban America.* The people enjoy their homes and feel that they need make no apology when they give their street address. They have adequate resources to maintain a satisfactory "American standard of living." Their social traits reflect their economic status. They think of themselves as substantial, responsible citizens. In contrast people who are in penury cannot live in such a favorable situation, in spite of their desire to do so; and on the other hand the restless and the aggressive, ambitious young couples, social climbers, and some of the wealthy prefer to move into newer homes in a developing area.

2. Since these are long-established communities, *the proportion of persons* — *past forty-five years of age is greater than for the city as a whole,* and consequently there are fewer small children. This is particularly true in single-family residence areas. Also the two sexes are rather well balanced numerically, for these are communities of homes, in contrast to the rooming-house areas, which cater more to single men and women. Here the family is the normal social group. This factor itself adds appreciably to the sense of permanency and social adjustment.

3. *Community consciousness and the sense of civic responsibility are* — *more marked than in other portions of the city,* although these traits vary with the amount of mobility and the extent of home ownership. The mobility rate is lower and the home ownership rate higher in single-family-residence than in apartment-house areas. Yet, regardless of the type of dwelling, men and women expect their streets to be clean and the parkways properly maintained. They grumble if children scatter papers on the sidewalk, and complain to one another if the janitor in the corner apartment house or the neighbor down the street fails to keep his grass trimmed. They turn out in large numbers when the public school holds its special exercises,

and respond to the request of churches and schools for clothing and food for overseas relief.

4. *The social institutions—schools and churches, libraries and the park recreation center—are generally adequate to community needs.* There is money for the development of their programs, and plants are in good condition. People are determined to give their children advantages. Organizations like the Boy Scouts and the Y.M.C.A. are well supported, and it is less difficult to secure volunteer counselors than in areas of underprivilege, where parents often feel incapable of exercising any leadership, or in areas of rapid growth, where people for one reason or another may regard themselves as too busy to undertake community tasks.

These stable communities have an important function to perform in preserving American culture. They are, in fact, replacing rural America as the main repository of the sense of civic responsibility and what has sometimes been condescendingly called "middle-class morality." For more than a century the rural community served as the conscience and mentor of the nation. It voiced and maintained the ethical standards and political principles which influenced national as well as local legislation. When rural society was most effective in this respect, it was least aware of the important contribution it was making. When, however, it began to lose its influence —because of its relative decline in size, loss of the family-farm idea, and the rise of urbanism—and to become more mobile and urban in pattern of thought, both it and the nation first became aware of the role it had played. Never again will rural society set the tone for American life. The conserving influence which it once represented must be exercised, if it is to exist at all, by the stable communities of the all-too-mobile cities.

Types of stable communities

The term "stability" may be applied to urban communities in two ways. When the city planner uses it, he ordinarily refers to the permanency of the physical structures in an area. Under this definition communities occupied predominantly by apartment houses or apartment hotels may be counted as stable. Since the buildings have been well constructed and are protected by zoning laws, it is anticipated that they will have a life span of not less than fifty or seventy-five years.

When the sociologist discusses community, he is thinking more in terms of population characteristics than physical structures, although the two are closely related. To him stability means either (1) the population is well established and has a low rate of turnover, or (2) the general *type* of population in an area will remain relatively constant over a period of at least two or three decades, that is, the people entering will have approximately the same social and economic characteristics as those who are leaving. In the first instance the people remain; in the second the population pattern is constant but the individuals change. In either case there is social continuity, the maintenance of the same population traits and institutional life. The definition of the sociologist is more comprehensive and is not inconsistent with the usage of the city planner. It calls attention to the fact that stability is a social rather than primarily a physical matter. For instance, even an apartment hotel can maintain the same character for several decades, in spite of the fact that the average length of residence may be less than a year.

Stable communities may be made up of single-family dwellings, two-flat buildings, or apartments. But in each the buildings are well constructed, will continue to perform their present function, and will over the years tend to serve the same type of population. However, when single-family residences predominate, tenure is generally longer and the mobility rate relatively low.

1. *The Single-Family Residence Area.* The most common type of stable community, found in small as well as large cities, is made up of single-family residences. More than half of the homes—frequently as high as 80 per cent—are occupied by their owners. The fact of possession makes people hesitant to move, and pride of ownership stimulates the desire to keep the property in good condition. There is friendly rivalry with others along the street to keep hedges, lawns, and flowers attractive. When one repaints his house, others follow suit.

The house was purchased in the first place to serve as a home, and it has become over the years the locus of family traditions and affection. Ordinarily the people who bought homes or moved into a community of this type either had a family at the time or expected to start one. As a corollary, the husband is usually the wage earner and the wife the homemaker. The children form a bond of common interest along the street. The women attend the same Parent-Teacher Association meetings and sometimes belong to the same church group. The men ride to town on the same bus and talk over politics as they work on the lawns on Saturday afternoons. They sometimes swap tools and rosebush cuttings with an openhanded friendliness which causes all to feel, "What a pleasant neighborhood this is to live in."

As years pass, children grow up and move away from home, but the parents tend to remain. Some younger families move into the community, although the higher the land values the more difficult it will be for young couples to establish themselves there. Usually the average age of the residents slowly rises, and the enrollment in the public school declines. The area becomes more sedate and the streets more quiet. In communities of this type the disturbing, disintegrating effect of our urban industrial society is least violent. Here there is little anonymity, and the social relationships of the people are most similar to those of the small town.

2. *The Area of the Two-Flat Buildings.* In many cities, particularly where land values are high, some neighborhoods are zoned and used for two-flat buildings or duplexes. A two-flat building is a two-story structure, the first floor occupied by one family and the second, similar in floor plan, by another. In the duplex the two dwelling units are divided by a wall through the center, one family on each side. A variant which is being increasingly used is a revival of the common-wall row house. In this case as many as ten or twenty dwelling units stand side by side, each dividing wall being shared by two units. In modern construction these units are generally staggered or are irregularly arranged to permit adequate lighting and variety in appearance. Frequently they are grouped about a common courtyard.

All of these devices permit a more intensive use of land and keep down the cost, while still giving the occupant most of the advantages of a single-family residence. The home ownership rate is as a rule somewhat lower than in single-family residence areas. Ordinarily the owner will live in the first-floor flat or on one side of the duplex and rent the other dwelling, although such structures are often owned in partnership by two families. Similarly some of the new party-wall houses are owned on a co-operative basis. Under such an arrangement each partner or co-operative member has the responsibility for maintaining his own dwelling unit, and also the privilege, within limits, of doing what he wishes with it. Although land use is more intensive and there is less privacy, areas of this type have much more in common with neighborhoods of single-family residences than with apartment-house districts.

3. *The Apartment-House District.* The apartment house is a device for still more intensive use of the land. A plot 50 by 150 feet which would be deemed suitable for one single-family residence may, in high land value areas of a city, be used for an apartment building containing from six to eighteen dwelling units. Such structures usually are three stories plus basement in height, as people object to climbing more than three flights to their apartment. Taller edifices are found in large cities, but unless land values are very high it is uneconomical to erect apartment buildings of five or more stories, since elevator service and many other facilities must be provided.

Only in a few of the metropolitan cities, such as New York and San Francisco, will whole communities be found which are occupied predominantly by apartment houses. In smaller cities they play a minor role. They are generally built in good residential districts which are either within easy walking distance of the center of the city or are served by excellent transportation. Preferably they are located on corners, which furnish a maximum of light and air—important advantages where families are crowded close together. Often single-family dwellings or duplexes occupy the rest of the block.

From the point of view of the apartment-house owner, whether an individual or a corporation, the structure is primarily an investment which must pay reasonable returns. It is to his interest to have it well constructed and maintained so that it will continue to rent well for fifty years or more. It is therefore a stabilizing factor in the community.

Few apartment-house dwellers—generally less than 5 per cent—own the homes in which they reside. An inevitable result of the low rate of ownership, except in a period of housing shortage, is a high turnover rate of occupants. This, however, varies with the apartment-house type and the degree of stability of the community as a whole. In one- or two-room apartments the turnover rate is much higher than in the five- or six-room units. In the former the major items of furniture are provided by the owner, and the tenant can assemble his earthly goods and move to another location with the aid of a taxicab. This type of apartment is preferred by young people in the city simply because it involves little investment in furniture and a minimum of responsibility. Change of occupancy is less frequent in larger apartments, which are as a rule rented unfurnished and to established families.

Apartment-house areas do not have a normal distribution of population, such as characterizes the city as a whole. Some landlords object to renting to families with children, although they will not dispossess established tenants if a baby is born to them. Further, apartment-house living is not particularly suitable for children,[5] especially after they reach the age of five

[5] Jane Sayre, in her poem "Apartment-House Crooning," has amusingly described the process of developing inhibitions in the apartment-house child:

> Hush, my darling, sleep and grow;
>   Be as quiet as a mouse;
> You are not too young to know
>   This is an apartment house.
>
> Hush, my little darling, please!
>   Mrs. Jones despises boys.
> She has trained her Pekingese
>   Not to make the slightest noise.
>
> Mrs. Smith, who lives above,
>   Tapped the floor. Oh, think of that!
> Can't you be, my little love,
>   Quiet as her Persian cat?
>
> Dogs and cats and boys, my dear,
>   Must in silence bear their woes.
> Tenants only want to hear
>   Sound effects—on radios!

From the *Saturday Evening Post,* Dec. 9, 1933. Used by permission.

or six. Parents of small children who have been living in an apartment house generally seek some other type of accommodations before the time comes when they must send their first youngster to school. The result is that in apartment-house districts there are many young couples who have only very young children or none at all, and older people whose families have gone out from the parental home.

Those who dwell under an apartment-house roof must make many adjustments that are not required of people in private homes. They must observe the rules of the building, keep out of each other's way, stay off the scanty lawn, usually forgo the keeping of a pet dog or cat, turn the radio off by eleven o'clock, and so on. In spite of the fact that they live in such proximity to one another, apartment-house dwellers commonly do not consider their near neighbors as intimate friends, and frequently do not know them at all.

Not owning their home, and having no permanent stake in the community, they do not possess the same sense of community spirit and responsibility which characterizes the people in private homes or duplexes. They are in the area but have no particular feeling of obligation to maintain it in its present physical condition—that duty devolves on the owner and the janitor. The majority of them will not give to the community charities drive unless pressure is exerted at the place of employment. The proportion of citizens who exercise their franchise is also low.

Here there is less community support for the institution of the family. Either the neighbors do not know about the marital conflict between the husband and wife in the third-floor-west apartment, or they simply shrug their shoulders. The community exerts little restraining influence on the vagaries of personality, except through the formal control of law and the rules of the house.

4. *The Apartment Hotel.* The apartment hotel is an extreme development of the large apartment building. In it the dwelling units rarely comprise more than two rooms with a diminutive kitchen cabinet built in a section of one wall; tenants are expected to take their guests to the hotel dining room. The apartment hotel, which may contain more than two hundred dwelling units, affords even less opportunity for family privacy than the apartment house. In fact, it is a high-class, expensive rooming house occupied by people who wish to escape housekeeping responsibilities. Elderly persons, especially women, single men, and childless couples enjoy living in these quarters. No children romp in the lobby, but instead sedate, elderly bridge foursomes will be seen. At the insistence of the women, barkless dogs are often permitted. These people, while perhaps living many years in the same apartment, have little sense of responsibility for community life

outside the hotel. Although they may frequently be lonesome and in need of ministry, it is difficult for the church to serve them.

Stability and change

From a consideration of the different types of stable community it is clear that there are two major variables influencing community life. The one is the extent to which the community seems to be permanent and fixed in its physical appearance, the other the degree of social continuity and integration. A stable community does not come into existence as soon as new housing is erected but only after most of the land has been occupied, the people have settled down in their new habitat, and social institutions have developed. It is not stable until it has had time to acquire a character, an integrated personality of its own.

The passage of the years brings physical and social changes. These may not be of any significance for many decades; then in some sections single-family residences may give way to large apartment houses, or, on the other hand, they may be permitted to deteriorate, and a general process of decline may set in. At first there are only a few signs of change. Some may not be noticed; others disturb the neighbors. No one innovation in itself seems crucial, but they are evidences of a gradual transformation in the community life. As they accumulate, many of the old-timers, once so proud of Chatham Square, talk of moving out to the new subdivision. Others quietly sell before an expected decline in property values occurs. Each of these changes sets others in motion. The process may take twenty years, or it may occur within two; but after it is well under way, the community may no longer be designated as stable.

CHAPTER EIGHT

Churches in Stable Communities

THE development of an urban community is usually as uneven as the growth of a child—everything does not happen at once or in a completely predictable fashion. However, by the time a community can qualify as "stable," that is, by the time it is largely built up and has a settled type of population, its social institutions are firmly rooted and flourishing. By then the public school has its traditional Christmas and spring programs, and a few of the older teachers remember when the parents of some of the present pupils were in school. By then the West End Businessmen, the official community boosters, have for many years sponsored Halloween parties to keep the youngsters out of mischief, and a fireworks display in the local park on the night of July Fourth.

The churches of several denominations are also well established. They have outgrown the tents and stores in which they began, and even the first small bungalow structures on their own lots. Now they are in their "permanent homes," though some are still in debt. Churches, like the other local institutions, are an accepted part of the community life and represent the interests and loyalties of the people.

The stable community the natural habitat of the city church

The well-established urban residential community, particularly when it is made up of single-family residences, furnishes an environment similar to that of the small town. Here urban restlessness and mobility are at a minimum. Most of the families live in their own homes, and renters, when forced to relocate, try to find a suitable house somewhere near by. This is particularly characteristic of the nucleus of the community—the portion which gives the area its distinguishing traits. Many of the businessmen went to high school together and played on the same teams. Now they are the strong support for civic organizations and the local churches. These people regard themselves as substantial citizens, conscientious, middle-of-the-road Americans. They are the upholders of community law and order, rather comfortably situated; radicalism of any form is far from them.

These people in overwhelming majority have a Protestant background. This may be taken for granted in the South, which, except for the area around New Orleans, is traditionally Protestant, and where until recently even a large city might have only one Roman Catholic church and a small synagogue. It is also generally true in northern and western cities. The non-Protestant whites—Roman Catholics and Jews, who in the main have arrived more recently from Europe and have a lower economic status—and Negroes have tended to be the predominant group in blighted and near-blighted areas, where rents are low, while whites with a Protestant background have been the dominant population element in the middle and upper-middle class or stable communities.

These communities, therefore, are the most congenial for the white, Protestant church, which moved in along with the people. Here it has been able to continue with the same type of program and attitudes that characterized it in the small town. It has not been forced to make serious adjustments to urban life and problems. In the stable community, if anywhere in the city, Protestantism should be able to make a comprehensive and vital contribution to personal and community living. Yet often, even in this most favorable environment, the church is not spectacularly successful.

Characteristics of churches

Protestant churches located within a stable community have much in common—like children reared in a family—although no two, even in the same denomination, conform exactly to the same pattern. They differ in location, membership selection, effectiveness of ministerial and lay leadership, and influence. However, most of the Protestant churches in stable communities had similar beginnings and now share a few significant traits.

1. *Initial Local Interest.* A vital church springs out of the desire of people within the community to have a religious ministry for themselves and their children. They may be fortunate enough to receive some skilled guidance and perhaps financial assistance from the city missionary society of the denomination to help them in the initial stages of organization. But no matter how alert and energetic the missionary society, if its overtures do not meet with a co-operative response from the people it cannot hope to foster in the community a strong, permanent institution. The reason that there are so many well-established churches in stable urban communities is that when they were being settled a generation or more ago the people regarded religion as of vital importance and took it for granted that they must have a church. The early history of churches located in what are now stable communities is marked with self-sacrifice and zeal. Typical is this account, taken from a "golden anniversary" booklet:

A great deal of the material for the church was donated, and much of the work was done by members themselves. Mr. L—— gave all the posts needed for the underpinning of the building. The lathing and laying of the floors was done by those in the community who could come and help.

Homes were mortgaged to meet the bills. Coal was carried from homes of members to heat the church, all through the snow, slush, and mud, in order that a great church might find its roots and a firm foundation be built where the word of God could be preached through the years to come. During the next spring, when the bills for lumber came due and the church had not received sufficient funds to meet them, Brothers P——, C——, and S—— mortgaged their homes to guarantee the payment and keep the credit of the church good.

2. *A Central Location and a Permanent Building.* Generally the church is situated within two or three blocks of the small business center of the community and is often near the public school. There is an advantage in having a central location, readily accessible to all. Occasionally a denominational official responsible for the placement of a church is parsimonious in his use of funds and buys a "bargain lot" toward the edge of the community or on lower ground. This usually proves to be poor economy.

The church in a stable residential area is as a rule housed in a well-constructed, durable edifice which approximates the quality of the better homes. If it is definitely inferior in appearance, its members are apologetic and have difficulty in winning new adherents.

3. *A Local Membership.* A church of this type is dependent on the people of the local community. Unlike the downtown church, which can attract adherents from the whole of the city, or an institution in an area of underprivilege, which can claim loyalty and support of outsiders on the basis of its need, this church must justify itself and find its support among people who live near by. Usually about three fourths of its active members live within walking distance. Ordinarily men and boys constitute a larger proportion of the membership—40 to 45 per cent—than in downtown or blighted area churches, where the figure frequently drops to 35 per cent. This is a family area, and husbands and fathers participate actively in community institutions.

4. *A Combination of Professional and Lay Leadership.* This typical church always has a full-time minister and usually some other full- or part-time paid staff members, such as organist, choir director, and sexton. Larger establishments may have, in addition, two or three full-time ministers, a director of religious education, parish visitor, and secretary. The size and compensation of the staff are limited by the strength and economic status of the membership.

Much of the work of the church, perhaps more than in other types of communities, is accomplished through the efforts of unpaid lay workers. The officers and teachers of the church school, counselors of youth groups, officers of the women's organization and the men's club, are all volunteers and constitute the living framework on which the program of the church depends. Some may have been reluctant to accept their responsibilities; a few may be poorly trained or socially inept. Nevertheless, there is no other agency within the community which receives such a generous gift of time and talents as the local church.

5. *A Conventional Program.* The typical residential church is less highly specialized than its sisters in the downtown and "mission" areas of the city. The main elements of its program are conventional, similar to those in the small town: a Sunday morning worship service and in some areas, especially in the South, a less formal evening service; a religious education program for children and youth—although by high-school age approximately half drop out—and a few adult classes, which are relatively well attended; a women's society, usually the most active group within the church, reaching some who have no other contact with organized religion; a youth organization for social friendliness as well as serious discussion; and a number of all-church functions—occasional dinners and programs which afford an opportunity for fellowship. In some churches this program is elaborated, with many committees and a wide spread of activities. Since the stable community consists chiefly of families, many phases of the program, including the church school, may be built around the family and parent-child relationships. The program is most effective when it grows out of the people's interests and efforts and constitutes the center for much of their social as well as their religious life.

Problems of churches

No living organization is free from problems, and churches even in stable communities are no exception. This is not a situation to be deplored, but a challenge to thoughtfulness and an opportunity for growth. Some problems they share with all other churches: the perennial tasks of reaching new members, training lay leadership, and raising adequate funds are not the exclusive concern of churches in residential communities. Each of these topics will be dealt with in a separate chapter.[1]

There are, however, several problems which rise out of the nature of the stable community, the common interests of the people, and their tendency toward social and religious conservatism.

1. *Parochialism.* Because the active members of the church in a pleasant community have so many interests in common, the church itself may be in danger of becoming ingrown. The people within the fellowship enjoy their church life and are content to keep it as it is. At how many churches would a stranger have an experience similar to the one described by a visitor to a small neighborhood church:

[1] See Chaps. XVI-XVIII.

Immediately following the benediction there was a general buzz of conversation in all parts of the auditorium. People obviously knew one another well and gathered in little knots to talk over matters of mutual interest. A number of women that I passed were talking about officers for their society. Groups of men, standing around waiting for their wives, were bantering one another, and a cluster of young people chattered gaily. As I walked from my pew to the door, I noticed two men counting the collection in a room just off the lobby.

No one spoke to me, although a few cast curious glances in my direction. At the door the minister shook my hand vigorously: "Good morning. Glad you were here. Hope you will come again."

This situation is serious enough while the community remains stable because, although the church is serving a small group well, it is not living up to its full potential. It is willing to receive any who ask to join its fellowship, but it does not go out of its way to gain new members. If it does not develop the habit of encouraging the outsider to participate in the church activities, an ingrown society will dwindle even though population increases. More unfortunate for the church will be the sequel: when population begins to move rapidly, the church is bound to lose membership at an increasing rate, even though the number of people in the area remains constant.

2. *Self-Centeredness of the Program.* A corollary of the parochial interest of members is seen in the program of the church itself. The people have heard many sermons on evangelism and the missionary enterprise, and, at least in theory, they believe in these aspects of the church's endeavor. They would be glad to see the church at large increase in size and influence. But for most of them the work of the denomination and of ecumenical Christianity is a far-off and tenuous affair. Their energy and practically all of the funds which they raise are expended on their own organization. Frequently the only monetary support given to the benevolent enterprises of their denomination comes from the women's society or the monthly "missionary collection" in the church school. Excellent as is the program of the local church in residential communities, it often needs to be expanded and vitalized, with more attention given to the civic responsibilities of members, the social implications of the Christian message, and the world-wide enterprises of the church.

3. *Long Leadership Tenure.* One unfortunate result of ingrowth is that the same persons exercise leadership year after year. This commonly occurs in churches in stable communities, where a few men and women continue to hold the principal offices. They are willing and capable, and so they are re-elected, as no one wishes to offend them, and qualified volunteers rarely assert themselves. In a more dynamic organization this problem usually does not arise.

4. *Movement of Leaders.* The church tends to elect to office persons who

have somewhat higher income and status. Yet it is these who are most likely to move out of the community into a developing suburb. They commonly continue to hold their offices and exercise much influence on the financing and planning of the church's program although they may have moved several miles away. This may have unfortunate results for the church, since people who live out of the community have divided loyalties.

These four problems become more acute as the community grows older, though the seeds of them may be seen even in newer areas. The marooned church in an underprivileged community manifests them in an exaggerated form.[2] It is important that they be dealt with while they are still of manageable proportions. To neglect them is to invite a situation which may in time result in the closing of the church.

Apartment-house people and the church

Few areas can be designated as apartment-house communities except in cities of 200,000 or more. But in many a smaller city apartment houses line one or two of the streets within what would otherwise be a single-family residence community. These composite communities manifest many of the traits to be seen in the more highly congested apartment-house areas of a metropolis; the difference is one of degree rather than of kind.

Understandably, the attitudes of apartment-house dwellers in religious as well as other matters are affected by their manner of living. This fact must be taken into account by a church which hopes to reach them. Many churches located in a community made up predominantly of private homes simply overlook the people in near-by apartments, assuming that if they wish to come of course they will, and if they come they will be welcome. Illustrative of the common neglect of apartment-house dwellers, and of the way in which the situation may be remedied, is the following case.

Trinity Church is located in a high-income suburban community. In the past twenty years it has grown rapidly and now has a membership of 1,200, who have comfortable incomes; most own their homes.

A recent study was made to determine whether it would be advisable to relocate farther west, away from the apartment houses which were crowding in around the near-by commuters' station. Analysis of the membership distribution showed that in the seven blocks of apartment houses the church at that time had 32 members. No special effort had been made to enlist the interest of the apartment dwellers. They did not live in the community for long and, since they were younger and had lower incomes, they did not feel particularly at home when they attended the church.

Leaders of the church, after studying the results of the survey, came to the conclusion that their present location was an advantage rather than a disadvantage.

[2] See pp. 98-99.

If it moved west, into an area which was being rapidly built up with single-family dwellings, the church would gain some new members, but it would surely lose others who would then be farther away. And it would be moving from a more densely occupied section where, the leaders became convinced, the ministry of the church was particularly needed. The decision was made to stay. The physical plant and equipment have since been improved and a church visitor has been employed who is giving her chief attention to winning the interest and participation of apartment-house people. The church and church school have both continued to grow, although the total population has increased little in the last few years.

To follow the earlier policy of this church and neglect the apartment-house residents is in the long run poor strategy for the local church and for the denomination. If the young married couples in these apartments have no vital contact with the church during their two- or three-year stay in the area, not only does the church fail to minister to their needs at the time, but they also become much poorer prospects at a later date and elsewhere.

If a church is surrounded almost exclusively by multiple dwellings and continues to disregard the families living in them, it will certainly, even though slowly, die of attrition.

The Palmer Park Methodist Church has had a long and varied history. Twenty years ago its membership reached a peak of 562 and then began to decline, as brownstone residences were replaced by brick apartment houses. In four years the church had lost half its members; financial support dwindled. Most of the leaders now lived two or three miles to the west. By the time the Reverend Robert R—— was appointed the people were discouraged, and many thought the church would have to be closed. Only a minority of the 250 members were active. The church school was a third its former size.

The new pastor, a hearty, vigorous man in middle years with a talent for pastoral work, plotted the membership on a map. He discovered that over half lived beyond walking distance, while less than two score came from the near-by apartments. With the aid of a few alert young people he canvassed the area within four blocks of the church and discovered more than three hundred persons who were members in some Methodist church or at least had had some Methodist background.

After two years of strenuous work the pastor could report only 117 active members. But they were people who actually lived in the community and participated in the church program. It was then that his labors began to bring more obvious results. In the next four years 295 persons were received from preparatory membership or on profession of faith, and 54 came in by transfer. Three more years have now passed, and the membership has been steadily built up until there are 476 members, most of them residing in the immediate neighborhood. Such is the mobility within the area that a minimum of fifty members must be recruited each year to make up for losses.

The erection of apartment houses always creates problems for a church accustomed to a permanent, home-owning population. Uncounted churches in such situations are closed because of loss of members and of financial support, when all about them are men and women who need the ministration of the church. For one reason or another these near neighbors do not themselves make contact with the church. Too often the minister, instead of taking advantage of the possibilities offered by the increased population, becomes discouraged because they seem unreachable, and seeks another parish. His successor receives a somewhat smaller salary, feels that the church is fighting a losing battle, and he too soon leaves. So a church limps from discouragement to discouragement until finally it totters into a church merger or directly to its demise. There are indeed circumstances in which it is necessary to close a church. But a great many of those which have been closed could have continued as effective organizations had there been vigorous pastoral leadership and wise planning and supervisory work on the part of denominational officers.

No urban area is static. *If it is to be effective, the church dare not be less dynamic than the community itself.* Only diligent canvassing of the community for new people, regular reviewing of the program, and wise recruitment and training of lay leadership will maintain the church as a virile institution.

CHAPTER NINE

The Downtown District
and "Old First"

EVERY town and city has a main business section which is in fact a summation of its economic, political, and social life and a sensitive barometer of its prosperity. The banks and stores, doctors' and lawyers' offices, hotels and theaters, reflect the standard of living of the people. The larger the population and the higher the living standard, the more extensive and prosperous this central district. A shabby, ill-kept Main Street, with many vacant stores, unpainted fronts, and dusty window displays, is a telltale symptom of civic apathy and economic decline.

The continued growth of a city is paralleled by a steady expansion of its downtown area. This expansion takes place in two directions, up and out. Taller hotels, department stores, and office buildings are erected along the main thoroughfare, since this is the choice and most accessible location. Simultaneously new, though less pretentious, structures fill in the adjoining blocks where old buildings have been cleared away. The process continues as the city grows larger until, in a metropolis such as Philadelphia, St. Louis, or Los Angeles, the downtown district may occupy a square mile, with the development along the most desirable streets extending even farther. When because of physical reasons—hemming in by rivers or hills, or scarcity of land—it is difficult to incorporate new downtown territory (as in Pittsburgh or New York), the incentive to erect higher buildings is all the greater.

The people who live downtown

Although it is crowded with workers and shoppers during daytime hours and again with entertainment seekers in the evening, the business district has a relatively small and highly selected resident population. Ordinarily there are no single-family homes and few apartment houses within its borders. Those who occupy its hotels and rooming houses are chiefly transients, visiting the city on a business trip, attending a convention, or enjoying a honeymoon. Most of the transients are men past twenty-five years of age.

Yet there are always some permanent residents. In a city of 25,000 a few of the proprietors occupy inconspicuous apartments above or in back of their shops: the men who run the Chinese laundry, the Greek confectioner and restaurateur and his family. Not many couples with children are found downtown; people who wish a well-rounded home life prefer one of the residential districts. However, some individuals enjoy the activity and even the noise and bustle of the city, and would feel lost in a quiet section of town. These may lodge for forty or more years in the same hotel room, perhaps six stories above the roar and jangle of downtown traffic. They generally are nonfamily people, more often men than women, persons who make up for a sense of deep loneliness by being in the midst of activity day and night.

The downtown church in the smaller city

The city was still in its infancy, a mere hamlet in size, when the first church was built, one short block from the main crossroads. Population multiplied; the number of houses and stores increased; and the church found itself first at the edge of, and then completely surrounded by, the hustling business district. A neat bronze plaque calls attention to the fact that here the first house of worship in N—— was erected in 1827. The present edifice, an impressive gray-stone building, is the third structure on this site. Other churches were established by different denominations, but, as land values rose and population moved away from the business congestion, several of these followed their members to pleasanter districts. One sold its site to an expanding department store, and another for hotel purposes. Now that the city has reached a population of nineteen thousand, "Old First" alone remains downtown near the courthouse.

There is no other church so well known. The pastor is called on to participate in civic affairs and is interviewed on controversial issues by newspaper reporters. He is requested by people from all over the city to conduct weddings and funerals. There are now three other churches of the same denomination in N——, located in as many different outlying portions of the city, but no one of them is known except to the people in its immediate vicinity.

First Church assisted in the establishment of these other congregations. Two of them grew out of Sunday schools conducted by its members. Later, with some financial assistance from the mother church, lots were purchased and small frame buildings erected. Two of the younger congregations, Brock Hill and Homewood, are now worshiping in attractive, substantial structures. Each has a full-time minister and a membership of approximately three hundred. The third, Brown Memorial, located in a low-income industrial area, has had a more precarious existence. For twenty years its membership has hovered around one hundred. It still occupies its first and now feeble frame building, and is served by a student pastor.

Old First is a strong, flourishing organization with more than twelve hundred members. Business and professional leaders of the city are on its board of stewards. It is free of debt and has no serious difficulty in raising $24,000 each year to meet its budget. It has an outstanding minister, known in the city for his preaching ability. An associate pastor assists with the calling and has direct charge of the young people's program and religious education. An organist-choir director, a secretary, and a sexton complete the staff.

1. *Its Membership.* The membership of the church, which fifty years ago lived within a few blocks, is now scattered through the city and adjoining suburbs. A large number come from the communities of Brock Hill and Homewood. Members of Old First are proud of their church and its long record of distinguished service. They find satisfaction in telling their friends that they attend there. A few of the men are aware that leadership in its activities "does them no harm."

On Sunday mornings each Main Street bus brings its complement of children for the church school, and the near-by streets are lined with parked cars during the worship service. There are elderly people in the congregation who have loyally attended and worked through many years of the church's history. Young people in their twenties, alone or in couples, make up a fourth of the congregation. Later, when they have children who are past kindergarten age, many of them will decide to send the children to the church school in Brock Hill or Homewood, where they themselves may join. Over half of the worshipers are in their middle years, from thirty to sixty. A few elderly widows from one of the downtown residence hotels, visiting businessmen, and other transients are scattered through the congregation.

2. *Relation to Other Churches in the City.* A friendly and usually unmentioned rivalry exists between First Church and the smaller community churches. Brown Memorial, to be sure, regards itself as permanently a mission church and has no hope of competing with the ministry of Old First. The pastors and congregations of the other two are located in communities where the downtown church also finds much of its support. In fact, some of the residents within the very block where Brock Hill is located are members of Old First; and the pastor of the Homewood Church was openly irritated when the best soprano in his volunteer choir accepted a paid position in the downtown quartet. These tensions are, however, minor. The relationship among the ministers is cordial and co-operative. The young people from the different churches occasionally have joint meetings, and the architect who drew plans for the Homewood Church donated his

services because, as a member of Old First, he had long been interested in the daughter institution.

A measure of competition is inevitable between the downtown and community churches in such a city as N——. If it is kept within Christian bounds, it may indeed prove a wholesome and stimulating influence. Occasionally, however, a downtown church develops a sense of proprietorship for the religious life of the whole city and struggles to prevent the establishment of any other congregation of its own denomination, even after the city reaches a population of 25,000.

The First Methodist Church of X—— was founded before the city itself was incorporated. The two have grown up together, although the church in recent decades has remained practically stationary. X—— now has a population of approximately 18,000, and the membership of First Church is recorded as 1,050. But the average attendance at the Sunday morning service is under 350.

There is no other Methodist church in the city or in either of its rapidly growing suburban communities. Each of the two most recent district superintendents has proposed establishing a new congregation on the outskirts and has sought to enlist the interest and co-operation of the pastor and laymen at First Church. These efforts met with a cool response on the part of the laymen, and outright objection from the minister. He has frankly said that he was fearful of losing many of his families. He foresaw greater difficulty in raising church funds and, the interviewer concluded, was concerned lest his own ministerial status, based on the size of his church, be lowered. It looks as though there will be no second Methodist church in or near the city of X—— until the present pastor is transferred to another charge.

In the meantime new churches of other evangelical Protestant denominations have been built in each of the two suburban communities and are attracting to their membership large numbers of former Methodist people.

A "first church" which desires to prevent the rise of a competitor will offer a number of reasons or excuses for its policy: (1) "Our church is well organized and can take care of all the people in our denomination in the city." (2) "We have a good building, centrally located and paid for. There is no need to put up another structure and go into debt." (3) "Should another church be started, it would be located where we now have many members. Probably a considerable number of these would leave our historic church and thus jeopardize its position." In a city of 25,000 where the Protestants make up a sizable proportion of the population these arguments have little validity for any major denomination. They represent a dog-in-the-manger attitude which, in the long run, has proved decidedly harmful to the individual church itself and to Protestantism as a whole.

Just as one church may prevent the development of new congregations, so another may cause the snuffing out of "competing" churches within the denomination that it may have a clearer field for itself. For example, in D—— there were four churches of a particular denomination in 1905, when the city had a population of 70,000. Some years later the strongest of them called an ambitious young man to be its pastor. Within the next twenty-five years he had merged all four and erected an impressive religious edifice in a fine residential community. His church had grown greatly in strength, but its membership was less than the combined membership of the four churches thirty years earlier. And in the meantime the population of the city had almost doubled.

The ministers and laymen of the churches referred to in the preceding illustrations failed to perceive what most merchants have discovered: it is not good business to prevent others from having good business. This does not mean that uncontrolled expansion and cutthroat competition either in business or in churching are good. On the other hand, while the downtown church in a city of 50,000 will probably continue to be the strongest organization within the denomination, it cannot perform the same function as a church located where the people live. The latter should be more effective in serving childhood and youth, whose friendships are formed in neighborhood play groups and at the local public school; the value of these ties is dissipated in the downtown church, where children come from every section of the city. Each of these church types has its own distinctive contribution to make to the religious life of the city, and neither can successfully take over the function of the other.

Marginal types of downtown churches

A few special-interest groups also hold their religious services downtown. The central business district is the logical and most convenient location for the French Presbyterian Church, where the French language is still used, and for the Church for the Deaf, which of necessity uses the sign language. These societies with special appeal may meet in the chapel of Old First, or they may rent a second-floor "public room" in a hotel for certain hours on Sunday.

Other religious societies convening downtown include such sects as the Christadelphians and the Rosicrucians. The Ethical Society rents a small theater on Sunday afternoon and maintains an office in the same building. An undenominational church, with chief emphasis on a fundamentalistic preaching service Sunday evening, meets in another theater. These marginal religious institutions are fractions of churches, carrying on only a segment of the functions performed by Old First. They generally have a small membership, with few if any meetings except on Sunday. A large proportion of their attendance is made up of curious "one-timers."

The downtown church in the large city

In smaller cities the First Congregational or First Baptist Church is essentially a religious society serving an expanded community. It has deep roots in the various residential areas of the city and is as much tied to those small stable areas as it is to the variegated life at the center of town. It is like a banyan tree with aerial roots reaching far out, striking the soil in many other areas and deriving its nourishment from them, receiving only a portion of its sustenance from the immediate vicinity.

The growth of the city is accompanied by a steady outward thrust of population, and a church which remains at the center finds its membership moving ever farther out, with a consequent weakening of ties. Although most of the old-timers continue to attend and support First Church until their death, many who are younger and have families transfer loyalty and membership to local community churches or become inactive. This tendency is perhaps less marked in southern cities where, in general, the churches have received better support and where even the downtown church has continued to be a family-centered institution, more like the church in the small town. However, the process goes on even in the South. Often the board of the church is for years unaware of what is happening. Membership figures remain high because scores who are inactive or nonresident are left on the roll. The finance committee recognizes that more difficulty is encountered in raising funds for the budget, but there are a few old families who can be depended on to make up the deficit. The attendance at the Sunday morning worship service shows some decrease, but the sharpest falling off is in the church-school enrollment.

It is at this time that the church is forced to make a difficult decision. Unless changes in the program are effected, the church will slowly decline in influence. The possibilities are: (1) The church may be relocated and placed in some community where there is a concentration of its members. Because its downtown property is valuable, the land can be sold for enough to purchase a large lot in a residential area and to erect a new building. If carried out, this action not infrequently causes serious tension, for in each of the residential communities other established churches feel that they have a prerogative. Under the comity programs of many large cities it is openly regarded as an unbrotherly, if not an unethical, act to locate within a half mile of another evangelical Protestant church.

2. It may merge with a church already located in a residential community, thereby avoiding possible inter- or intradenominational friction. This stratagem as a rule involves the loss of not only one church organization but, more important, many members of Old First, who wish neither to affiliate with the new merged congregation, because it is too far away or uncongenial, nor to join some other church nearer home.

3. The church may decide to remain where it is. In this case it must choose between two emphases: (*a*) It may continue what is essentially a family-type church program, not greatly different from that to be found in a small town or a stable community. If it is to remain a family church, the families must be sought out. Special buses may be furnished to bring the children to the church. Calling must be conducted in the residential districts, where the callers compete with representatives from local community churches. Such a church will survive only with difficulty—unless some friends provide an endowment—for it is out of its natural habitat. (*b*) It may study the downtown community in which it finds itself and determine what distinctive contributions a Christian church can make. On this basis its program may be more or less completely revised, in order to render services not easily performed by any other religious institution in the city.

This adaptation of program is the logical procedure if, in a large city, the denomination intends to maintain a strong downtown church. This means that it must be unafraid of creative venturing in an effort to bring the Christian message to the men and women who work in its shadow or hurry past its doors.

Functions of the downtown church

When Old First begins to look for the distinctive opportunities for service which are about it, it will discover that no other Christian fellowship in the city has so many and important functions to perform. There are services to long-time members and the transients, people in family units and solitary men and women, and its obligations for religious and civic leadership.

1. *A Church for the Old-Timers.* Difficult though it may be to accomplish it, the pastor and the central church must strive to maintain an established membership. These people furnish a stability and continuity which is important, not only for the sake of financial and organizational strength, but also from the standpoint of the transient. If all in the church are strangers, it is about as difficult to create a sense of Christian fellowship and at-homeness as among the crowd that leave a movie house.

Any religious society which has ministered to people for several decades has developed for itself a place in the affection and loyalty of hundreds of men and women, many of whom will never feel so completely at home in another congregation. The church owes much to these people and is under obligation to continue to serve them. Should it ever intentionally or unintentionally permit its membership nucleus to be dissipated, the warmth of its fellowship would disappear; then only with the greatest of difficulty could it re-establish the atmosphere and character of a church. The ushers, the people scattered through the congregation who speak to strangers, the smile, the handshake, the invitation to return—these are assets for which there is no adequate substitute.[1] An increase in the number of professional workers cannot compensate for the lack of interested volunteer laymen.

An important segment of the regular membership consists of business and professional women, most of them unmarried. They are in the main well-educated people, and many of them hold positions of considerable responsibility. Some are leaders in the church, and the majority are generous in their support of it. Whereas the average church has a few such women, in Old First there are enough to constitute a separate evening circle in the women's society.

For all these regular members, even if not for others, the basic essentials of a local church organization should be maintained. The church school seldom has more than a small enrollment of young children. However, its classes for youth, young adults, and also for businessmen may be larger than in any other church in the city. The women's society may not have as elaborate a program as in a residential church, and some of its daytime meetings will be held in the homes of members far away from the sanctuary where they worship. Nevertheless, it is in such groups as this, the young people's society, and the men's club, that friendships are formed, leadership developed, and interest aroused in the other, perhaps more distinctive, aspects of Old First's program. A church which offers nothing more than congregational worship on Sunday morning lacks cohesiveness and permanency, and cannot achieve a sense of fellowship which is necessary for the building and confirming of Christian character.

2. *A Sanctuary for the Transient.* Not every person who spends the week end away from home wishes an opportunity to worship on Sunday morning. But some do. For them the sight of a familiar church bulletin board announcing divine worship is itself a heart-warming experience. It helps to confirm within them the influences for good. The sound of the chimes, the illuminated stained-glass windows are a friendly invitation to a person alone in a strange city.

No one can realize how far reaching these quiet influences may be. Recently an elderly man informed the preacher in a large downtown church that forty years ago when he was uncertain how to spend Sunday evening in the city he dropped in at that church. The then minister preached on the Christian way of life. The young stranger proceeded on his journey. But

---

[1] Regular members of the church might well be urged by the membership committee to sit in different sections so that in every portion of the sanctuary there will be a few friendly persons to greet others about them. Even if a transient is in a city for only one Sunday, the service and church will be more meaningful for him because of such a greeting.

before he reached home, the comments of the pastor had produced in him a deep conversion experience. He joined the church in his home town and became an active layman. Not for twelve years did he find opportunity to return to that city to express his appreciation. He told the story to the pastor's successor. The man to whom he was indebted had died, not knowing the contribution he had made.

Because the congregation of a downtown church will have many transients in it, representing a wide range of viewpoint and experience, it is often helpful to introduce an informal touch in the Sunday morning service to make people feel at home. The pastors of some metropolitan churches occasionally ask for a show of hands: How many are worshiping with us for the first time? How many are from out of the state? And so forth. While this and other "folksy" techniques may displease a few who attend, most will feel more relaxed and participate more completely in the service because of it.

3. *A Center for Young People.* Every large city draws to itself thousands of young men and women from smaller towns. These youth, generally from eighteen to twenty-five years of age, find an inexpensive place to stay in one of the rooming-house districts on the edge of the business center. They spend little time in their room, with its shabby furniture and stained walls. But they soon learn downtown well. Naturally First Church is more attractive to them than a run-down church located a few blocks from the room.

First Church, if it has a dynamic program, not simply on Sunday nights but on weekday evenings as well, will prove a rich boon to them. They tire of the movies, museums, and "hot spots"; the parks are attractive only in good weather and for a short season. The job offers little contact with other young people. With seven nights a week on their hands they are on the search for something interesting to do. Therefore the church should be for them more than a morning worship service and an evening fellowship on Sunday. It ought to provide opportunities for inexpensive, clean recreation and social life. Many youth would gladly spend two or three evenings a week in such an environment.

The church can provide a reading room and lounge, where current magazines, some good books, and a radio are available. In one church daily concerts of recorded music are held from six-thirty to eight in the evening. On some evenings classical music is played; on others, opera, light classical, or popular. Some churches sponsor various hobby groups: photography, stamp collecting, and radio engineering. These clubs customarily meet on the same evening, and afterward the members join in a social time. Pressing and mending equipment, made available by one church, is used by young men as frequently as by young women. Included are an electric sewing machine, two ironing boards, and electric irons, as well as an assortment of needles and thread. These items are available only at specified periods during the week. Another metropolitan church has a field trip for its young people once a week. They may have an evening in Chinatown, visit a museum, spend a Sunday afternoon with a consulting engineer to learn how skyscrapers are planned and erected, or hold a theater party. In short, these varied activities can create a friendly, homelike atmosphere and furnish young people with time-filling as well as educational experiences.

4. *Ministry to the Hotel Population.* Residents of downtown hotels are not likely to be touched by any church unless it is Old First. These people in the main give the impression of being sophisticated, completely self-sufficient, and rather hardened individuals. Their appearance and manner will frighten off a timid minister. Nearly all are nonfamily people, and a church which functions primarily as a family institution makes little provision for them. Their hours are irregular; they are hard to reach; and they are wary of any person, whether bond salesman, insurance agent, or minister, who would intrude on their privacy. Some are there for one night only; others are long-time residents.

The Christian Church has made little effort to reach these people, except through the formal announcement of services on the hotel bulletin board. While it is obviously not feasible for a minister to spend one or two afternoons a week calling from door to door in a hotel, he might proffer his services to the manager as hotel chaplain. It is as appropriate for a hotel to have a chaplain as it is to have a "house physician" to meet the emergencies which arise in the lives of the hotel guests.

The experience of one downtown pastor is significant. The managers of two of the large hotels near his church welcomed the idea of having a hotel chaplain. On the advertising blotter placed in every room they printed his name, office hours, and telephone numbers (office and home), along with the names of others on the house staff. Scarcely a week goes by in which guests do not seek the minister's aid. An elderly woman becomes seriously ill and calls for a minister. A young man is overwhelmed with a sense of guilt. A girl who left home to be "on her own" becomes nervous and frightened. With such personal crises as these neither the hotel manager nor the house physician is prepared to cope. Hotel dwellers often desperately need the insight and fortifying power which the Christian faith can give, at the hands of an understanding minister, and the logical person to perform this service is the pastor of Old First.

5. *A Counseling Center.* People who are confronted with a serious life problem frequently prefer to consult a stranger—doctor, lawyer, or minister —who is trusted because of his position, rather than their immediate friends or even the family physician. The pastor of the downtown church, if he has skill in counseling, will receive more calls for advice than any other minister

in the city. Near-by hotels and rooming houses furnish a disproportionately large number of lonely, unadjusted people. Persons from other sections of the city, members of local churches, also come because here in the center of things there is a certain anonymity which protects them from the gossip of the home neighborhood. Here it is easier for them to relax and "tell the whole story." Further, they feel that the minister does not know all about them and their family background and will not have any prejudgments in their case.

Harried, nervous, unhappy people come at all hours of the day and night, asking for material and spiritual help. A few may be panhandlers, begging money for a meal but spending it at a saloon. Some wish vocational guidance; others are troubled by the behavior of a husband, wife, or son. An occasional fear-ridden man who feels "irresistibly tempted" to commit suicide asks help in a last desperate effort to free himself from the terror that haunts him. The variety is endless. If the downtown pastor is to help these people, his office must be accessible and adequate office hours indicated.

No one man is competent to meet all the problems set before the minister at Old First. He therefore should acquaint himself with specialists in related fields to whom he can refer many of the cases that come his way. He will often need the help of a case work agency. On his telephone pad should be the names and telephone numbers of medical specialists, or at least of a general practitioner. Serious mental cases he should never attempt to deal with by himself, but should direct to a competent psychiatrist or consulting psychologist. He should be prepared to use the services of Alcoholics Anonymous. In other instances he will need legal advice.

Certain churches have established counseling clinics. A panel of specialists meeting one evening a week usually includes, in addition to the minister, a doctor, a lawyer, and a social worker. Often a psychologist or a sociologist is added. Generally interviews on these evenings are by appointment, and the person fills out certain forms in advance to supply information regarding himself and to save staff time. In a relatively simple case an interview with one of the staff members may suffice. In more complicated situations the interviewee may be referred to one or more other members of the staff as well. In this event he may be asked to wait until later in the evening or to return at the time of the next clinic to secure advice. Staff members discuss the more serious issues in a staff meeting and reach conclusions on the basis of their joint wisdom.

A man who has a pastoral concern for people and who will avail himself of the opportunity of studying counseling methods will discover that he can render profound Christian help to distressed men and women. Often these people leave his study never to return. Frequently they do reappear and become staunch members in the church.

6. *A Center and a Voice for the Denomination.* Old First is the one church in the city that all within the denomination know about. It is the mother, as well as the central, church. It is the focal point for denominational thinking and, because of its convenience, the logical place for city-wide meetings, whether evangelistic or fund-raising in nature, and for the sessions of the teacher-training school. Other churches copy its worship services and study its educational program.

The minister is generally a leader in his own right, but the traditions and prestige of First Church add to his stature. He is invited to address the state conference of social workers, and give the invocation at the banquet of the state dental association. On occasion he is appointed to a committee by the mayor, and what he has to say about housing and welfare legislation is listened to with respect. The minister at First Church is a personality of civic importance.

7. *A Symbol.* Trinity Episcopal Church at the foot of Wall Street, in New York City, with its old brownstone steeple surmounted by a cross, provides startling contrast to the buildings round about, a reminder that there are matters more important than the rise and fall of stock prices. The clamor of Broadway traffic, the bustle and self-importance of the financial district, are challenged by the old church and its quiet, ancient cemetery. Death is a reality which cannot be shut out, but the church also proclaims the assurance of the resurrection.

The downtown church represents the timeless in the very midst of the contemporaneous. People of every faith step inside its doors, and a few forgo lunch in order to meditate in its sanctuary. Some central churches have an organ recital of religious music from twelve to one o'clock; others play recordings over a public-address system, using simple hymns as well as more elaborate religious and classical music. It is interesting to note the difference in facial expression of the people when they come in, tired from a morning in the office, and when they leave, refreshed.

Old First, whatever the city, is a symbol, not simply for people of one denomination, or even for all churchmen. It is a visible evidence that there are eternal values in life which dwarf the importance of industry and commerce. The Chicago Temple, the only remaining "first church" in Chicago's Loop, raises high above the crowding office buildings the symbol of the cross. Catholics and Jews, as well as Protestants, have expressed their satisfaction that the symbols of religion have not been completely crowded out. And when at five o'clock, as the office workers are rushing and pushing toward streetcar, subway, and elevated in a hurry to get home, the chimes ring out from its tower, one can see people pause and the expression on their faces change before they hurry on again.

CHAPTER TEN

Areas of Transition and Underprivilege

In every American city, small or large, there are sections which show signs of deterioration and shabbiness. If the population is small, these sections may be only a few blocks in extent; in the metropolis the area may include several square miles. As a rule it is an old part of the city, near or contiguous to the central business district; sometimes it almost constitutes a belt surrounding it.

Portions of this area are so seriously blighted that even the casual observer is impressed by the tumble-down appearance of the houses and the evident poverty of the inhabitants. Other sections are relatively well kept and, whether judged by rents, condition of housing, or the appearance of the people, could almost be classified as stable communities. Some precincts of the inner city have throughout their history been regarded as undesirable places to live, because the land was swampy or the railroad yards were near. No "substantial" homes were ever erected in this vicinity, only low-cost frame structures with inadequate plumbing and often, even in northern cities, without central heating. Frequently, however, areas which are now dowdy have been grand ladies in the past. Streets still lined with three-story brownstone houses, which once witnessed the coming and going of fine carriages and the town's elite, have become the playground for the children of the poor. Gone are the servants, and the mansion of long ago now shelters ten families instead of one.

From the standpoint of the people who live in a stable community such an area is not only depressing but disorganized. Actually, except in the homeless-man and rooming-house districts, there is a great deal of social organization, formal and informal—families, cliques, gangs, churches, clubs, and so forth. Each individual has many ties which affect his social standing and influence his behavior. But because of the desire of the people to get away from the unpleasant physical aspects of the area, it is difficult to achieve community stability.

The community in transition

Some deterioration takes place in all structures with the passage of time. However, the pride of home owners and the managerial concern of investors holds this to a minimum through the judicious use of paint, new stucco, and tuck pointing. In some sections of the city houses maintain their air of well-being decade after decade. These are the stable communities. Yet with a shift in population these same communities can undergo rapid deterioration with corresponding changes in social organization.

The beginnings of this change are frequently almost imperceptible. Apparently insignificant signals begin to appear. An owner dies, and his widow posts a sign, "Rooms for Rent." A family on the corner, hard pressed for funds, rebuilds the first floor and rents it out for a store. Some of the older families sell, feeling that the bottom may drop out of land values. Others move to the suburbs, convert the old home into small housekeeping apartments, and turn the task of rent collecting over to a real-estate agent. They spend no more money than is absolutely necessary on remodeling and upkeep, since they may not be able to secure a satisfactory return from their investment.

More significant but less observable than the physical changes is the breakdown of community morale. Old-timers who once knew everyone in the block by name now feel that they are marooned in a sea of strangers. The old sense of pleasant, comfortable security which is associated with neighborliness has gone. Rapid turnover of property and the appearance of people who have strange customs and noisy children produce a sense of confusion and alarm.

The new population—perhaps of Italian background—may in time again create a semblance of stability and neighborliness but the buildings are older and the houses more crowded. Consequently they too, or more likely their children when they marry, will move on if finances permit. This may open a new cycle of community change, with Mexicans or Negroes following the Italians. As succession takes place, there is continuing deterioration of the property. Each group that moves out leaves the homes a little more dilapidated for those who take over the premises.

Evidences of deterioration

In physical characteristics areas of transition vary from the "conservation area"—so called by city planners because the earmarks of transition are already present, but deterioration is staved off through city planning and the co-operation of home owners—to the "blighted or slum area," where the process of deterioration is almost complete. The traits described below are representative of the so-called blighted area.

No area becomes blighted suddenly. Evidences of decline accumulate slowly. More people crowd into the old buildings. The humble, one-story frame houses are raised and an additional brick story placed underneath, with an outside wooden stairway provided for the upper floor. Although the lots are small and often shallow, an additional house is erected on the rear to bring in extra income. Back and front yards are very small, if they exist at all, so that there is scant play space for children except in the street, where truck traffic is a hazard, or in the alley.

The structures themselves show unmistakable signs of age and neglect. They are dingy, having long since lost all of the original paint. Porches and stairways are sagging, and broken windows with rags stuffed in the openings may occasionally be seen. Zigzag cracks show in some of the brick walls. Fences stand awry. An abandoned and tottering building, with broken windows and much of the woodwork pulled off for use in local cookstoves, adds to the general shabby appearance of the neighborhood. The much-used streets are covered with dust and litter, which is blown up into the face of the passer-by with each gust of wind. Garbage accumulates in the alleys, and, since much of it is not kept in cans, it is scattered still farther by rats and stray dogs. In the hot weather inadequate garbage collection results in a heavy smell of decayed food hanging over the alleys and rear yards.

Many of the structures have been subdivided, and basements and attics are utilized for living space. Commonly a family of three or four lives in a two-room "housekeeping apartment," the larger room serving as kitchen, dining and living room, and at night as bedroom. Cooking facilities may be a gas plate in one corner of the room, or perhaps an old range used not only for cooking but also in the winter as the sole source of heat. Many dwelling units have no running water, and toilet facilities are shared with two to six other families. Even in the heart of some of the largest cities of America many outdoor privies are still in use.[1]

The prevalence of these conditions of bad housing and underprivilege is far greater than most citizens realize. Table IV illustrates the extent to which urban America is inadequately housed. This poor housing is not evenly scattered through the city but is concentrated in the areas of underprivilege. The old houses which are in need of repair are generally the same ones which are crowded and lack satisfactory plumbing facilities.

The few trees which once grew in this area have been fighting a losing battle. They die off branch by branch and are not replaced. Pathetic efforts are made each spring by a few of the householders to grow a small plot of

---

[1] The U. S. Public Health Service reported in 1947 that there were more than four thousand privies within the city limits of Chicago.

grass and some flowers back of a wooden fence, but the results are poor, as the soil is worn out and beaten hard, and the beneficent rays of the sun reach it only through a smoky haze.

Table IV
CONTRASTS IN HOUSING WITHIN REPRESENTATIVE CITIES BETWEEN SUBSTANDARD & SUPERIOR HOUSING AREAS, 1950 [2]

Type of census tract		PER CENT OF DWELLING UNITS			
		Having 1.51 persons or more per rm.	No private bath or dilapidated	No running water or dilapidated	Median monthly rent
Akron:	substandard	7.0	46.2	25.6	29.40
	superior	*	*	*	83.14
Atlanta:	substandard	28.7	78.9	55.8	16.52
	superior	*	1.4	*	63.36
Austin:	substandard	27.6	56.4	36.8	22.35
	superior	*	2.5	1.1	60.34
Des Moines:	substandard	10.9	49.6	22.5	31.53
	superior	*	1.5	*	81.68
St. Louis:	substandard	15.1	70.9	26.2	15.96
	superior	*	1.6	*	90.52
San Francisco	substandard	22.3	84.2	4.6	18.74
	superior	*	7.6	*	92.76

* Less than 0.1 per cent.

When the now substandard areas were first settled, the people were close enough to the country to satisfy their desire for open spaces. Before the need for park space was recognized, the land was fully occupied. Now there are almost no parks, although small grassless playgrounds adjoin a few of the public schools. School facilities are often shabby and antiquated. Even churches have a down-at-heels mildewed appearance which repels rather than attracts the passer-by.

[2] These six cities were chosen from different sections of the country (U.S. Census, 1950, Housing, Vol. V) and do not represent the worst or best conditions. A dwelling unit with 1.51 persons or more per room is termed "overcrowded"; it means, for instance, that at least five people live in a three-room apartment or seven in a four-room dwelling. A dwelling unit is "dilapidated" when it is "run-down or neglected, or is of inadequate original construction, so that it does not provide adequate shelter or protection against the elements or it endangers the safety of the occupants."

The costs of deterioration

The financial cost of deterioration is great to the original owner, who may lose heavily as he sells in panic to escape lowering prices; to the renter, who pays an absurdly high price for limited facilities; and to the city, which suffers losses in taxes.

Generally people leave the old neighborhood, not because they have been offered a tempting price for their property, but because the altered physical condition and social composition of the community have made it less attractive to them. The decline in land values may be either gradual or precipitate, depending on the degree of prejudice against the newcomers and on the rapidity of their entry into the neighborhood, but it does stimulate fear on the part of the old-timers and speeds up their leaving. Unscrupulous persons often buy up such property cheaply from frightened owners and, by a policy of deliberate exploitation, derive at the expense of the poorest citizens a high return on their investment. They do not expect to maintain the property, but to secure a maximum income from it while there is demand. They often permit it to become tax delinquent, expecting eventually to forfeit a thoroughly deteriorated house to the city.

The drop in land values produces a decline in the city's income from the area, even though the population is increasing and the local costs of government are rising. More teachers may be needed in the public school; additional policemen must be employed; and public welfare expenditures mount. Old housing plus overcrowding creates serious fire hazards and may involve tragic loss of life as well as property. Witness the following account of a fire in a slum section of Chicago in 1947:

Fire inspectors uncovered "flagrant violations" today in the jammed tenement where 10 trapped women and children burned to death early this morning. . . . Fire Inspector W. F. Cotter called the whole structure where nearly 300 persons lived in 22 apartments "a bad fire hazard." . . . There were only two front entrances to the four-story building and no rear exits.

More serious than occasional deaths from fire are the discouragement and depression which people feel when they live in the midst of dirt, decay, and dilapidation. Some become dulled and hopeless, accepting their drab existence without complaint. Others nurse a feeling of suspicion and hatred against the respectability and privilege which they see in other sections of the city and seek release by defying authority, stealing a car, swiping fruit from a wagon, or engaging in illicit sex behavior. A few, repressed and unhappy, become mentally ill. The highest mental disease and delinquency rates in American cities are usually found in the areas of deterioration.

Economic insecurity and low morale produce and aggravate family tensions. If there is to be family loyalty, it must arise from the strength of character of the parents themselves, as there is little in the immediate environment to encourage or support the customary virtues and ties of American family living. The highest desertion rates in the city are found in the areas of underprivilege. This is not because poorer people necessarily have less affection for their spouses. Often it is an expression of the desire to escape from anything which seems associated with the disagreeable environment.

Personal and economic insecurity lays a foundation for the political machine to build upon. Worried and impoverished citizens are happy to find a friend in the ward boss or the precinct committeeman, a man who is acquainted with the city, knows how relief agencies are operated, and can "get things done." This politician knows the people of his precinct more intimately than many ministers do the members of their congregation. It is his function to be friendly, to know the names of the children, to have candy in his pocket, to stage an outdoor picnic, to get coal for Widow Jones when the winter is cold and she has no funds, to get a bed in the crowded county hospital for a tuberculous child. He helps his friends secure jobs; and when a boy becomes delinquent, he frequently will appear with him at court to sign his bond. It is understandable that the people in the precinct are glad to follow his guidance in political matters at election time. Votes are rarely bought with an outright money payment; they are secured through a much more informal and subtle method of giving favors. One would make a serious mistake if he assumed that these politicians did not have a genuine interest in the welfare of many of their neighbors in the precinct. However, the effect may be devastating on urban and even on national politics.

The social costs of community deterioration are not measurable in dollars. When judged in terms of unrealized hopes, thwarted personalities, and the public welfare, the cost is appalling.

Types of underprivileged areas

The areas which can no longer be classified as stable range from humble but livable homes to tumble-down firetraps, and, in social adjustment, from well-knit family units to the disorganization and anonymity of the homeless-man district. In general there is greater mobility and less homogeneity —and consequently less community consciousness—than in the stable residential communities. In cities of twenty thousand and over a measure of specialization may be observed in different sections of the underprivileged area. Some cater to the homeless men, others to roomers, and still others to racial or nationality groups. Each of these presents a special challenge to the church.

1. *The Homeless-Man Area.* Near the railroad tracks, usually on one of the

older downtown streets which is bordered by decrepit, unpainted buildings, is the homeless-man district. Here in musty lodging houses unattached men live or, rather, spend the night. Into this convenient pocket of the city drift a few hundred or, perhaps, in the midwinter and in larger cities, tens of thousands of "floaters." Some are out for adventure and a good time, and intend to take up their old pursuits in a month or two. Others have deliberately chosen the hobo way of life. They get a job and work for a week or a month and then with some cash in their pockets return to their urban "hangout," where a few dollars will cover expenses for a month or more and in the meantime they may enjoy the sense of freedom and leisure which is dear to the hobo's heart. A third group have come here to hide themselves. Life for them is an unsolvable and bitter riddle, and they have felt inadequate to meet its demands. Here they can lose themselves, and no one will pry into their unhappy past. These men, and some from the other two classes, soon or late degenerate into bums. In the homeless-man area each person is a unit by himself, with no sense of community, no family tie.

This section of the city has its own characteristic social institutions. Cheap restaurants flourish, with emphasis on the quantity of food served rather than the quality. Their windows are plastered with large signs, "Stew, coffee and rolls, 30 cents," and the men wander along the street window-shopping for the best bargain in meals.

It was only five-thirty, but the light had gone from the sky and an even colder night was following on the heels of a sharp, blustery day. I entered a cafe located between a pawnshop and an employment office. The window was covered with moisture and the air was heavy with the smell of frying grease and stale coffee intermingled with the odor of unwashed humans. About fifteen men were ahead of me, seated on stools in front of the long lunch counter. Not a woman or boy in the group. The men were poorly dressed and ate with their hats on. Faces were grimy and apparently innocent of soap and water.

A few of the men ate quickly and went out into the night, but most took plenty of time, stirring and sipping their coffee. There was no conversation among them. They just sat—apparently preferring the warm, lighted, though stuffy restaurant to the cold and loneliness of the winter night.

"Flophouses" and cheap hotels are numerous. A flophouse is usually simply a loft where a man can buy a "flop" for ten or twenty cents—space to spread out on the floor the newspapers he has accumulated during the day as a bed for the night. Accommodations are primitive, and the hall, even in summer, reeks with stale body odors. The hotels offer slightly more privacy. The rooms, which may rent for fifty cents a night, are not more than five by seven feet in size, and the walls, which are simply thin metal panels, do not reach the ceiling. Sheets are changed once a week—less frequently than the roomers.

Employment offices, recruiting for construction, railroad, and seasonal work, are located along the street. Whitewash signs on the front windows describe the jobs. Hoboes refer to them as "slave markets." The pawnshop, the hobo's bank, is another prominent institution. Here men borrow on an old watch or overcoat, hoping to redeem it when "the world gives me a break."

I saw a man walking up and down slowly between a restaurant and a pawnshop with a banjo under his arm. The man was old and haggard, white-haired, slow of step, poorly dressed. Finally he sold his banjo and went into the restaurant to order an egg sandwich and coffee. He told me that that banjo was the last thing he had to pawn. He had been a vaudeville player with a banjo company; but he had not been good enough consistently to make the grade. Now, broke and hungry, he pawned his banjo to get food.

Along this street the tawdry burlesque show and the all-night movie are to be found. Western thrillers and sexy shows are preferred; either provides an escape from the drab unsavory dullness. Near by are houses of prostitution. These are the final houses of degradation, the place where a prostitute ends up when she has lost her earlier youth and charm. Saloons with cheap liquor—another escape device—sprinkle the area, and at almost any time of day a few drunks can be seen swaying uncertainly along the sidewalk or sitting on the curb, head in hands.

The one contrasting element in this dismal picture of battered and exploited humanity is the little mission which is near by. Unfortunately its windows are sometimes as dirty as those of the pawnshop. The efforts of organized religion to solve the problems of these people will be discussed in the next chapter.

2. *The Rooming-House Area.* A deteriorating area of single-family homes is a logical place for the establishment of rooming houses. Especially appropriate are the ancient residences on a few of the main streets just beyond the business district. Here a young man recently arrived from a small town rents a hall bedroom. A childless couple seeking to get a start in the city takes the "second-floor front, with running water." Two girls attending art school use half of the attic. And so the old building is filled with ten or twenty people who have different interests, standards of living, and social and religious attitudes.

The rooming-house district has a different atmosphere from the habitat of homeless men. More women live here. The street looks shabby but respectable. Most of the roomers regard their present situation simply as a way station on the road to a more congenial mode of living. There is little that can be called home or family life and almost no sense of community solidarity or concern for the general social welfare. These are individuals, each interested primarily in his own personal problems. They commonly do not even become acquainted with others in the same building. Often the housekeeper does not know the names of her roomers, who are there for a few weeks or months and then move on. The post office and credit companies have constant difficulty in tracing clients who have left inadequate addresses. In this area of high mobility and anonymity the social influences which uphold the proprieties of life are almost nonexistent.

Rooming-house people from force of circumstance are isolated and have little opportunity to form pleasant associations. The loneliness and efforts to build up substitutes for friendship are seen in the following partial report of a contact with a young roomer in a restaurant.

INTERVIEWER: Do you live near here?
MAN: I used to. But at Christmas I moved to————[a better rooming house area].
INTERVIEWER: Why do you still come back here to eat? The food isn't any better.
MAN: Well, frankly, the woman here is so mother-like. . . . Say, if you don't have anything to do tonight, come up and listen to my radio.

His apartment was one room with a rollaway bed, bath and kitchenette. On the wall were a picture of a girl in an old straw hat, and a full-length painting of another girl, in a frame made by himself. The furniture consisted of a desk, cabinet radio, a parlor suite of conservative color, a showcase of trinkets, an end table. In addition there were three ash trays. On the desk was a photograph of a girl, a picture of a second girl in a photographer's frame, and a boudoir lamp of a girl curtsying with a red light inside it.

He rented his apartment for a month at a time because employment was uncertain. He spent his money on his apartment rather than on shows, and so forth. He had very few friends, none in S—— (where he had lived for four years, since graduation from a small-town high school). He moved on an average of once in two months during the first year he was here. Since then he has not moved so often. He has few amusements, mainly reading magazines and smoking. He does much of his own cooking. During the summer he likes to walk in the park. During the winter he stays in his room. His magazine reading is all of the light short-story type. "Serious things make my head ache." He is now twenty-two years old.

The rooming-house area is a small eddy in the life of the city. Into it float people out of the main stream. Then after swirling about for a time, often counter to the main current of social life, they are swung back again into the stream. This is probably the most difficult area of the city for the church to serve, and yet here, because of the disorganization within the community, its contributions are particularly needed.

3. *Racial and Nationality Colonies.* Larger in extent than the homeless-
man or rooming-house areas are the racial and nationality "colonies." Immigrants from Europe long ago settled in the low-rent slum sections of
northern and eastern cities. The Italians did not spread evenly throughout
Paterson or Bridgeport, but concentrated within a few blocks, the people
from Palermo in one block and those from Naples in another. In a land
where they were regarded as foreign and inferior, and where few understood their language, it was pleasant to come home at night and meet friends
from the old home town. They felt a homesickness for their fatherland and
exalted the symbols which tied them to it. They supported newspapers in
their native tongue, stores which imported favorite foods, restaurants preparing native dishes, and clubs and churches which might well have been
lifted straight out of the old-world environment. The Greeks had their coffee
shops, the Czechs their *Sokols,* or calisthenic and social clubs.

Within these colonies there is considerable social control. Children are
sent to the parochial school where Italian or Polish nuns teach them in accordance with old-world standards, much of the instruction being in the
mother tongue. And, until recent years, the Italian father and older sons
in the family exercised supervision over the daughter's or sister's courtship
with the same strictness that obtained in Italy.

The tide of European immigration was stopped by the first world war
and has not flowed swiftly since. With the passage of time, the death of
older members, and the Americanization of the younger generations the
distinctiveness of these colonies is slowly being lost. The younger people,
as soon as they can do so, move into a better community, usually an "area of
second settlement," which they enjoy because so many of their friends also
reside there that some of the flavor of the old colony still remains. The
traditional loyalties to Sweden or Germany or Poland, though now dilute,
are still in evidence.

Negroes moved from the rural South into southern cities and, especially
from 1917 on, into northern and western ones. They and the Mexicans established other colonies. Because of the strong prejudice against these groups
in the North as well as in the South, and because of their low income status,
they could gain entrance to only the most disorganized, deteriorated communities where rents were lowest. Frequently as Italians or Jews moved out,
Negroes moved in. They also have their own institutions and by necessity
live much of their life within their own community. While segregation is
not legally sanctioned in northern cities, it does exist in fact, and, with
a relatively high birth rate and a continued in-migration, Negroes live in
some of the poorest, most congested housing in American cities. With their
extreme poverty, bad housing, overcrowding, and weak family structure it

follows that personal disorganization and inner tensions are widespread and delinquency rates high in the Negro slum areas.[3]

The homeless-man area, the rooming-house district, and racial and nationality colonies all have marked differentiating features and also their own distinctive types of religious institutions. However, in smaller cities as well as larger ones, block after block which cannot be considered "stable" still cannot be classified under one of these heads. They are midway between the anonymity and mobility of the rooming-house district and the closely knit family and community life of the nationality or racial colony. These are "conservation" communities whose inhabitants, though on a lower economic plane, look to the adjoining stable communities as their pattern. One of the chief contributions which the church can make in such an area is to shore up or help rebuild sagging community morale.

Social welfare agencies in blighted areas

Many forces are at work to improve the physical and social conditions in areas of underprivilege. Here most of the city's welfare agencies are located and the largest proportion of the community chest funds is expended. These agencies range all the way from the scientifically organized family welfare society to the free-lance mission which is opened in a vacant store and closes after three months. However, numerous as they are and in spite of the earnest work of their leaders, little more than a beginning has been made at removing the blight of the slum.

1. *Group Work Agencies.* Social settlements are foremost among the organizations seeking to develop a constructive social and recreational life for children and adults. A settlement is a building, a staff, and a program. The building is located within the underprivileged area. There, among the people whom they wish to serve, "settle" the men and women on the staff, sharing in the life of the neighborhood, getting to know the people and their problems, and assisting as good neighbors in the establishment of a more wholesome community. South End House in Boston and Hull House in Chicago have been held in high regard by three generations of slum dwellers. These and other social settlements have not only served the people of the neighborhood but have been a training ground for thousands of men and women who, after a period of residence, have become leaders in social work and civic reform.

The program of such "houses" consists chiefly in organizing groups of youth or adults about some common interest. There are drama clubs and basketball teams, art classes, mothers' circles, English classes, and craft-shop

[3] It is necessary to keep in mind that, in spite of the handicap of racial barriers, many Negroes have achieved a relatively high economic status and have established pleasant, middle-class communities in or suburban to most large American cities.

work. The aim is never to impose a program or a culture from outside, but rather to assist the people of the neighborhood in self-realization, to build up a neighborly spirit within the community, and to quicken and direct the latent interest in community improvement. Many of the best of social settlements are sponsored and financed in whole or in part by various churches. In some of these considerable attention is given to religious instruction, while others hold no formal religious services whatsoever. An important feature of these houses is that they aim to remain in the area, serving each new population group as it moves in. At this point they stand in contrast to many churches which tend to follow their congregations as the members move out.

The American Boys' Commonwealth, the Boys' Brotherhood Republic, the Y.M.C.A. and Y.W.C.A., and other agencies also maintain centers in areas of underprivilege. In some cities businessmen's organizations sponsor a program for boys, conducted in a vacant store during the winter and on vacant lots or a school playground in better weather. In the summer many agencies send mothers and children to a camp in the open country. Some of these campers have never before been out of the city or seen a live cow or pig.

The alderman from the ward may underwrite the expenses of the "Fitzgerald Club." He furnishes not only a meeting place, with occasional refreshments, but also baseball and basketball uniforms—with his own name on the back of the sweaters—and the other necessary sports equipment. He has, of course, a political as well as a social interest in the organization.

The leadership in group work agencies is in many instances thoroughly trained, wise, and skillful. Too often, however, the institution limps along with an inadequate, underpaid staff, with much of the work done by well-meaning but inexperienced volunteers. In the latter event there is rapid staff turnover, and the impact on the community may be negligible.

2. *Family Welfare Agencies.* These organizations sometimes have their offices in one of the social settlements, but do not sponsor any group activities. Their approach is that of the case worker, and they deal either with families as units or with persons. They may find it necessary to give financial assistance, but no longer think of this as their most important function. Through counseling with persons and families about adjustment problems they are able to relieve many of the strains of living in the area and may prevent desertion or delinquency. Their burden is heaviest in periods of depression, but even in prosperous days hundreds of families need their assistance.

3. *Child Welfare Agencies.* Many settlements and churches maintain nursery schools for the care of preschool children during daytime hours while the mothers are at work. In some situations this is a particularly

valuable contribution, although in terms of the number assisted it is one of the most expensive forms of social service, because it is necessary to have two workers for twenty or twenty-five children, and the program runs from seven-thirty in the morning until the latter part of the afternoon. Much space and equipment are required.

Public and parochial schools as well as the church and settlement at times reach into the home to help in the adjustment of the child or the improvement of his health. Child placement and foster home agencies, frequently working in co-operation with the Juvenile Court, are found in every city. Other organizations are concerned with aid for dependent children and give assistance to families with young children where the breadwinner has died, deserted, or become incapacitated. The federal government makes grants matching state or county funds on a fifty-fifty basis for mothers' pensions. These are intended to help the mother maintain her family as a unit, on the commendable theory that it is better for children to remain with her than be removed to an orphanage or a foster home while she earns the living.

4. *Health Agencies.* Health hazards are greater in areas of underprivilege. Infant mortality is higher than elsewhere in the city, and so is the general death rate. There is more sickness, caused in part by lower income and poorer housing. The Visiting Nurse Association has most of its patients in impoverished communities. Parts of the area in transition—though not the homeless-man or rooming-house districts—are characterized by a very high birth rate. Philanthropists, shocked by the high infant and maternal mortality rates, have in some cities established lying-in hospitals to serve these people. Some of the social settlements furnish space for clinic purposes. These clinics are of many types: dental, lung, prenatal and infant, or general medical.

In spite of the work of the many social welfare agencies, life goes on in the blighted areas of American cities under heavy handicap. Courageous work here and there seems only to highlight the greater need, and, as a resident in one settlement house has stated, "The more effective we are in our work, the faster we lose our capable people from the area. They do not remain to improve the community."

Large-scale rehabilitation housing within the city

For over half a century public-spirited citizens have been concerned with the effects of unwholesome housing conditions. Jacob Riis and Washington Gladden claimed that the government had as much responsibility to tear down health-destroying tenements as it had to drain off a miasmic swamp. No piecemeal improvement will suffice. The deteriorating influences overwhelm any small oasis of new, decent housing and drag it back to the old level.

The prerequisite for rebuilding the health and social life of the community is a comprehensive program of physical rehabilitation. A few ambitious building projects of this nature were undertaken by private capital before the depression of the 1930's. Although these were a great improvement on the housing which was replaced, they were not located in the most needy communities. Private companies hesitated to take the heavy financial risks involved in actual slum clearance.

Beginning with 1933 the federal government has taken the lead in promoting and financing extensive housing developments in badly deteriorated areas.[4] Inexpensive, low-rent units designed to meet at least the minimum standards for health and decency were erected according to a single comprehensive plan. Some of these projects take care of as many as a thousand families. The houses are not only new and bright in appearance, but are spaced so that sun and air can reach each apartment and children have ample play space. It is not surprising that the people who manage to secure a place in a government housing development are willing to make almost any sacrifice to remain in it. In 1939, when pay rates were low and unemployment an ever-present threat, the proprietor of a barbershop remarked concerning the families in a near-by project:

The people who live there are so anxious to remain that they skimp and save every penny they can so that, in case they lose their job, they can stay on until they find another. Before the project went in, I used to do a fifty-dollar-a-week business, and now I seldom do thirty dollars a week. Those folks don't eat enough, they want so badly to stay in a good place like that.

These large projects, sheltering as many as five or six thousand people, have had a profound effect on the whole community in which they have been located. Owners of near-by residences have sought to give a face lifting to their own property, tuck pointing brick and stone structures and painting frame ones. Many of them are envious of the more fortunate people who can live in the plain, small, yet new apartments in "the project." As one man remarked, "It must be nice to have a window in each room the way they do."

The future of the blighted area

The area of underprivilege is too extensive ever to be taken over by expanding business or industry, which means that people will probably live

---

[4] During the war the government's efforts were turned to building acres of "temporary" houses near the massive defense factories, which were generally on the outskirts of the city.

there for decades to come. The question is whether it will continue to be a source of physical ills and social disorganization or whether it can be redeemed as a place for wholesome living. Even now it has two advantages: proximity or easy access by good transportation to downtown, and low land values. Yet under present circumstances few who can afford to live elsewhere will elect to buy or build there. The congestion and dirt, the disorganization of the community, the poor educational facilities, and perhaps the uncongeniality of the dominant population deter them.

In many cities the planning commission, chamber of commerce, and other public and private agencies are struggling with the problems of public safety, traffic movement and parking, slum clearance and low-cost housing. In a dynamic city change is continuous: an old bridge is replaced; building fronts are clipped off to permit widening a street; or a new freeway cuts a swath a block or two wide through miles of humble houses. These activities, beneficial for the total urban population, are demoralizing to the neighborhoods which are thus disturbed. A new superhighway elevated on a twenty-five-foot ramp will not only metamorphose the appearance of the area, but will destroy many familiar landmarks and institutions which have had a stabilizing influence. Even the construction of attractive large-scale housing projects creates a temporary disorganization of the community, as old shacks are reduced to piles of rubble, and as former tenants scurry to find other cheap tenements nearby where they can afford to live.

Yet in spite of the temporary displacements and social upheaval, efforts at improvement are bearing good fruit in cities throughout the country. Whole tracts of shabby, dilapidated structures which have been firetraps and health hazards for a generation are being replaced with neat, utilitarian, fireproof multiple housing, sometimes ten or more stories in height, and surrounded with plenty of open space where children can play in safety or mothers can wheel their baby carriages.

The fundamental improvement of areas of bad housing is contingent on: (1) an educational process, getting the people in the area and throughout the city to understand the need for unified action and large-scale physical rehabilitation; (2) financial assistance, either from the government or from other sources, including the rising earning power of the residents themselves, with resulting ability to pay higher rents and demand new and decent housing; and (3) the gradual rebuilding of community morale, so that the people will have a sense of sharing in a wholesome community life. Only by drastic and heroic measures can the steady physical and social erosion which is still taking place in areas of deterioration be halted. The last of these three tasks presents a particular challenge to the church.

CHAPTER ELEVEN

Religious Institutions
in Areas of Underprivilege

THE people in the areas of underprivilege, poor and often exploited, belong to the class to which Jesus devoted much of his ministry. Here live the masses of unskilled laborers who perform the drudgery of the city. Their houses are overcrowded; the birth rate is high; and gangs of children and youth swarm on the streets looking for something exciting to do. Families are often loosely knit and have little rootage in the community.

Significance of the underprivileged area for the Christian church

There is little in such a community to encourage high standards of personal, family, or civic living. Consequently the ministry of the church is all the more needed. Its teachings on social as well as personal righteousness should arouse its special concern for these people. In no other section of the city is there a greater urgency for the inculcation of Christian standards as a basis for good citizenship.

Yet in this area of special need the church has had most difficulty in maintaining a foothold. Because the income of the people is low, they by themselves can scarcely support a Protestant church with a full-time minister. The local Roman Catholic church, sustained by small gifts of perhaps a thousand families and served by a celibate priesthood, can meet its expenses and erect a substantial building. But a Protestant church ministering to thirty or eighty families has a desperate struggle to finance even a modest program without missionary funds or other outside aid.

Few local residents have developed leadership ability, a further handicap and challenge to the Protestant church. The people, embarrassed by their lack of formal education, evade leadership responsibilities. Actually many of them have as great native ability as people in the residential suburbs. Too often the minister does not know how to develop the potential leaders in his congregation, preferring to rely on "imported leaders"—men and women who have been successful and have moved out of the area.

It is also difficult to secure capable ministerial leadership. It requires as great zeal and concern for people to dedicate one's life to the service of a blighted area as it does to volunteer as a missionary to a foreign field. These churches do not offer a minister much prestige. He will have a higher status if he serves almost any other type of congregation. The salary is generally low and perhaps uncertain. If he lives in the community, as he must do if he is to identify himself with the people, he subjects his wife and children to all of the physical and social hazards and discomforts which characterize the area. The church members, if they can afford to do so, move out of the community. He must remain to serve the unsuccessful remnant of God's people.

Further, in these areas the church has most difficulty in maintaining an adequate local membership. Albert Rasmussen, in a study of the Congregational churches of Chicago, has shown that the lower the economic status of the community, the smaller the proportion of the membership living near the church. In blighted areas only two in ten dwelt within a mile of the institution, as compared with nine out of ten in the growing section of the city. These figures are probably representative of the situation in other denominations and cities.[1]

Table V
PROXIMITY OF MEMBERS TO CONGREGATIONAL CHURCHES BY TYPE OF COMMUNITY, 1945-46

TYPE OF COMMUNITY	Per Cent Members Within One-half Mile	Per Cent Members Within One Mile
Blighted	13.7	19.6
Near-blighted	53.3	63.9
Conservation (tending to decline)	50.5	69.3
Stable	61.0	82.3
Growth and progressive development	67.5	88.9

This is the dilemma which confronts the church in its ministry to areas of underprivilege: In the very places where the message of the church is most needed the difficulties in presenting it are the most acute.

The process of deterioration and the churches

The city is always changing. Some areas now blighted were once prosperous residential communities. What happened to the churches in the process?

When, many years ago, merchants and white-collar workers were erecting their comfortable houses in the neighborhood, they built a church of suitable size and appearance to match their homes. For a time it grew in membership

[1] Albert T. Rasmussen, *Comparative Study of Congregational and Other Protestant Churches in Chicago, 1945-46,* p. 89.

and influence, but as the years passed most of its members died or moved away, and other groups took over the community. Now the majority of the church members live at least two miles away. Some old-timers continue to return to worship, and a number of them still hold leadership positions. The membership is declining, and it is harder to raise the necessary funds—unless perchance some wealthy person has provided an endowment. The length of the pastorates has declined, as ministers realized that the church was on the "down grade" and wished to leave before it slipped further.

At some time in this process the governing board of the church is compelled to face the question of its future. Should it remain and continue with its present program? Should it move out into the newer territory where many of its members now live? Should it change its outlook and program while remaining at the same location, and seek to reach the people round about? In every such church each of these positions has its advocates.

Usually it is the first of the three options which receives major support. If the minister is an exceptional preacher and pastor, or if the church has a number of alert, aggressive lay leaders, it may continue strong and influential even though it is "unfavorably" situated. But often the church becomes "marooned" or socially isolated, and the newer residents are scarcely aware of its presence. A number of moribund churches may remain physically in the community but spiritually far away, limping along until finally the mortgage cannot be renewed and financial necessity compels reconsideration.

A sizable minority of the churches choose the second option and eventually sell their property to another religious organization, usually of a sectarian type, or to a business concern. In any large city some of these old structures can be seen, still with their Gothic windows and steeple or tower, now in use as a garage, night club, or warehouse. A church which follows this option also has a number of difficulties to face in finding a new niche for itself.[2]

The more difficult procedure, but the only one which will assure the continued vitality of a church, is constant recruiting of new members from the local area and orienting the program toward them. This calls for capable and imaginative ministerial and lay leadership. Often an institutional program is developed emphasizing social, educational, and recreational group work as a means of serving the people near by. Such an undertaking in an area of underprivilege must receive generous outside financial support from denominational agencies and perhaps the community chest.

The problem in the small city

In a city of less than twenty thousand population the area of deteriorating housing is usually not large enough to constitute a distinct zone by itself. Nevertheless, the process which is clearly evident in the metropolis is al-

2 See p. 75.

ready manifest here. Surrounded by poor housing or industry, a church may maintain its strength for a long period of time, but it experiences increasing difficulty in adding to its rolls newcomers to the city.

In the smaller city such a church may, under effective leadership, serve as a "bridge" institution. That is, it may be more cosmopolitan than other religious agencies, bringing together people from every economic plane and cultural level in a common public worship and religious experience. Where there is no downtown church of the same denomination, it may, if not too adversely located, perform the functions of the central church for that communion. However, if it is in the shadow of a strong downtown church, it can rarely hope to develop comparable strength or prestige.

Religion in the homeless-man area

In practically every city there are at least a few blocks along one of the streets near the railroad where the homeless men and the wanderers congregate; the larger the city, the more extensive the section. The religious institutions which are located here are as definitely a part of the picture as is the flophouse and the cheap restaurant.

1. *Missions.* The most characteristic religious agency is the mission, usually set up in a small store, whose windows permit the men to see who is inside and what is going on before they enter. It may be supported by one of the established denominations or, in a smaller city, by a group of the downtown churches. Most missions, however, are conducted by "free lances." Occasionally a man who has been down-and-out undergoes a profound conversion experience in a mission and decides that he himself will carry on the work which helped change his own life. Generally these "superintendents" must raise their own funds, in part by a door-to-door appeal in the residential districts; very little is ever contributed by those who attend. The tax exemption privilege of religious institutions keeps the store rent much lower than would otherwise be the case. A baking company may furnish day-old rolls for use in the customary free meal after the religious meeting.

Missions vary greatly in leadership, policy, and cleanliness. Practically all of them provide "coffee an'" (coffee and doughnuts or rolls) after the services. About half of them have a few rooms or a loft where a limited number of men are permitted to sleep. Meetings are often haphazard and dull. A visitor from outside the area, even though unknown to the superintendent, may be called upon without warning to sing a solo, to testify, or to "preach a sermon." The following is a description of a typical mission.

There has been an independent mission at this location for twenty years. The present management is in its fourth year. This mission has no denominational connection and is a "faith" work.

Mr. Y——, about thirty-five years of age, is a wholesale meat salesman who operates the mission at night. He was ordained by the "Grace Witness" group and speaks much of being a born-again Christian. Very pleasant and co-operative in spirit.

The interior of the mission is neat and clean, well painted and decorated—one of the better places. Indirect lighting softens the appearance of the wooden chairs and wall mottoes. Two pianos are in evidence. Behind the pulpit platform is the prayer room and office.

The services are led by various groups from the fundamentalist churches in the city. The wholesale meat men take one evening a week. The preliminaries and the early part of the meetings are invariably long and drawn out. Of the time between 7:30 and 9:00 o'clock only the last half-hour is given to the message, altar call and closing song. The music, instrumental and vocal, is usually of an inferior sort. The dog-eared song books are of the "gospel and full salvation" type.

No drunks who are boisterous, too drunk to know where they are, are allowed to come in. No sleeping during the service is allowed, nor is walking about or disturbing the meeting permitted. The doors are locked during prayer. The men are given coffee, sandwiches, and doughnuts at 9:00 P.M. The average attendance is around fifty. Of these, about fifty per cent are repeaters. This figure is arrived at by placing a pile of song books near the door. If a man takes one on his way in, he is a repeater. If he has to be given one or shown where they are, he is a new customer.

Whether the missions are effective is a question that is often asked. No simple answer is possible. It seems generally agreed that the men sample one mission one night, another the next, seeking primarily such immediate and physical benefits as "coffee an'" and a bed on a cold night.

Nevertheless, profound changes do take place in the lives of some. In practically any mission at least one person may be interviewed who has been led to a changed life by a religious experience in a mission. Even police officers and local merchants, who generally are quite skeptical about the work of the missions, know the story of one or two men in whose life a dramatic change has taken place. The men on the street, below their hardened surface, have an appreciation for "this religion stuff," in spite of their exploitive attitude toward the missions. But they dislike being forced to expose their inner and secret yearnings, which they manage to keep quite well covered most of the time. As one hobo remarked:

The guys in charge of these missions think the Catholics are bad because they have this here confessional. And yet they want us to get up and tell our sins before the whole d—— bunch. I believe in what they preach, but I'm not going down in front and get saved and have to tell a hundred guys about it.

The mission is at best only a partial answer to the church's responsibility for these homeless men. It does reach a few individuals effectively, but in the

majority it reinforces an already cynical attitude toward organized religion. Men need more than the haphazard song-and-preaching services of the missions, topped off with coffee-an'. They must be seen as whole personalities, and a broader and integrated ministry provided for them.

2. *Denominational Programs.* Nearly all of the churches which once existed in the area while it was still used for residence purposes have long since closed. The Salvation Army and the Volunteers of America are the two oldest organizations designed to aid down-and-out men and women. In practically every large city the Army operates a hotel or hostel for homeless men. It is in a position to give medical aid or clothing when it is needed, and will also help a man get a job. In larger cities it has developed a sizable, well-staffed social work organization supported in part by the community chest.

Some Protestant denominations maintain a combined mission and social service program for homeless men. Religious meetings are held nightly in a more worshipful setting than the store-front missions can provide. Church-like pews replace the wooden chairs. Stained-glass windows are an impressive substitute for the cheap chromos that decorate mission walls. The altar and cross, even the extra entrance vestibule which diminishes street noises, all add to the churchly aspect. The real drawing card for the men is the superior reputation of the establishment. These are known as the best places to go. Like the missions, they regularly offer those who stay through the meeting coffee-an' and generally can provide a night's lodging for those in need. Much emphasis is placed on getting the men to abandon drink and secure a job. Frequently an ordained minister is in charge of the work, assisted by a corps of lay volunteers. The emphasis is always evangelical, and the technique, except in some of the Episcopal missions, is evangelistic.

The Goodwill Industries of America, first established by the Methodist Church in Boston and now in many cities conducted on a nondenominational basis, has made one of the most substantial contributions toward rehabilitating men and women. This organization, which solicits discarded furniture and clothing, maintains workshops located in the areas of underprivilege, where these goods are reworked for later sale. Its chief function is not to provide salable secondhand merchandise, but to give employment and guidance to persons who would otherwise find it almost impossible to get a job: a blind man, a woman with a heart ailment, or a down-and-outer for whom regular employers have no time. The aim is to rebuild physically or spiritually handicapped people and help them where possible to fit again into normal society. Daily chapel meetings are held in the plant, and, without any high pressure, religious awakening often occurs.

The better supervised agencies, in spite of the discouraging aspects of their work, are more successful than the missions in changing life patterns.

Their emphasis is not simply on saving the man's soul, but also on re-habilitating his body and re-establishing his self-respect. Time is needed for this, and wise guidance.

Religion in the rooming-house area and the "port of entry"

Compared with the homeless men, the people of the rooming-house district seem like a relatively stable population and certainly cannot be classed as vagrants. They are busy in offices or stores earning their living during the daytime, seeking to maintain, especially after they first arrive in the city, the evidences of respectability which characterized them in their old home town. However, the rooming-house district itself is a moral and spiritual depressant for them. Few are the agencies designed to undergird weakening morale or inspire to higher living, and, as one of these, the Christian Church has not been particularly successful.

1. *The Downtown Church and the Roomers.* Roomers do not care to spend much time in the neighborhood of their sleeping quarters. Since they are foot-loose and all transportation leads to the center of the city, they can often be effectively served by downtown churches.[3] This is especially true if the church is not thought of as "high hat" by the roomers, who are hungry for personal recognition and fellowship. Sensitive as they are, because of their own social insecurity, they will probably not return if they feel that the church is cold and formal.

2. *The Neighborhood Church.* Within the rooming-house district there are usually a few marooned churches which have survived from the time of the community's prosperity. As a rule they are struggling simply to maintain their existence. They have a declining membership, and at the Sunday morning worship service only a small fraction of the seating capacity in the sanctuary is used. The program, still designed for the people who used to live in the community, has little appeal for the roomers. The church, down-at-heels, is too much like the community from which the roomers would like to escape.

Quite different is the situation of a church which is located in a border-line area between the rooming-house district and an established residential community. In this case the church will frequently maintain its full vigor and have a well-developed program, ministering to the people on either side of it. Yet here again, because of his sensitiveness, the rooming-house dweller has a tendency to feel he is not wanted unless others of the congregation go more than half way to overcome his reticence and encourage him to share in the specific fellowship activities of the church. This takes much time and personal cultivation, which unfortunately most churches are not in a po-sition to provide.

[3] See pp. 78-79.

3. *Attitude of the Roomer Toward the Church.* When people first arrive in a rooming-house district, they bring with them not only their luggage but also their conceptions of right and wrong, and the place of religion in life. Frequently they seek early to affiliate with some church. But if the results of this effort are disappointing to them, they soon lapse into the typical state of mind of the community. A rooming-house proprietress questioned on this subject probably spoke for the average roomer:

HOUSEKEEPER: There is neither an attitude of antagonism toward the church nor interest in it. I would say that most of the roomers have forgotten about religion. They have learned to live without it, and other things have been substituted.

INTERVIEWER: Suppose a church with a good program should be started. Would the roomers be interested?

HOUSEKEEPER: Here on L—— Street they might, because there are more families here. But as a whole I do not think they would, though I suppose everyone needs a church.

INTERVIEWER: Do you, then, go to church?

HOUSEKEEPER: I used to, but I don't any more. When I lived in E——, I was a Baptist and went every Sunday. When I started to the Baptist church here, they began pressing immediately for money. I didn't like that. Then in their program there is too much Bible and not enough application. So I went to the Presbyterian church, but common people don't fit in there. Then I tried the Four Square church, but they were terrible. So I stopped going.

INTERVIEWER: You said that most people here have substituted something else for religion?

HOUSEKEEPER: Yes. I go to the movie, but mainly I work. I have forty-five rooms to take care of.

No mere observer can understand the deep struggles that are going on within the life of a young person who lives in the anonymous and demoralizing atmosphere of the rooming-house area of a large city. The following conversation reveals some of this struggle in the mind of a young man. Obviously he needs the support which the church should be able to give, but it is equally clear that he is not finding the assistance he thinks he needs. Only the relevant parts of the conversation, held in a local restaurant, are recorded.

INTERVIEWER: Do you get home often?

ROOMER: About once a month. A fellow has to keep a grip on things some way.

INTERVIEWER: Why, is it so hard to keep going here?

ROOMER: You must be new. Say, boy, if you are, move out. There isn't a place in M—— where it is harder to keep going than right here. . . .

INTERVIEWER: Say, where's the best place to go to church here?

ROOMER: That's the first question I asked when I got here, too. And no one had anything but wise cracks for the answer.

INTERVIEWER: Why, don't people go to church?

ROOMER: Not here.

INTERVIEWER: Why not?

ROOMER: Well, at first I thought it was because the people had no use for the church. But now I think it's the other way around. The church has no place for these poor devils.

INTERVIEWER: How's that?

ROOMER: Well, I was nervous and tired and fed up with this d—— city. Then I remembered what my folks used to say about the church. So I went. But there was nothing there for me. Beautiful music, fine sermon, lots of people. But I didn't feel right. In these churches everyone seems to have made their friends before you arrive. They are interested in having you make friends and feel at home, but they want someone else to do it. They had me sign a visitor's card; but it was about as personal as though I had signed a check at the bank. A few days later someone came to call. He sat on the bed. I sat on a chair. I asked him to take his coat off. But he said, "No, I can only stay a few minutes." Do you think he persuaded me to come to his church? No sir! There was nothing personal. It was just a hurried, routine call.

Many of these judgments are evidently unfair to ministers and church members. This minister had probably worked hard to develop a calling program so that every stranger who left his address would receive at least one visit. Yet these are representative attitudes and can be understood as a logical outcome of rooming-house living. If the church is to help these people "keep a grip on things," it must recognize their fears and furnish the personalized ministry which they so much need. For example, the minister in his preaching should stress the personal implications of the Christian message, using illustrations applicable to the people of the area. He should be available for personal counseling and be prepared to use the resources of the community to help solve in a tangible way the problems of roomers and others who come. The church might well maintain a list of reputable rooming houses and dependable health services. The pastor and his laymen need to take every opportunity to individualize the ministry of the church, through the friendly greeting before and after service, a call at the rooming house, an invitation to drop in some evening at the parsonage, and through well-planned social and recreational activities conducted weekly.

The outside bulletin board might properly carry a permanent message: "Calls will be made on the sick on request." The pastor should be prepared to administer Holy Communion to persons who are ill. It is often through aid received in times of weakness that men and women are most deeply touched.

4. *The Family Port of Entry.* Family groups moving into a city and having little money often locate in the one- or two-room, low-rent apart-

ments or "housekeeping quarters" in or near the rooming-house district. These sections of the city are often referred to as "ports of entry" because the highly mobile newcomers settle here until they can become financially secure and discover adequate housing.

Being a family group diminishes the disorganizing effect of the unstable community. Even so, these folk experience the typical difficulties of the roomer in discovering a congenial church and a new circle of friends. One reason is that they usually come from a small town where they felt much at home. The near-by church, if they go at all, seems strange to them in its membership and order of service. These people, if they arrive in large numbers and come from an ardently evangelistic background, may establish a little religious circle of their own. Or at least they will be a ripe field for an alert missioner who stresses revivalistic methods. Sometimes the newly formed congregation is able to buy one of the old buildings whose membership has scattered. Such a religious society is usually almost indistinguishable in its worship services and program from the rural churches which were left behind.

The Protestant church which is already there in the community, if it is willing to make some adaptations in its program and employ some of the phraseology which the transient groups enjoy, can count on a much heartier response than it would otherwise receive. This, of course, would transform it from a stranded to a neighborhood church and continue both its life and its usefulness.

Religions in nationality and racial colonies

A major portion of the underprivileged areas has been occupied by distinctive nationality and racial groups, chiefly immigrants from Europe and Mexico and Negroes. Here where the rent was low they established colonies in which their traditions and institutions were preserved. These helped them make the difficult adjustment to a new setting.

1. *Imported Churches.* Family ideals and religious beliefs are among the most deeply cherished of man's possessions. The need for the comfort of religion and the guidance offered by the pastor or priest is particularly felt when people break away from their old home and move to a new land, where life is strange and values are different. The Scandinavians and the Germans established Lutheran churches wherever they settled. Services in the mother tongue were heart-warming in a city where only English could be heard on the streets. In Irish, Italian, or Polish settlements the Roman Catholic church founded a nationality parish and imported priests from the old country. Most of these churches were built while immigration

was still at its height and preserved even in their architecture and decoration the flavor of the old homeland.

The minority churches of European countries were also represented among the immigrants. Indeed, America, traditionally a Protestant and "free church" country, seemed especially congenial for German Baptists or Swedish Methodists. Although these churches had much in common with American congregations in the same denominations, they maintained their own identity and held services in the native tongue. The strength of such churches depended largely on the size of the nationality colony, but all—Catholic, Lutheran, and Evangelical alike—have undergone change with the passing decades.

2. *The Bilingual Church.* To the distress of immigrants to America, their children show little eagerness to be identified as Germans, Czechs, or Italians, or to master the language of their parents. Educated in the American public school and playing on the streets with children who speak only English, they wish to be thought of as Americans. In the church an outcome of this was that the mother tongue would be used for the morning service and English for the evening. In effect the church became bilingual. The lack of new recruits for the colony, because of the stoppage of immigration, and the mounting opposition of the second and third generations to the use of a "foreign" language have, after a struggle, resulted in a gradual disappearance of the bilingual feature.

Even so, however, these churches have had difficulty in extending their fellowship to include others outside the old cultural group. The people in the congregation know one another so well that they unwittingly are cool to chance visitors, and a newcomer must be persistent if he is to become a part of the fellowship. Further, he will need to accept the little traditions and practices which have held over. For example, the Swedes will continue to enjoy their smorgasbord dinners.

The church with a foreign-language background often becomes marooned when its people move on. Its membership declines as its young people drop away, and few outsiders are attracted. Unless the bilingual church is willing to minimize the ties with its European culture, in fact as well as in name, its future is not promising.

3. *Religion in Communities of Various Races.* The social disorganization in areas of transition not only reduces rents but also makes it easier for members of non-Caucasian racial groups to locate there. It was inevitable that the Chinese, Japanese, Mexicans, and Negroes moving into a city should establish their colonies in the poorer areas. Even though the older inhabitants may have prejudice against the newcomers, they are not able to maintain a solid front against them. Each of these racial colonies has its own distinctive religious institutions. Many Chinese continue ancestor worship in

their own homes and attend special services in a Buddhist temple, which may occupy part of the tong or "business association" building. Some Oriental-Americans, particularly those of Japanese descent, have become Christians, usually attending a church sponsored by a Protestant denomination or by the council of churches.

The Mexicans are nominally Roman Catholics. If there is a large colony of them in the city, that denomination will establish a special "national" church for them. Otherwise they will be expected to go to the local parish church. Because of their extreme mobility and the fact that many men come to American cities without their families, it is more difficult for a family-type Protestant church to minister to them. Nevertheless there are scores of Mexican Protestant churches. Worship services are generally conducted in Spanish, but the program as a whole is bilingual.

Negroes usually are in one of the Baptist or Methodist denominations. To a greater extent than members of other races they have supported their churches with enthusiasm and generosity. Generous though they are, low-income Negroes have difficulty maintaining the church building and paying an adequate salary to their pastor. Some of the ministers are as well trained and as capable as any of their brothers in the white churches. Others have had little opportunity for schooling and present the message with a fervor and often an incoherence which is more acceptable to the older people than to young educated men and women.

Almost as numerous as the congregations of regular denominations are the free-lance, store-front churches found especially in the poorer Negro communities. An aggressive man who has been a leader in one of the churches feels that he does not receive proper recognition and withdraws, along with ten or fifteen other families. They set up a new church, and he is elected and ordained in accordance with congregational custom; or he may even be "self-ordained." The next step is to secure a meeting place. This will probably be a vacant store where the rent, because of the tax exemption provision, is quite low. The new movement receives a name, such as "God's Heralds," or "The Independent Mount Zion Baptist Church." There are many reasons for the establishment of these little schismatic groups, but certainly one of the chief is the struggle for recognition and the perquisites associated with being a pastor.

The increasing race consciousness of the Negro has led, in the minds of many, to an identification of some of the old-line Protestant churches with the subordination from which they are seeking to escape. The noisy, emotional, revivalistic service is also an irritating reminder of primitivism. Consequently young Negroes, particularly those with more education, are leaving Protestant churches in large numbers; some have joined the Roman Catholic Church, in part because it was not identified in their minds with days of humiliation, and in part because at least nominally there is no segregation in it. This movement is now a cause of grave concern to Protestant Negro religious leaders.

World War II gave great impetus to mobility not only of whites but of Negroes as well. The pressure of the flow into many northern and western cities has weakened the bars of segregation in community after community. The typical pattern is still for the white residents to sell out and flee from an area at the first signs of the approaching wave, and for the "white" church to maintain its whiteness until it has practically expired, and then sell out to a Negro congregation. However, there are encouraging evidences of a changing attitude. This has been stimulated by the very fact of Negro mobility and by the Supreme Court decision of 1954 and the enlightened position taken by labor unions, governmental bureaus, and professional groups. It has also followed from the discovery by certain more daring social groups, including church people, that association with various members of the Negro race is rewarding and pleasant. It is significant that census information in a northern city indicated that with the inflow of an upper-income Negro population to a particular area the average educational attainment in the area was raised.

For several years an increasing number of churches with white Caucasian membership have welcomed to their worship and to their membership people of other racial groups. Chinese, Japanese, Nisei (second-generation Japanese), Mexicans, or Negroes are members or attenders in over a thousand "white" churches. While most of these are in the North or West, some are found in the South. For example, some white churches in Texas have a few Mexican and Negro members. Nor are these churches limited to areas of underprivilege; in 1947 the First Baptist Church of Chicago called a Nisei to be its full-time pastor. The people of nearby historic St. James Methodist Church voted in 1954 to invite Negroes (who constitute three fourths of the surrounding population) to join their fellowship. Within a year sixty-two Negroes have become members. Morale is high. Attendance has risen, including attendance of whites. And the newcomers are generously supporting the budget. This type of integration is being carried on with little publicity in a good many Protestant churches. The testimony is that since persons of other races have been admitted to membership, the spiritual tone of the whole congregation has been raised and their consciences have shed a burden. There is a basis for hope that Protestant churches will, before it is too late, achieve color blindness.

The institutional church

Perhaps the most significant adaptation of the Protestant church to the changing or disorganized community is the development of an "institutional" program. Instead of maintaining services primarily for the benefit of members who have left the area, it deliberately remodels the building, employs a professional staff, and develops a seven-day-a-week program. It is in effect both a church and a social settlement. The usual religious activities—Sunday worship services, church school, and youth fellowship— are retained. But in addition any or all of the following elements may be added: a nursery school to care for children of working mothers, handicraft classes, playground groups, basketball teams, drama groups, discussion forums, a library, low-cost movies, Boy and Girl Scouts, citizenship classes for adults, mothers' clubs, a family adjustment center, counseling service, community betterment clubs, and a summer camp. The aim of the church is to serve the people who live within its shadow, to help them with their daily problems of living, and to be a character-building force in the community, filling the lives of children and youth with wholesome, creative interests and combating the influences which make for bad health, delinquency, and despondency.

On the desirability of such a program there is general agreement. However, there is not a clear consensus among Christian people on three important questions concerning the role of the institutional church: (1) What is the relative weight which should be given to the distinctively churchly or religious activities as compared with the more secular educational and recreational program? (2) Should missionary money be used for the benefit of Roman Catholic or Jewish children, who, with few exceptions, will continue in the religious practices of their parents? (3) Should the financial assistance of the community chest—which involves making the program open to all without any religious requirements—be sought? No one of these three interrelated questions can be readily answered in simple terms. Confusion exists in some institutions concerning them—with the board of directors and often the professional staff in serious disagreement—resulting in tension, misunderstanding, and inefficiency. A first step in wise programming is to establish a clear policy on these points.

Churches in underprivileged communities, especially those aiming to serve people of the area, are necessarily dependent on substantial missionary support, except in rare cases where there is a large endowment. Just as the city government cannot expect to raise enough money in taxes locally to maintain the essential services in blighted or near-blighted areas, so the church cannot expect these low-income people to finance adequate religious services. It rests with the denominational missionary society and the churches in more privileged communities to see that necessary resources are provided.

Capable professional leadership is at least as important as financial support. The demands on the pastor and director of the institution are diverse and specialized. He needs not only the skills of pastor and preacher, but also a knowledge of group and case work. He must be able to supervise and preserve harmonious relations within a staff of paid and volunteer assistants. Often much of the burden of raising funds devolves on his shoulders, and contact must be maintained with the many civic agencies which are interested in his community and with which he should co-operate.

Although ministers generally do not have special training in group work and social service, they can, with patience, imagination, and some effort, acquire the understanding and skills necessary for success. The major Protestant denominations have departments of city work with superintendents who can give wise counsel. Directors of social settlements and other institutional churches, staff members of the associated charities and community chest—all will welcome an opportunity for conference and the sharing of experience. Members of college and university departments of sociology and social work are another resource.

The following account describes what has been done by one minister who had little specialized training in urban church work until after he was appointed to a run-down church in an underprivileged section of a southwestern city.

For several years the new pastor received little assistance from his denomination and consequently became discouraged. During a short course in urban church problems he gained an understanding of the processes which produced such communities as his, and a determination to analyze and solve his own local problems. He presented his findings graphically to his supporting members, to the denominational officials, and other public-spirited citizens, demonstrating that the blighted area where his church was located needed much more than the customary church services.

Within five years, under a revised program, six members have been added to his staff, hundreds of additional boys and girls have been reached, three community buildings and chapels have been erected in as many of the slum "pockets" located in the river bottoms. In spite of the fact that this is the area of broken homes, beer joints, and houses of assignation, the delinquency rate has steadily declined, until now there are fewer truants and juvenile delinquents here than in some of the so-called better residential districts.

The minister, in co-operation with a radio station, has organized the "Crusaders." Under his direction children from different clubs and churches plan and present a weekly radio broadcast. The Bible and religious teachings are kept central. Protestant, Catholic, and Jewish boys and girls, whites and Negroes, share in the programs. The Crusaders work for community betterment, agitate for clean streets and garbage collection. As many of them have discovered, "religion can be fun."

The problem and the future

The church itself cannot be expected to eliminate the slum. The responsibility for basic physical change falls outside the church's domain.

Nevertheless, with its message of redemption the Christian Church has in many communities boldly essayed to change the moral climate. The methods employed have been adapted to the needs of the people and also to the circumstances: it has tied personal rehabilitation to mission work among the homeless men; it has created employment opportunities for the physically and socially handicapped; it has sought to reach the almost inaccessible rooming-house dwellers with a personal ministry and with opportunity for Christian fellowship; people with foreign tongues have received the message in their own language; and boys and girls have found wholesome fun and character-building experience in a Christian environment.

Yet the church in most impoverished communities has been only partially successful. The reasons are numerous. Many congregations have sold their property as members moved away, and have opened a new sanctuary farther out. Others have hung on with steadily diminishing membership until debts accumulated, and, with nothing left to sell, the church finally "flickered out." Some have remained physically in the community but have withdrawn psychologically. In general, Protestantism has faced its responsibilities here in a piecemeal fashion. Each church has struggled over its own problems and reached its own decisions without reference to what was happening in other churches near by. So, one after another has been closed, until in some of the dominantly Roman Catholic communities in northern cities no evangelical church has remained to serve the diminished but significant non-Catholic population.

If the responsibilities of evangelical Christianity are to be adequately met in communities of this type, it can only be on the basis of intra- and interdenominational planning and support. The churches of the entire city have an obligation to these older areas, from which much of their own leadership has been drawn. Both ministers and laymen in prosperous communities should be quickened to a sense of their own obligation. They can underwrite a program which will make possible the forging of new leadership within the community and the transformation of its moral climate. City planning will determine in considerable measure the future land use of these poorer sections, but only an alert clergy and laity can take advantage of the opportunities which are offered, either under present conditions or in the event of community rehabilitation.

CHAPTER TWELVE

The Growing Edge of the City

UNCOUNTED urban Americans long for the pleasures which accompany life in small, simple residential communities. That is why suburbanites on Long Island or in Westchester rise early to catch the train which will take them twenty or thirty miles into Manhattan, where they work through seven or eight hours before catching the commuters' train back home. In all probability there are more than a million employed people in America who spend two hours a day going to and returning from work, so that they may live far removed from the job. In fact, the transportation system is an intricate set of pumping devices to move people from their homes, where they cannot earn a livelihood, to their jobs, where they do not wish to live, and back to their homes again. At the cost of five hundred travel hours per year these Americans are attempting to have their cake and eat it too.

Stable, "mature" communities of the city and its suburbs house a large proportion of the population, but there are always others who desire and can pay for a new home in less crowded surroundings. These account for the continued outward thrust into new territory. The older, sedate communities are not so attractive to the ambitious young city family. When they think of a new home, they have in mind a modern dream house, fresh out of *Better Homes and Gardens* or the *Architectural Forum,* in the optimistic surroundings of a rapidly developing subdivision. They find romance in the quest for a house located on a curving, tree-bordered street, with ample play space for the children. However, they are kept from being too impractical by the ubiquitous fact of cost and the cool eye of the mortage company.

This longing for a "home in the country" is widespread among city people, and, while most who talk about it will never have one, the very discussion of the subject whets the desire and increases the likelihood that they will use their savings for such a purpose. It is not simply the rich who desire such a residence. On one side or another of every metropolitan city will be found housing developments designed to fit almost any purse, from ornate estates with elaborate gardens to small building lots cut from one corner of a farmer's pasture, with no facilities other than the farm pump and outhouse.

The suburban trend [1]

The impersonal statistics of the census reflect this desire to live in less congested surroundings.[2] The population *around* metropolitan cities (fifty thousand or more) has been growing two and a half times as fast as the population *within* those same cities[3] and more than twice as fast as the rest of the   population of the United States—that is, outside the metropolitan areas. This trend is continuing, and the lion's share of postwar development is on the fringes of medium-sized and great cities.

Table VI
COMPARATIVE GROWTH IN SELECTED CITIES
AND THEIR SUBURBS, 1940-1950

METROPOLITAN AREA	Per Cent Increase in Central City	Per Cent Increase Outside Central City
All metropolitan areas	13.9	35.5
Dallas, Tex.	47.4	73.7
Detroit, Mich.	13.9	54.8
Portland, Me.	5.4	28.5
Seattle, Wash.	27.0	94.2
Winston-Salem, N. C.	10.0	25.0

Illustrative of this movement is Table VI, which shows the rapid suburban growth around five representative cities selected from different sections of the country.

Types of new residential development

The development of new tracts for urban and suburban residential use has proceeded in accordance with the American tradition of free enterprise and individual initiative. While the size of lot and the type of housing construction may be controlled within the municipal boundaries, few regulations govern land use and construction outside the incorporated areas. The regional planning commissions of most metropolitan districts perform only advisory functions, and individual builders may not even know of the

---

[1] The population movement referred to in this section is chiefly to the *outlying undeveloped portions* of the major city and its older suburban municipalities. The older incorporated municipalities which adjoin large cities are often and properly referred to as suburbs. Many of these suburbs have experienced only slightly faster growth than the metropolis and would classify as stable communities rather than areas of new growth.

[2] See Table I, p. 20.

[3] This contrast would be even more marked were it not for the fact that some cities, such as New York and Los Angeles, have such far-flung boundaries that they include in "city" statistics much population growth which is really suburban.

existence of such an agency. The result is that while some suburban residential communities are wisely laid out and form coherent, architecturally harmonious sections, others represent extreme disorganization in land use and type of construction.

1. *Small Sporadic Developments*. In a period of prosperity money jingles in the pockets of industrial and white-collar workers. Then, if ever, they can secure homes of their own in desirable surroundings. So they cruise through the countryside looking for a likely plot. Farming land, three or perhaps twenty miles from the city along a paved but secondary road, looks inexpensive and attractive to many of them; and frequently the farmer decides it is advantageous for him to cut up the south edge of his farm into quarter-acre plots, which he can sell for three hundred dollars each. This brings a comfortable profit on his original investment—much better than growing corn or cotton.

The prospective builder then finds himself with a piece of land large enough for a house, garage, garden, and a few fruit trees. For water he must either go to the farmhouse or sink his own well. For a sewage system he will install a septic tank. The hookup with the lines of the electric company can be made at small cost. City gas is not obtainable, but his wife can cook with electricity, "canned gas," or some other substitute. He will probably first build a double garage, in which they will live while they labor to construct their much-anticipated house. (Some never get beyond the garage stage.) Other like-minded families purchase adjoining plots. And finally there emerges a little neighborhood of a dozen houses, strung side by side along the highway, illustrating the advantages and disadvantages of un-co-ordinated development in a small subdivision.

Occasionally such little settlements are artistically laid out through the joint efforts of the householders. Their homes are built just as they wish, but they help one another in construction and together plant rosebushes along the shoulder of the highway. They take pride in the appearance of their homes and prevent the accumulation of litter which so often mars the rural landscape. However, even under the best circumstances the advantages of independence and low tax cost must be balanced against the lack of sidewalks, street lighting, and fire and police protection; and eventually the problems of water supply and sanitation may constitute a serious hazard.

In most cases these hit-or-miss small real-estate developments prove a disappointment. The wife is removed from nearly all social contacts. The husband takes the car to go to work, and she is stranded, with her children and a few neighbors, but without the usual responsibilities and interests of a farm woman. The buildings which were laid out on paper are difficult to erect with amateur labor, and the more elaborate plans are compromised for something less expensive and easier to construct. The dream may fade quickly and the family move into a half-finished house, which remains in that condition for a decade. Or, disillusioned, they sell to some other venturers. A neighborhood of this sort can easily take on the appearance of a shack town, which, if the city ever does expand far enough to touch it, will serve as a source of blight to any new better-class settlement.

2. *Large-Scale Peripheral Developments.* More important than this random building is the planned subdividing of large tracts on the edge of the city. This development is usually near a major transportation artery and spreads out into the territory on either side, along the crossroads, reaching first a block or two back and then, as more population moves into the region, still farther. This outthrust is much like the wave pattern created by the prow of an advancing ship.

Tracts of land, usually five or ten acres in extent—but sometimes as large as fifty acres—are acquired by a real-estate company which subdivides the property, lays out streets, and installs water, sewer, and street-lighting systems. Then, to the accompaniment of an advertising campaign, it proceeds to sell the lots to any parties it can interest. Some buyers intend to erect a home. Others, with no intention of building, may purchase the land speculatively, hoping to sell later at a profit. Such lots may remain vacant for five or even twenty-five years. In some cases the real-estate company itself constructs the houses and then sells the finished homes. This was a common practice during World War II, when a person who desired a house had almost no chance of securing building materials for himself. With government support large-scale builders opened up extensive tracts for war workers, constructing as many as five hundred homes at one time. In this type of project no lots are left vacant, and the houses are of a similar construction, often so uniform as to be monotonous.

The foresighted subdivider realizes that most of his prospects will come from the sector of the city in which his development is the newest outthrust. So he can forecast to a certain extent the characteristics of the population which will move in. This will determine many phases of his plans, from the size and price of his lots to restrictions written into the deed on the type and minimum value of the construction. The shrewd developer takes into account the particular background, prejudices, and loyalties of the people even when he is naming the new streets in his subdivision.

The suburban expansion suddenly stops and becomes congealed when a business depression looms. Risks are greater; money is harder to borrow; people hesitate to buy land or build. But as soon as another period of prosperity seems assured, realtors and construction companies again set out their stakes, string flags around their tiny offices, and advertize in the newspapers concerning the gala opening of the Ogden Park Subdivision.

3. *The Metamorphosis of the Rural Village.* Along the railroads which

long since have connected every American city with other urban centers are numerous small stations strung like beads on a necklace. These "whistle stops" grew in importance as the farming community developed, and slowly some of them became prosperous villages. They were aware of the large city ten or twenty miles distant, and glad that it was such a convenient market for their produce, but were anxious to maintain their own independence.

As the population of the city increases, a significant change begins to occur in these towns. City dwellers, usually of the middle- or upper-income class, charmed by their quiet, tree-lined streets and attracted by the combined advantages of rural living and lower taxes, begin to buy some of the older homes. Others build houses for themselves, thankful that local wage rates and often materials are lower. These newcomers maintain their tie with the city. Some commute to work by train; others drive in. As the traffic becomes heavier, the railroad improves its suburban service. After the town is recognized as within commuting distance, a real-estate company may stake out a subdivision on its outskirts, and the in-movement is augmented. Slowly but certainly the town which once looked to the surrounding countryside now faces toward the big city. It may never be incorporated within the city boundaries, but its economy and even its habits of life are being transformed. Some of the old-timers who at first rubbed their hands with satisfaction at the higher prices which city folk were willing to pay for real estate are wishing now for the old tranquillity. The population slowly takes sides: the rural-minded versus the commuters. This division is seen in the debate over political issues—whether to broaden Main Street and increase the parking area at the railroad station. The old-timers say, "No," and the new ones, "Yes." The question "Should the ban on Sunday movies be lifted?" demonstrates the same cleavage. The difference in viewpoint may be seen in the Parent-Teacher Association, in the town chamber of commerce, and in the local churches.

Not all of these towns remain beyond the boundaries of the city. Most metropolitan centers have achieved considerable growth through the incorporation of one such former rural town after another. This has not occurred in the environs of Boston, since other sizable cities adjoin it and wish to maintain their identity. But Philadelphia, Memphis, Los Angeles, and other major cities have incorporated scores of towns over the decades. With the passage of time the distinguishing marks of these absorbed communities disappear; the land between the former independent town and the city is used for residential purposes; and rows of apartment houses may now replace the former single-family homes.

The smaller city is not always incorporated by the metropolis. Within the city of Indianapolis, not far from the Circle, are a few blocks of old homes. For more than fifty years the residents of Woodruff Place (1940 population: 1,434) have steadfastly refused amalgamation with the larger city. Los Angeles has completely surrounded no fewer than nine such incorporated cities and many unincorporated patches of county, which still carry on their independent existence inside its borders. Except for taxing purposes, educational standards, and police and fire protection, these political divisions are more nominal than real. The stranger crossing the city boundaries cannot detect the difference, either in the type of residential construction or the cultural life of the people.

4. *New City*. Recent years have produced an entirely different type of suburban development. Instead of building ten or even a hundred homes on a meadow adjoining the city, a few well-financed organizations have laid plans to establish in the open countryside a new and complete suburban city. A large acreage is procured near high-speed transportation. A comprehensive plan is drawn up; streets are laid out; and utilities provided for. The business district is planned, and property is set aside for schools and parks. Land-use restrictions (zoning) are incorporated in the deeds. A new city begins to spring out of farm land.

Park Forest, which will eventually care for at least forty thousand people, is an illustration of this ambitious type of town planning. It is now in process of development on a pleasant, semiwooded tract of 2,400 acres, including a little lake, located in the open country twenty-five miles south of the center of Chicago. The plan calls for the construction of ten thousand dwelling units in addition to necessary stores, offices, schools, and churches. Three thousand row and twin houses (sharing a common wall) are in process of construction. Not more than two hundred out of the ten thousand dwelling units will be in the nature of apartments. There is to be plenty of space, grass, and trees—a garden city for young, middle-class families.

So great is the desire of American families to live in pleasant, semi-rural surroundings that large-scale undertakings, protected with adequate safeguards to ensure attractive community development, are meeting with eager response. Certainly in a period of acute housing shortage a project carried forward on this gigantic scale is particularly likely to succeed.

5. *The Inner City as a Development Area.* City planning commissions usually classify the federal low-cost housing projects and similar large-scale developments as "new growth." The construction is indeed new, although it replaces older and deteriorated buildings instead of filling in previously vacant land. Since these projects rarely involve an appreciable increase in population for the community, and usually occasion little change in population composition, they do not properly fall within the same category as the preceding types of new-growth communities. They and the problems they present for the church are discussed in Chapters X and XI.

Hazards in urban expansion

The rapid, unregulated extension of urban residence areas in periods of economic prosperity entails certain risks—for real-estate developers, for people who buy the land and build, and for community institutions such as the church. The entrepreneur must invest or borrow large sums of money. His chances of securing a good return will depend in part on his own wisdom and foresight but also on other factors beyond his control, such as the competition of other subdividers and the general economic condition of the nation.

For the prospective home owner there are also uncertainties involved. Many subdivisions are carefully planned, and contract promises are conscientiously kept: streets and sidewalks are laid; utilities are installed; and parkways may be beautifully landscaped. In other cases all that remains after the lots are sold off are the corner stakes and the promises. If most of the lots are held for a later rise in price, large tracts of the subdivision may revert to a weedy, uncultivated state. Sidewalks in time are tipped and broken, and street lights shattered. The appearance of desolation creates a feeling of dissatisfaction on the part of those who have built and repels prospective buyers.

Unless the area is properly zoned, persons who think they are building in an attractive, homelike community may some day discover a factory being erected on an adjacent street, or the corner lot may be acquired for a roadhouse. Whereas most cities are now completely zoned, relatively few states provide for zoning unincorporated territory where much of the urban growth is taking place. The values which suburbanites envisage for their children may quickly fade because of the lack of such protection.

Another problem arises when too much land is set aside for commercial use. Since business lots can be sold to the public for considerably higher prices than residential lots, subdividers often lay out a larger proportion of the land for business purposes than can ever be justified by the population which will be housed in the adjoining residential sections. If an owner, eager to secure some return on his investment, should erect a few small stores, he may find it almost impossible to rent them because there is not the economic base in the community to support additional business ventures. Empty stores with dirty windows and vacant lots with weed patches and billboards are unsightly nuisances which detract from the appearance of the neighborhood. The first signs of community deterioration make their appearance at such points.

Serious health hazards may exist in the uncontrolled random developments on the fringe of the city. Communities with as many as two thousand inhabitants and no adequate water supply or sewage disposal system are numerous. Each residence has its own outdoor privy or septic tank, and nearly every house its own well. There may be no inspection or quarantine against communicable diseases. The dangers to the health of the local people and to the residents of the near-by city are obvious.

Moral hazards also exist where there is more interest in immediate profit and selfish advantage than in community welfare. An extreme example is Calumet City. It began as an uncontrolled settlement decades ago, exploiting commercially the leisure-time interests of a certain portion of the men in the great steel mills and manufacturing plants of South Chicago and Gary; and it has continued to follow the same pattern, as described in *Life* magazine:[4]

Planted just inside Illinois, Calumet City has 14,000 inhabitants, no railroad station, no Protestant church, no traffic lights, no central telephone system, 308 night clubs and seven policemen. Its ratio of one bar for every 46 persons is highest in the U.S. Forty years ago Calumet City was the home of a prosperous white slave ring. Twenty years ago it was headquarters of a rumrunning outfit. Today it is the nocturnal hotspot, the busy Barbary Coast of Lake Michigan's booming industrial plain.

City and regional planning commissions are keenly aware of such sore spots. The church also needs to recognize the serious problem and challenge involved. Its work with individuals and groups, even though excellent, cannot by itself overcome the demoralizing forces in the community. Therefore it must be interested in and support constructive legislative controls.

Social characteristics of the new community

Suburban residential developments are as varied as the American population, ranging from the attractive and well organized to the dismal and disintegrating. Nevertheless, the people moving into these areas of rapid growth tend to have a number of traits in common.

1. *Family Organization.* When young couples have been married for five to ten years, they feel that they should begin to achieve their long-cherished goal of acquiring a home of their own. For the sake of their children, also with an eye to their social position, they would like to locate in a pleasant, uncrowded suburb. New-growth communities, therefore, are made up typically of family units, with a disproportionately large number of young married people between twenty-five and forty years of age and with an approximate balance between the sexes. The number beyond fifty is relatively small. There are many young children, most of whom are under ten when the families first settle in their new homes. Where the core for the suburban community was an older rural village, there will be another important

4 Jan. 20, 1941.

element in the population group. The old-time residents will show a higher percentage above fifty than the national or state average.

2. *Economic Status.* Every urban community exercises a selective influence, drawing to itself persons who have approximately the same economic status and living standards. This is particularly true of new-growth areas. When the subdividers stake out small building lots, they are aiming for a relatively low-income clientele. When the tract is divided into quarter-acre plots and a high minimum construction cost is stipulated, a higher-income group is attracted. Each community tends to be relatively homogeneous in so far as economic status is concerned.

Regardless of differences among communities, it may be safely assumed that the new settlers will feel a degree of financial stringency after making the required down payments on a new house, buying suitable furniture, and beautifying the yard. The move to the suburbs generally comes when the need for play and living space for the children is most keenly felt. This also begins the period of heaviest family expenditure, which usually will last until the children are through college.

3. *Social Institutions.* The institutions which people establish are a cue to what they conceive to be important, and in turn attract similarly minded people. A Dutch Reformed or Roman Catholic church draws people of that faith to the area. A well-appointed school building and a public library will raise the community's status. On the other hand, most prospective home builders do not wish to rear their children where a number of taverns or roadhouses are operating.

Whether one looks at Cincinnati, Dallas, Denver, or Phoenix, the most impressive sights about the city are the peninsulas of new home construction reaching into hitherto open country. On the outlying newly laid-out streets one will see the foundations in place; a block nearer displays a row of almost-completed little square houses; while one block closer in new families have just taken possession and got curtains up at the front windows. So block after block is filled in; washings go up on clotheslines; fresh grass gives a green cast to the yards; and tricycles, little wagons, and sand pails decorate the walks.

These rapidly growing communities around American cities are particularly appealing to alert, ambitious young men and women who earn their income in the big city but wish to live in the environment of a small town. Here are to be found the majority of the future business and professional leadership of America. If it is to be a significant institution in these communities, the church must pioneer along with the new homemakers.

CHAPTER THIRTEEN

Churches in Developing Communities

TURNING away from the old and toward the new always involves both anticipation and uncertainty. This is notably true of families which move out from a long-established community to a new home. Many of their closest friends and perhaps relatives remain behind. The children must be introduced to another school and must discover new playmates, and other members of the family will also need to find their place in the new environment. Every social institution to which they once felt attached is now beyond walking distance: the playground, the park where they strolled on Sundays, the public library, the social club, the "juke joint," and the favorite bakery.

The new community is itself in a state of flux. Houses are being erected along the street; the school is expanding to take care of a larger enrollment. Some adventurous entrepreneurs are hopefully establishing small businesses, a few foredoomed to failure, but now bright and attractive. The entering family may not realize it, but others about them feel almost as unsettled, strange, and insecure as they. In such a developing community there is inevitably a lack of organization. The residents, all of them relatively recent, are hesitant to assume leadership. These social characteristics, common to areas of rapid growth, confront the church.

The maintenance of old church ties

In this residential development there is at first no organized religious life; but as new homes spring up here and there, some alert churchman with the help of a few local families initiates a Sunday-school program, and later on a worship service, in the living room of one of them. The project may be on a volunteer, part-time basis, designed primarily for children. If the leader is sectarian in viewpoint, it will have a restricted appeal. Usually the major denominations do not get around to establishing a new congregation in the area until the population is further augmented.[1]

If the religious life of the majority of the people is to remain vital, they

---

[1] Problems and procedures involved in establishing a new church are dealt with in Chaps. XV, XXI, and XXII.

will have to keep in touch with their old home churches. This is at first the natural inclination of church-minded families, and in spite of the distance they make the trip back each Sunday. The very thought of maintaining this long-established relationship is something of a balm to their spirits wounded by the severing of many ties. Consequently they plan to continue in regular attendance, and not a few families actually do keep in close touch with the old church over the years. Others, however, gradually form new local interests or decide that the trip is too arduous and, when there is a change of pastors, cease attending. However, in the numerous situations where no church of the same or similar denomination is located in the near-by community, the old church has a continuing responsibility. It should not make it easy for the suburbanite to forget his religious affiliation, but by visitation and perhaps an adjustment of the program keep him in vital relationship.

Religious life in Jakes Corners

The little sporadic suburban developments opened by enterprising farmers or small-scale realtors attract people who have a yen to live in the country. This urge is perhaps the only bond among the new householders. Common religious interests are lacking except in so far as one eager young couple may have persuaded others with a similar background to come along and buy some of the lots. Isolated as these people are, they soon develop a sense of neighborhood, but this is rarely supported by membership in the same church. Jakes Corners, with its twelve families, is too small to have a church of its own—even if all were of the same faith—and is too far from the nearest town for the children to walk to church school. Two of the Roman Catholic families still conscientiously drive the three miles to Sunday morning mass each week. But the rest of the settlement is content to "sleep in" and, after a late Sunday breakfast, work on the house or grounds. The adults, even some who were fairly regular in church attendance when they lived in the city, readily develop a secular attitude toward Sunday. A few of them still hold nominal membership in a church, but in that institution they are eventually placed on the nonresident list and forgotten. They and their children, in effect, are living in a secular, non-Christian environment. The rare exception may be when some devout mother, at no small inconvenience to herself, seeks to conduct a Sunday-school class for eight or ten youngsters of assorted ages.

To minister to these people is not easy. For one thing, until life crises arise they have little sense of need for or obligation to the church. For another, since they are in small, rather isolated clusters, it is not possible to organize a church especially for them. However, it is just as appropriate for the Baptist or Methodist church in the nearest village or town on the highway to call on these people and seek to enlist them in the fellowship as it is to send missionaries to China. In actual fact the churches in such suburban towns are likely to restrict their ministry to the people who live within or just outside the incorporated city limits. Families which live a mile or more from such a town are in an interstitial area which tends not to be included in the recognized parish of any church. In rare cases church members use their own cars to drive out and bring in the children from Jakes Corners and adjoining farms, or a bus may be employed for the purpose. Generally this is an unmet responsibility.

Religion in Manor Park Subdivision

No religious institution is placed within the new subdivision until a considerable number of homes have been erected. In the meantime the people are without any local ministry. The lack is not as marked as at Jakes Corners, for they are adjacent to the city and usually on a familiar highway leading back to the old community and church. Public transportation facilities are convenient, so children can be sent in to the church school, and young people can return for evening meetings without using the family car. If there is a church of their own denomination in a settled community within walking distance—a mile or less—and with alert leadership, a number will transfer their church letter to it.

When, with the passage of time, a church is established near by, many of the community will, if its teachings and leadership appeal to them, join the new congregation. Or, if they have become part of the secularized mass, the church will need to begin what is often the long and difficult process of rewinning them to religious loyalty and participation. The shorter the gap between the surrender of interest in the old home church and the development of the new congregation, the better will be the chance of conserving earlier religious attitudes and training. The church which roots in well is the one that begins its life when the community itself is in the process of making. Many of the strongest urban churches in America were founded years ago when their communities were young. Though once they needed all the assistance which a missionary society could give, they now have achieved a maturity and financial stability which makes them the chief source of strength for the church extension program in their own city.

Religious life in the former rural village

Some of the most successful suburban developments cluster about a long-established village. For a score of years or perhaps a century the village has been the shopping center for the farmers for miles around. It has had time to develop a full complement of rural institutions: an Odd Fellows hall, a Grange, a woman's club, elementary and high schools, and several churches. This is a setting in sharp contrast to the open fields which, when subdivided, form a base for a new settlement with no traditions, no institutions, and no loyalties.

The commuters who move to such a village generally plan to drop most of their organizational ties in the city and enter into the social and religious life of the new community. The first few migrants from the city are heartily welcomed and invited to join in local activities. These urbanites are alert, friendly, and enthusiastic about their new, semirural surroundings. Some of them may soon be asked to assume a measure of leadership in civic affairs and in the church. As the number of commuters increases, however, certain of the old-timers become irritated at the way the intruders seem to be taking possession of "our town" and begin to erect a defensive barrier.

The church which had functioned smoothly and conservatively for decades gradually finds that in some important respects the "city people" have different standards and tastes. A number of the newcomers have joined, and a few of the wives have taken an active part in the women's society. The fact that they are better dressed and have a little more self-confidence than the older members may be the reason for some tension. However, more serious conflict will develop if the urban women propose changes which startle or shock their associates. They may urge that the choir be robed, or that the chancel of the church be rearranged and a cross and candles be placed on the altar table. Perhaps they suggest a bridge marathon as a means of raising money instead of the conventional cake sale or strawberry festival. One of the commuters, now on the official board of the church, may propose that the young people be permitted to dance in the church basement—an idea repugnant to most of the older members.

On the other hand the suburbanites, who planned on a new home in an idyllic community, have discovered that the people in Stevensville have some definite ideas of their own, as well as a possessive feeling about the community institutions and in fact the whole area. While many of the newcomers are in hearty accord with the traditional standards and are easily incorporated into the community life, others who join the church soon become provoked at the "narrowness" of those in control. They may drop out or bide their time until the majority is on their side, so that they can effect the changes which they desire. In any case there is likely to be more or less tension as members cluster about leaders who represent different viewpoints concerning church life and practice.

Fortunately in typical suburbanized rural villages the tensions which customarily are found between the old residents and the outlanders are resolved without bitter conflict. In most cases the Protestant church, after a period of disagreement and uncertainty, accepts its responsibility, enlarges its sanctuary, and proceeds to serve what is by then a dominantly urban community. This process of readjustment can be accomplished without personal hurt or institutional damage if there is imaginative, skillful, and consecrated ministerial leadership.

Religious life in New City

When an entire city is laid out and built as one project, the developers often set aside one or more plots as sites for churches. The inclination of the planners seems to be to locate all of these sites close together and near the prospective business district. While this may be a good arrangement if all parts of the development are within walking distance, it is unwise if provision is being made for as many as twenty thousand people. The actual placement and erection of the churches, of course, must be left up to the various denominations or to a central planning body, such as the comity commission of the council of churches. The approved procedure among comity commissions is to assign to one or more of the member denominations responsibility for building a church in New City, with the expectation that it will welcome and serve all Protestants within its natural parish.

In New City the church must be built from the ground up, not only physically but also socially and spiritually. The people, most of whom arrive within a year or two, are strangers to one another. There is no organization, and the minister himself is a newcomer. The situation offers many advantages: None of the families has rootage, yet all expect to live for many years in their new homes; therefore they are eager to make friends and to establish a wholesome community life for their children. They take for granted that there will be a church. They tend to be young married people in their active years, and many will be ready to assume a measure of leadership in community endeavor. Lacking, however, are a sense of community, a suitable meeting place, and a body of practicing Christians which the newcomers can join. This situation calls for unusual organizational skill on the part of the minister who is appointed to create a local congregation and build a church.

The significance of new-growth areas for the church

The most important population movement in America is from the cities into adjoining suburban areas. The people who are making their homes in these nascent communities generally have a Protestant heritage. The wisdom displayed by ministers and laymen in adapting old churches or establishing new ones to serve the religious needs of this population will greatly influence the course of Protestantism for the next fifty years.

Part III

CHAPTER FOURTEEN

The Church Discovering
Its Community

MOST people take their city for granted. In similar uncritical fashion laymen and even ministers commonly accept their church and its program without asking whether it could be a stronger force in the community. If the issue is raised, they will agree that the primary function of the church is to bring the Christian message to the people who live near by and to build them into the fellowship of the church, gradually extending the Kingdom of God in that particular area. Yet rare indeed is the congregation which deliberately seeks objective answers to such questions as: Are we living up to our opportunities? Is our program adequate for the needs of our people? Are we developing Christian leaders and giving them opportunity to exercise their skills? Are there neglected groups in the community whom we should serve? Can we improve our location or utilize more completely the resources of our building? These and related questions and the techniques for answering them are discussed in this and the following chapters.

The minister is—or should be—too busy to spend his time assembling figures or making charts and graphs unless they can be used to strengthen the program and the fellowship of the church. Techniques are not ends in themselves. However, the alert pastor will learn all he can about his people, his church, and the life of the community, in order to increase his own and the church's effectiveness. To this end the digging out of facts, the preparing of significant graphic materials, and their skillful presentation may be important means.

The function of research

Ministers and administrators frequently profess to be "fed up with surveys, as nothing ever comes of them." Unfortunately there is some basis for this complaint. Surveys, often involving the expenditure of much money and effort, may result in only a routine report and stacks of cards gathering dust in some back closet. The trouble in these cases is not only that no use is made of the data, but that the objective of the project was not specifically defined to begin with.

The function of research is to supply the information necessary to the solution of a problem. The steps are (1) definition of the problem; (2) delimiting the scope of study; (3) selection of appropriate techniques; (4) gathering, interpreting, and presenting of data; and (5) decision and action by those who are responsible for the formation of policy. It is sometimes assumed that a survey should result in an exact prescription for action. This is not its function. Its purpose is the assembling of information requisite to making a wise decision. It is never an end in itself, and is incomplete until it is utilized by policy and program makers.[1]

Of first importance is the definition of the problem. The more explicitly this can be stated, the more wisely and efficiently the study can be planned. Two closely related questions are: Why do we desire a study? What is its scope to be? Two illustrations will make clear the way in which the problem and scope determine procedure.

1. In the present period of rapid suburban development a common problem is, Should a church be established in a new subdivision? For an answer to this question, information should be secured on (a) the present churching of the community; (b) possible plans of other denominations, as recorded in the minutes of the comity commission;[2] (c) the present population of the area and prospects for future growth; (d) the religious affiliations and backgrounds of the people; (e) the location and distribution of memberships of other churches within the denomination which are in the same sector of the city; (f) available financing; (g) relative advantages and disadvantages of possible sites. With these data in hand the administrator can decide whether a new church should be established and if so, having cleared with the comity commission, where to locate and how to start.

2. A new highway is being constructed, and the church must be set back or removed to another location. In this case the present distribution of members and their attitudes toward the old building and site are of paramount importance. Other factors also are significant: (a) How much land will be taken by the city or county, and what indemnity will be offered? (b) What is the physical condition of the present building, and can it be

---

[1] There are a few other limitations on research. It cannot readily measure certain subjective factors, such as the loyalty of the members of the church. It can point out that the present disagreement in the board of directors of an institutional church is a handicap to the program and to fund raising and will undermine the loyalty of the staff. But it cannot predict how serious the conflict may become nor measure the full extent of its repercussions. Neither can it predict detailed events, but only general trends and probabilities. Careful study will reveal the possible rate and extent of population movement, but cannot forecast which particular individuals will leave the area. If a number of generous givers are past sixty-five years of age, it is possible to forecast—on the basis of mortality expectation—a decline in contributions over the next ten years; but research cannot reveal which of the donors will die in any given year.

[2] See below, Chap. XXI.

moved? (c) Is it now well placed to serve its membership? (d) What are the population trends, and how will they affect the church in twenty years? (e) Are other churches of the same or similar denominations near by? These and related items of information are essential to a far-sighted answer to the problem.

A church, like a person, may have an organic weakness and not know it. Therefore periodic checkups, which will reveal impending problems before they become too serious, are desirable. For example, a church may be maintaining its membership and have no difficulty with finances. Apparently all is well with the institution. Yet membership and financial analyses[3] may show that in a few years the church will be in trouble. Is the church as effective as it might be? This question cannot be answered by protestations of loyalty or conclusions based on casual observation, but only by patient, detailed study.

Getting acquainted with the city and its communities

To understand any community it is necessary to see it in relationship to other parts of the city, especially the other communities in the same sector.[4] It is along the transportation lines within the sector that population—including church members—moves. In larger cities basic information for the entire area should be assembled by a central denominational or interdenominational office where it will be available for pastors. If necessary a minister may, by doing some scouting, secure the needed information for himself.

1. *Sources of Information.* Knowledge of the city and community can be gleaned from sources as diverse as informal conversations with the old-timers and the cold statistical reports of the United States Bureau of the Census. The public library, the historical society, and the archives of the city hall offer rich mines of information which a minister should exploit in preparing the historical pamphlet for the fiftieth or hundredth anniversary of his church. The department of sociology in the college and the school of social work, if one exists, will be informed concerning community characteristics, trends, and institutions. If additional information is needed, students from one of these schools can perhaps be assigned to gather it. Planning commissions of the city and region, the council of social agencies, the family welfare society, juvenile protective association, community chest, and church federation are all repositories of information. Maps of the entire city and perhaps of local wards can be secured, often without cost, at the office of the city engineer, the election commissioner, or the bureau of streets and alleys.

[3] See pp. 150-54, 176-79.
[4] See pp. 29-30.

For the sake of economy and efficiency the religious leader should discover the resources which are at hand, and avoid unnecessary labor. The organizations mentioned above either can furnish copies of the material or will permit the needed information to be taken from charts, maps, and other records.

2. *History of the City and Community*. An excellent place to begin in making a survey is to become acquainted with the history of the city or local community, not simply as a matter of general interest, but because it gives an understanding of the background of the people, a knowledge of their traditions, and an insight into trends. Older residents will enjoy having an opportunity to talk about the history of their community—the people who have lived there, outstanding events, tensions, changes in the institutional life and physical appearance of the area, and so forth.

If the pastor can feel the drama and the vitality of the city's history, he may, by sharing these insights, arouse in his people a keener interest in their own community life. And interest is the first step in the development of loyalty and a feeling of belonging. As people think of themselves as participants in community life, they establish roots in the social soil—a goal much to be desired. A by-product is a more stable community and a more loyal membership.

3. *Basic Current Information*. The next step is to discover the present characteristics of the city or community and any changes which may impend, in order to plan for the future of the church. The data described in the following paragraphs have a value for all churches in the city and, when once assembled on a series of maps, will be useful in discussion of present problems and future prospects. The city missionary society or the church federation may wish to assemble copies of these maps and to keep them and certain charts on file showing basic population, housing, and other data. These can be used again and again as a background in analyzing different types of church problems. In fact, maps gain value with the passage of time. For example, population density or nationality and racial distribution maps from 1930 and 1940 will not lose their value after 1950, but can be employed to show population shifts which have occurred in the intervening years. On the basis of these trends future movements may be predicted.

a) Transportation: A map which shows the street system of the city and adjacent territory, bus and streetcar lines, and, in the case of larger cities, rapid transportation—subway, elevated, and commuters' services. The latter are particularly important in dealing with the suburban communities. Projected superhighways and similar developments (see the planning commission) should also be included on the map.

b) Use of Land: A map showing the major classifications of actual current use, including the present location of parks and cemeteries, railroads, industry, business, and various types of dwellings. Each class can be shown in a different color or type of crosshatching. In larger cities fire insurance underwriters maintain relatively up-to-date, detailed use-of-land books. However, unless the study is of a small local community only the dominant usage for each block should be shown. This and the transportation map will make evident the barriers in the city and indicate the natural communities and the lines along which growth will probably occur.

c) Zoning: A map showing the legal limitations on land use. Zoning is a device to protect residence and other areas from invasion by less desirable types of structure and usage. Practically every American city now has a zoning ordinance, and the zoning commission has maps available showing these restrictions.[5] Zoning is important because it furnishes a cue to the future of community development. Where use-of-land maps are not readily available, a zoning map will often suffice.

Maps may also be prepared portraying other social traits which are useful in describing and classifying communities.[6] These may be already available in the office of some agency such as the realty board, united charities, or sociology department of the college.

4. *Studying the Local Community.* An acquaintance with the whole city is a proper background against which to study the local community and its churches. Indeed, these maps not only reveal specific facts concerning the community in question, but also show the relationship of it and its people to the surrounding area—an essential for forecasting trends. More detailed information for the local area on zoning, use of land, and population characteristics may be needed. In addition it is important to learn about its institutions and the religious attitudes and preferences of the people.

a) Community Institutions: The public schools, churches, playgrounds, library, theaters, settlement houses, and so forth can be plotted on a map of the local community—perhaps a ward map secured from the office of election commissioners—to show their spatial distribution and variety. The more important and pertinent of these can be studied to discover their program and influence in the life of the people. An interesting project for

[5] The "highest" land use is for single-family residences. Only a few other types of structure, such as schools and (generally) churches can be erected here. Other zoning classifications provide for two-family buildings, apartment houses, small commercial structures, large hotels and commerce, light industry, and heavy industry, each type less restrictive than the one preceding. No lower classification can intrude on land zoned for higher usage, although the reverse is permitted, i.e., a private home may be erected on property zoned for industry.

Some cities exclude churches from highest-class use. Often the work of organized religion is seriously handicapped because religious leaders paid no attention to zoning legislation when it was in the formative stage, and only after the enactment of the law did its implications dawn on them.

[6] See Appendix A.

a young people's group in a local church is to analyze the part played by these various institutions, each member of the group being responsible for observing and reporting on one agency. What is the purpose of the agency, and who sponsors it? What functions does it actually perform for the people of the community? What is their response to it, and from how wide an area do its patrons come? Is adequate opportunity now being provided in the community for wholesome fellowship for people of different age groups? What are the churches doing apart from the conduct of worship services? Are there unmet needs to which the church might direct its attention? Are there problem areas in the community? All of these questions properly have a bearing on the church, whose program never exists in isolation but only as one of many influences touching the lives of its members and con- stituency.

b) The People of the Community: More important than the institutions are the people for whom they and the community itself exist. If the church is to win adults and youth to its faith and fellowship, it must probe back of the general information which is available to discover the religious back- ground, church affiliation, and measure of participation of the people. The same investigation may reveal the length of their residence, the areas from which they have come, and the ages and religious training of their children. The only way to unearth these facts is to make a house-to-house canvass.

Family canvass or religious census

The most important single technique for studying the community and building up the membership of the church is the door-to-door census of the families who live in the vicinity. From the standpoint of recruiting new members best results will ordinarily be secured by canvassing within a half mile of the church, depending on population density. For a more general knowledge of the whole community, the canvass should cover, at least by a sampling process—perhaps calling on every fifth family—other sections of the territory as well. If churches of several denominations co-operate in the canvass, better advance publicity can be obtained, and more homes can be reached. In any case a committee should be in charge of the project and should decide the extent of the area to be covered, the type of information desired, and the general procedure. One person may be in charge of publicity; another, the preparation of cards and maps for the canvassers; a third, the recruiting of callers; and a fourth, tabulating the results. A summary should be prepared and a final report, with interpreting charts and maps, made to the participating churches.

The success of the canvass will depend on several factors: (1) the choice of questions, (2) the selection and training of canvassers, (3) the faithful- ness of the calling, and (4) the prompt return and utilization of the results secured. The committee responsible for the study should decide on the questions to be asked. These are then incorporated in the card to be used by the canvassers. The most convenient size is four by six inches. Following is one card which has been used widely.

Name _____			No. in Family _____		Tract ____
Address _____			Yrs. Lived Here _____		Block ...

		Attends What Church Name and Denom. Address	No. Times Last Yr?	Member What Church?	Religious Background
Husband					
Wife					
Relation to Head of Fam.					
Other Adults					

Children Under 18 At Home	Age	Receives religious instruction, where?			Not at Home Date:
					Refused Info.
					Date of Completed Call
					Visitor

Former Address _____

Information Over	Own Present Home? Yes _____ , No _____

The items generally included are the street address, family name, number in family and number of children, the church which the persons attend or, if they do not attend, the one they prefer, the church in which they have their membership, which may be different from the one attended. It is helpful to include a question on frequency of attendance; this gives an indication of participation and loyalty. Many "church members" do not attend even once a year. The religious background of the people will be of interest; comparison of that with membership will show the extent to which there has been transfer of affiliation and will in some instances—as where there is no other church connection indicated—furnish a point of contact for a local pastor. In some situations—for example, an area of high mobility—it may be desirable to ask other questions as to home ownership and years of residence, in order to discover changes that may be occurring in the community. The caller should be on the watch for additional information which will be helpful to a pastor, making notations on the back of the card. For instance, if there is sickness or an expressed desire for some pastoral ministry, this should be indicated and the minister informed as soon as possible.

The canvassers or census takers should be carefully selected. Persons who are argumentative, incoherent, or undependable certainly ought not be included. Intelligence, tact, dependability, interest in the church are the traits desired. As a rule it is better to have a large number of visitors so that only a moderate amount of work is requested of each. If people are expected to make more than forty calls, the probability is that many will not complete their assignment. It is better to have more workers, each making fewer calls, preferably about twenty per worker. If the load is light, canvassers will be more willing to make the recommended second call where no one was at home the first time. This will result in a more complete return, and the workers themselves will be better pleased with their achievement.

The committee or person in charge should first secure a satisfactory map showing the entire district to be covered. On this the territory may be divided into tracts of several blocks each, using census tract boundaries or else the natural division streets. A "captain" may be placed in charge of each tract. For assignment purposes number the blocks in each tract, and also indicate on the map the approximate number of dwelling units in each block. The term "block" is here used to refer to the total area which is bounded by four streets, and *not* simply one side of one street between two cross streets.

With this information before him the director can lay out assignments of proper size for each canvasser. In an apartment-house district the assignment may cover only half a block. In other cases, even in the same community, population may be so sparse that four blocks can be covered by one caller. For each visitor prepare an assignment card, perhaps using the back of a canvass card. On it draw a small map or diagram showing the block or blocks he is to cover. Note the names of the bounding streets and the approximate number of calls he will need to make in each of these blocks. In the upper right-hand corner of the card indicate the number or letter of the tract in which he is to work, and also the numbers of the blocks he is to cover in that tract. These numbers he should record on every card which he turns in. Attach this map or assignment card to a bundle of canvass cards for the use of the visitor, having a few more cards in the bundle than the expected number of calls. All of this material should be ready in advance of the first workers' meeting.

Convene the religious census takers for a brief instruction meeting at the church. This is best held early Sunday afternoon, preferably after a church luncheon. Describe the purpose of the study and explain how the assignments have been worked out. A detailed instruction sheet developed for use with the sample canvass card is found in Appendix B. The leader should go over the questions which appear on the card, explaining the reason for each and the best sequence in which to ask them. Conduct a sample interview so that the prospective callers can see how some problem situations are handled. Make it clear that householders are almost without exception polite and friendly; very few refuse to give information. Help the callers realize that once they are started they will find the experience significant and enjoyable. Stress the importance of the caller's initialing and turning in all cards, whether completely or partially filled in or blank, together with the assignment card. This encourages accuracy on the part of the workers.

Then, after a period for questions, send them out to begin the calling. If the weather is inclement, so much the better; more people will be at home. It is a good plan for the director and captains to take assignments themselves. If all start at the same time, morale will be higher, and better results will be secured. This is one reason for holding the meeting on Sunday afternoon, so that calling can begin at once. Generally each caller should take an assignment of his own. Most churches do not have enough willing and able persons to permit their going two by two.

Push the canvass through as rapidly as possible, allowing not more than two or three weeks for the completion of calls and turning in of cards. Keep in close touch with the workers through the captains, and preserve a sense of organization in the project. Do not let it ravel out. Announce a date at the time of the first meeting when a final report will be made on the whole project—not more than six weeks off. One person should be made responsible for handling the cards as they come in and preparing summaries of the information. Draw up a tabulation sheet for each of the tracts, with appropriate horizontal and vertical columns. Record on it the significant data for all of the families in the tract, noting the number of calls completed, incomplete, or refused. The tracts can be compared with one another and their totals added to obtain the figures for the entire community. These summaries will furnish an insight into the religious life and attitudes of the residents, show the relative strength in the community of different denominations and local churches, and indicate how large is the number of adults and children who have not been effectively reached. The major value of the canvass is the discovery, through the calling, of persons who are not actively related to any church and the development of a live prospect list of new members for the church and church school. Other uses for the religious census will be discussed in later chapters.

The primary function of the church is to minister to people. Those it can serve best are ordinarily the ones nearest at hand, within its own community. If it is or is to become a vital institution, it will not be indifferent to these people.

CHAPTER FIFTEEN

Placing the Church in the Community

OF all the factors on which the success of a church program depends, the most obvious and permanent is the physical location of the institution itself. Until the site is actually purchased, the location is the aspect most completely within man's control. This is a more crucial period in the history of a church than is often realized. A thousand dollars more in the original investment often makes the difference between a good site and a poor one. No similar expenditure of money can affect the work of the church so vitally or for so long a time after the building is once erected. A lighted cross on the steeple, a redecorated interior, or a larger salary for the minister cannot overcome a disadvantageous location.

Present status and future prospects of the community

Antecedent to the consideration of a site for a church is the question, Should a new church be placed within the community at all? A first step is to see the area under consideration as a part of the total city. It will make a difference whether it is an old, established community, a rapidly developing suburb, or the fringe of a suburb which has a central stable core. What is the present population, and what are the prospects for future growth? Who are the people who are likely to move in, and what are their religious backgrounds? Is the residential section protected by zoning, or is there risk of industrial infiltration which will deteriorate the neighborhood for housing purposes? If a church of more than temporary character is to be established, these are all pertinent questions.

Present churches in the community

It is important to discover what religious organizations are already conducting work among the people of a community. While few Protestants will become members of or attend a Roman Catholic church simply because it is convenient,[1] there is evidence that Protestants are increasingly casual

[1] Three recent studies showed that in each of the communities the number of Roman Catholics who joined a Protestant church was equal to or greater than the number of Protestants who became Roman Catholics. Most of the exchange was between the Lutheran branches of Protestantism and the Roman Catholic church.

in their denominational loyalty. Even the old cleavage lines between Lutheran and non-Lutheran Protestantism are less definitive than they used to be. For example, some United Lutheran churches have attracted scores of former Methodists and Presbyterians. Even greater is the exchange of members among the non-Lutheran churches such as Baptist, Congregational, Episcopal, Methodist, and Presbyterian.[2] If churches of one or two of these latter denominations are present, it may not be feasible—even if further population growth is expected—to found a new congregation.

Churches in adjoining communities must also be taken into account, since they will reach into any near-by growing area for new members. Such an institution is already a going concern with a developed program. Often its building has been paid for, and there is no undue pressure on the membership for financial support. Therefore it is attractive to new residents, especially if they are already members of that denomination.

In short, because a given denomination has no church in a community of five thousand inhabitants does not in itself prove that it can successfully establish a new congregation. A satisfactory answer to the question can be worked out only by means of a religious census, properly conducted and interpreted.

The religious census and church location

A well-planned religious canvass of all the householders, conducted by one denomination or several in co-operation, will disclose their religious affiliation and preferences. It will reveal whether there is a religious vacuum in the territory and whether the people will respond to the program of a new church.

After calls have been made and the results tabulated for the different blocks and tracts within the community, a number of crucial questions can be answered. What proportion of the population claims to be Roman Catholic or Jewish? How many state that they are members of specific Protestant denominations? With what local churches are they associated as members or attendants? How loyal are they, as indicated by the frequency of attendance? How many are now not actively related to any church? What is their religious background and current preference? What about the children? How many of them are receiving no religious instruction in a church school? As a rule the total figures on church membership and attendance for the area tend to be overoptimistic. That is, householders who send their children to

---

[2] This exchange is well illustrated in the study of Congregational churches in Chicago made by Dr. Rasmussen. He found that in one out of four Congregational churches there were more persons who had previously attended a Methodist church than had attended a Congregational church, and in one out of five cases there were more persons with previous attendance at a Baptist or Presbyterian than a Congregational church.

a church sometimes report themselves as members of it, and those who say they attend may, on inquiry, admit that it is several years since they were present for a service. Therefore there probably are more unchurched people than the statistics indicate. To be sure, many of these latter will not be easy to enroll in a new church.

The religious census sometimes reveals an ideal combination of circumstances, which makes the answer to the question of a new church perfectly clear: There are already a hundred families in the area; the homes are new, and more are being built; people are in family groups and eager, for the sake of their children, to have a strong church established. They are chiefly evangelical Protestant in background and have been active until recently in their old home churches. There is now no religious society in the area, and the comity commission of the council of churches[3] is willing to give the denomination a clear field, so that it need fear no early competition from other related Protestant groups. The denominational authorities have some funds with which to purchase lots, and can also supply a trained religious leader to begin the work. In such a case the sooner the project is initiated the better. Enthusiasm gradually wanes, and religious interests cool if neglected.

More commonly there is some conflicting evidence as to procedure. In such a situation only careful weighing of available data can lead to a wise decision. If half of the householders are nominally Roman Catholic or Jewish, it will take a much larger total population to support a Protestant church. Ordinarily it is desirable to have a present or prospective population of at least a thousand non-Roman Catholics and non-Jews as a field for the new church. Of this thousand about four hundred on the average will be practically unreachable by any church. Of the remaining six hundred, at least a third will not respond to the program of any particular church which is established, many preferring to attend their old home church—it may even be of the same denomination as the new one. Or they may belong to a group— for example, Pentecostal or Christian Science—which will not associate with any other body. This leaves a maximum constituency of not over four hundred persons of all ages, representing approximately a hundred households —and budgets. A church may be started with a smaller prospective constituency, but the financial burden of building a sanctuary and conducting a program will be proportionately heavier and the chances of establishing a strong church smaller.

Not only is it important that there be an adequate population, but the denomination which is to open the church must also be appropriate. The canvass itself will give information as to the religious affiliation and back-

[3] See pp. 199-204.

ground of the population and therefore will indicate which denomination has the greatest chance of success.

The religious census will help determine the best site for the church. One tract may have a larger proportion of congenial prospective members than another. Other things being equal, it is better to locate the church toward the far side of the community if population is likely to increase in that direction or if there is a church of the same denomination in an adjoining community on the near side. A spot map showing the block-by-block location of members of the denomination and of other persons who state a preference for it will assist in visualizing this distribution. Other evangelical Protestant families who are not already served by a church of their own denomination and might therefore respond to the new institution can be spotted on the map with dots or pins of a different color. Preferably the church should be located in or near the greatest concentration of dots. However, account must also be taken of the as yet undeveloped territory.

The tendency is to locate all of the churches of a community near its central shopping district. While the community is small, this is a convenient arrangement. However, if it continues to grow and subcommunities form on its edges, the best opportunity for a church frequently will be in the midst of a subcommunity surrounded by family residences and within easy reach of children and youth. There are times when it is a mistake to place a new church on Main Street instead of Park Place.

Criteria for locating a church

On the assumption that a church is to be placed within the community, there are certain general rules that should be observed in selecting the exact site.

1. *Reachability.* A residential church, as distinguished from the downtown or the institutional type of church, should ordinarily plan on drawing two thirds of its membership from within a radius of a half mile. In a rapidly growing suburb where houses are close together the percentage may be higher; in a smaller city, somewhat lower. Those near at hand can walk to the church. For the others transportation facilities are important. The larger the area the church is designed to serve, the more significant are streetcar and bus lines and convenient highways. Since the membership of a church gradually spreads with the passage of time as people move, it is desirable to locate even a new church designed for the immediate area near such lines.

2. *Convenience of Access.* In terms of distance a church may be reachable, but it may not be convenient of access. For example, if a church is located on an important street, the traffic may constitute a barrier for young children and elderly people living on the other side of the street. Unless stop lights

are installed at the nearest corner, an underpass is built, or a policeman is present on Sunday mornings at the church-school hour so that protection is afforded in crossing the street, attendance will be diminished. An underpass is less satisfactory for elderly people, because of the stair climbing which is involved. In some instances the police department will be willing to deputize a young man in the church to act at certain hours as a traffic officer at the designated corner.

Parking facilities for cars must be given consideration. It may be easy to drive to the church, but it is also important to be able to park on arrival. Certain cities, such as Los Angeles, now require that before new churches can secure building permits they must make adequate provision for off-street parking.

3. *Prestige Position.* If a church is to serve the whole community, it is unwise to place it in one of the less desirable or less attractive sections, even though a site in one of them may be convenient of access. It is easier to draw people from a less privileged area into a more privileged one than vice versa. The proximity of a railroad or industrial plants, the presence of a number of old, run-down buildings, small narrow lots and cheap housing, create a disadvantageous setting for a church. They should be avoided unless the church aims to minister almost entirely to low-income people who live in the immediate neighborhood. It is well for the church to be so located and built that the members can have pride in it.

4. *Visibility.* The very presence of the church should turn the mind of the passer-by to thoughts of God and things religious. To do this, it must be highly visible. One advantage of the village church is that it is usually conspicuous, with its steeple high above the other structures; in the city it is often lost among its neighbors. If it is on a corner lot with plenty of open space about the building and good landscaping, the visibility is increased, and the church electrically amplified transcriptions, catch the ear and therefore the attention of the people in the community, just as the tower and stained-glass windows catch the eye.

5. *Where Not to Locate.* The temptation to select a site which will cost less money is frequently so overpowering that a church, at a saving of a few hundred dollars, is poorly situated for all its years of work. A realtor offers at a bargain two lots that have been left on his hands. Or he may, to improve his chances of selling property in a less desirable section, even donate a piece of ground if a denomination promises to build. An unsatisfactory lot will prove expensive in the long run, no matter how low its original cost.

It is almost always unwise to erect a church near the natural boundary of the community, for then one half of the total territory from which a church can draw may be cut off by the barriers in back of it. The one exception is where the church is located on the prestige edge of a community—facing a beautiful park or lake shore. Here the disadvantage is not as serious, since people will travel farther to reach a high-status area, but for many, especially children, the increase in distance makes it less reachable.

A church should not be located on a dead-end street, where people can gain access from only one direction. Here parking and getting cars out again present a serious problem. If a railroad cuts through a community and it is necessary to locate near it, the church should be on a street where there is a railroad crossing or underpass. Otherwise the effect is similar to that of a dead-end location.

A church built on a steep street is inconvenient of access; everyone must climb either going to or coming from it. This is a handicap for elderly people and those who drive. In the winter in northern cities icy slopes are definitely hazardous.

Unless it is absolutely unavoidable, a church should never be erected in the middle of a block or on a narrow lot. Either of these decreases its visibility. Strangers can drive past the end of the block or even down the street on which it is located and be unaware of its presence. With neighbors on either side elbowing and often overshadowing it, the structure cannot have the status in the eyes of the people which even the same building could have possessed had it been placed on a corner with adequate spacing.

The size of the church and the area of service

After it is decided that a church should be established, it is important to develop a nucleus of people who are interested and will support it. The religious canvass will have furnished a list of prospects. They may meet for a period of time in one of the homes, a local store, or perhaps the public school or library. While the desires of these people should be considered in the selection of a site for the new church, they should not be the determining factor. The initial group of members might by chance have been drawn from only one of the sections of the community, a fact which could bias their judgment. The city missionary society is also involved, as is the future of the entire community which the church should serve.

After the site is selected and a church with its charter membership is duly organized, another problem remains: For how large a congregation should the prospective church building be planned? There are at least four factors to be taken into account: the present number of prospects, the religious congeniality of future residents, the extent of denominational support, and the skill of ministerial leadership.

The family canvass should reveal the approximate number of persons who are not now attached to any church within the city and may be brought into the new organization. How many new families can be expected to move in, and to what extent will they be prospective members? The increase in population is affected by the ease of transportation into the area, the activity of the real-estate promoters, and the phase of the business cycle. In periods of prosperity, when more money is available, the outward push of population to the new community is at its greatest. When a depression occurs, the city population is quickly frozen in its tracks, or moves back into a lower rent area. More than half of the people who will settle in this vicinity in the next ten years are now living along the same transportation lines nearer to the heart of the city. A knowledge of these groups and their religious interests, through general city-wide studies, will furnish an intimation of what the community—and therefore the opportunity of the church—will be like in ten years.

The amount of assistance—financial support and advice—from denominational headquarters will determine the speed and effectiveness with which the new church gets started, and therefore will influence its membership size. Ministerial leadership will also have an important bearing on the size of the prospective institution. As a woman in a growing community remarked to a church extension executive: "I am so glad that we did not attempt to open a church two years ago, because if we had, and the man you mention had been put in charge, I know we would have failed. It was better to wait two years and have Arthur M—— as our pastor. Now we can develop a real church." The size of the church is determined as much by the type of professional leadership which is furnished as it is by the number of people who will ordinarily look to a particular denomination.

If the total church edifice is erected while the community is in its infancy, superhuman wisdom will be required to decide its optimum proportions. An initial saving of money is effected by planning a small structure, but this may soon be outgrown. On the other hand, an oversize building not only is excessively expensive, but may exert a discouraging influence. The size of the sanctuary should not be gauged to accommodate the maximum Easter attendance.

As a general principle it is good strategy to erect the educational building first, and leave the sanctuary to be completed at a later date. The former is less expensive for the floor space provided. It will furnish suitable facilities for the church school and for other meetings of youth and adults throughout the week, and one of the large rooms can be equipped for the worship services. The advantage of postponing the erection of the main building is that in a few years the community will be somewhat stabilized, and a more accurate estimate of the size of the future congregation can be made. Further, there will be a larger membership nucleus to carry the higher costs for the sanctuary.

CHAPTER SIXTEEN

The Church Membership

WHETHER it is recently founded or rich in historic tradition, every church—provided it is alive—has a membership. The building and the organization constitute simply the setting and framework for its life. If the church is to maintain its influence and grow, more new members must be added to its rolls than are lost through death and removal. There are three aspects to the study of a church's membership. The first is concerned with the historical perspective—gains and losses of members over the years; the second with the location of the present members and also their age distribution; the third with the present program for recruiting new members and incorporating them in the fellowship.

Historical perspective

What has happened to a church in the past has bearing on its present condition. The fluctuations in membership and church-school attendance, and the changes in ministerial leadership are a key to its history. This information can be secured and presented graphically by the following techniques.

1. *The Life-Line Chart.* The life line shows the numerical changes in church membership over a period of years. To prepare it for a local church all that is necessary is to secure the number of members—preferably using the active membership figure—on the rolls year by year for a long enough period to gain historical perspective.[1] There is no need of going back of 1900 or 1910. Data on the church-school enrollment or attendance—the latter figure is usually more accurately reported—and changes in the pastorate may be recorded on the same sheet.

A chart can be prepared with appropriate horizontal and vertical scales. The base line represents the years from 1900 to the present. If some space is left on the right-hand edge, figures for subsequent years can be added later. The vertical scale represents the number of members, beginning always

---

[1] The assumption is that the reported statistics are reasonably accurate. The reliability of the findings is contingent on the correctness of the data. One will occasionally find a typographical error in published reports. In a sequence if one figure is far out of line with the rest, it is best to omit it.

with zero at the base line.[2] The membership figures can be plotted for the different years and the dots connected with a solid line. Similarly the church-school enrollment or attendance can be recorded, using a broken line. It is often a good idea to indicate changes of pastorate by a short vertical line cutting across the membership at the appropriate dates.

CHART II
LIFE LINE OF AN URBAN CHURCH

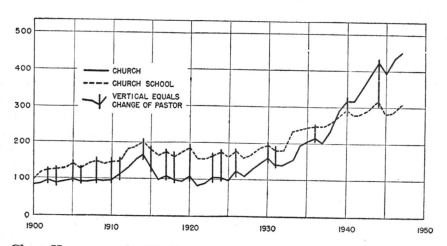

Chart II presents the life line of a church on the outskirts of a city of eighty thousand. Until the early 1920's the community was a small town, more rural than urban in type. During the twenties population increased rapidly, and in 1929 it was annexed to the city. The church had sixteen short-term pastorates from 1900 through 1926. Perhaps this is one reason why it grew so slowly, even after hundreds of commuting families moved into the town. Since the population has not increased as much proportionately from 1930 to 1945 as in the earlier ten-year period, the strengthening of the church during that time apparently is due to more skillful leadership and longer pastorates. The slow but continued increase in the church school is in contrast to the national average, which reached its peak prior to 1920.

Historical data may at times be presented more advantageously by showing, not the *numerical* change which has occurred in the membership of a church, but the *proportion or rate* of change.[3]

2. *Membership Accounting.* The analysis of accessions to and losses from

[2] If one arbitrarily assigns any other number, such as 200, to the base line, he in effect cuts off the bottom of the chart and magnifies, and therefore misrepresents, the rate of gain or loss in membership.

[3] See p. 208.

membership over a period of years may be termed "membership accounting." The procedure is simple and the necessary information usually available in the records of the local church or in denominational yearbooks. Determine the time interval which is to be studied, as, for example, 1940 to 1949. Look up the number of members, distinguishing if possible between active and inactive, reported at the close of the year 1939. Next determine the number of persons added to the membership roll in each of the next ten years, 1940 to 1949 inclusive. A distinction may be made between those received by transfer from other churches and those received on confession of faith and from preparatory membership. Only the latter two groups represent new growth for Protestantism as a whole. Add the figures for the ten years and then add the totals to the membership at the beginning of 1940. From this combined total it is necessary to subtract the recognized losses in membership: deaths and transfers to other churches for the period. If exact records of all members have been kept, the final figure should equal the present active plus the inactive membership. Rarely, however, do these figures coincide. Studies of churches in different denominations and sections of the country show that ordinarily there is a sizable discrepancy, which represents the people whom the church for one reason or another has lost track of during those years.

The information may be presented in the form shown in Chart III,[4] which pictures membership changes over a period of sixteen years in a church located in a developing community of an eastern city. In 1931 it had a membership of 703 persons, of whom 51 were inactive. In the next sixteen years it received 538 new members, almost one third of them by transfer. It lost 69 by death and transferred out 170. However, in 1946 there was a net gain of only 40 active members, and 9 more were on the inactive list. In sixteen years 250 persons dropped out of sight—no one knew where.

In this chart the area of each circle represents the number of people in a classification. The circles are drawn to scale, so that the area is proportionate to the number of persons.[5] For the preparation of the chart no special equipment is needed except a good compass, a centimeter ruler, and a protractor for determining the angles of the segments in each of the first four circles. The centers of all circles should be kept on the same horizontal line.

A simpler device for showing the difference between gross and net membership gains is illustrated in Chart IV. Each person added to the membership in the interval studied is represented by one square. This chart records the membership gains and losses for a church in a middle-class residential

---

[4] Charts III-XI appear on pp. 161-68.

[5] For a description of the scale which should be used in drawing circles see Appendix C.

community. In the autumn of 1940 it had on its rolls 418 persons. In the next six years 215 persons were received into the membership, but in 1946 the total membership was only 427, a net gain of 9. During the interval many long-time as well as recent members disappeared from the rolls. Twenty-one were taken by death; 58 were given letters of transfer to other churches; and 127 persons could not be accounted for.

The large mass of crosshatched squares on the chart shows impressively the fact that there is unnecessary leakage in membership. The presentation of this chart brought life and purpose into the membership committee of the church concerned. Records are now being kept more carefully, and the address list is maintained up to date. More important than record keeping, however, is the new determination on the part of active members to keep in touch with those who are less closely related to the fellowship.

The preceding techniques match losses for the entire membership against the accessions. An interesting study may also be made of what has happened after an interval of several years to the identical members received into the church in a given period. For example, one church, puzzled by the fact that it received many members but showed little net growth, checked up in 1946 on the membership status of the 124 people who had been received during the three-year period 1940 to 1942 inclusive. It was found that 40 of these persons had continued active; 10 had moved away from the community; 2 denied that they had ever been members. Inasmuch as they had not shown any interest by attending or contributing for two or more years, 60 had been transferred to the inactive list; and there was no record whatsoever of the remaining 12. The pastor in charge during this three-year period won a quick response from the community, but he and his laymen failed to build the new members into the fellowship, and the institution did not benefit by his efforts as it should have.

It will astonish a congregation to discover how much work is involved in maintaining a city church. So great are the losses due to mobility that some churches must receive as high as 20 per cent of their total membership each year in order to break even. As a rule ministers are far more active in recruiting than their laymen realize. The failure of Protestant institutions to grow as rapidly as might be desired is due, not so much to a lack of potential adherents or original effort to reach them, as to inadequate attention once they are enrolled. Often they feel they are not welcomed into the inner circle of the church, or that there is nothing vital for them to do. And when they move away or cease attending, the church makes little effort to revive their interest. The responsibility for this situation must be carried by the members as well as the minister.

The present distribution of members

Perhaps the most commonly employed technique in the study of the local church is the preparation of a spot map showing where the members live. A spot map is made by placing a pin or a small ink dot on a map for each member or family at the location of his residence. It is basic to the answering of many questions: Is the church in the center of its membership? Do many members come from a long distance, and do these participate actively in the program? Do the majority of members live within walking distance? Has the church in the past few years, as shown by dots of recent accessions, been able to win people living in the immediate area? How does the distribution of the church school compare with that of the membership? Are the same families reached, or does it represent a different group? Such a spot map will aid in dividing the membership into geographic or neighborhood units for purposes of calling or organizational contacts.

If an ink spot map is used, the church has a permanent record of the distribution of its members at a given time. Such a map is valuable, not only when it is first made, but five or ten years later, when it can be compared with a new map showing the current membership spread. This will reveal whether the church is holding its own or gaining in its immediate neighborhood. It will also show the direction and extent of membership movement and will indicate whether the program needs to be adapted so that the local community is adequately reached. For a description of the preparation of spot maps see Appendix C.

Churches in different types of communities tend to have characteristic membership distributions. The membership of the downtown church is spread over the whole city, with few coming from areas of underprivilege or lower middle income. Some live in downtown hotels, a few in old residences near the heart of the city, but the majority come from the middle and upper-class residential communities. In contrast the membership map of a family church in a residential area will show that about four fifths of the people are within walking distance. Ordinarily the newer the community, the larger the percentage of members living in the immediate vicinity.

A church in an underprivileged area which is reaching its own immediate community will usually have a concentration of membership about the church and another concentration perhaps two miles away made up of old-time members who have moved away from the area but maintained their loyalty to the institution. The pattern may be like a dumbbell, one end at the church, the other some distance away, with a scattering along the transportation line in between. If the church in such a community has made little effort to reach near-by people in recent years, its membership will be scattered like the dust from a comet, a small nucleus around the church and the rest out beyond it, away from the center of the city, along the main transportation lines of its sector. It may have more members in a suburban community two or more miles from the church than in the immediate vicinity. One can learn much about a church by studying a spot map of its members and church-school attendants.

The geographic distribution of members can also be presented in chart form. Chart V compares the membership spread of four churches in an eastern city of 150,000 inhabitants. All are in the same denomination, and all are located near the central business district. The geographic distribution of their members is shown on a percentage basis.

Church A, which has the smallest membership of the four, actually has twice as many members within five blocks as any of the others. The other three churches all have 75 per cent or more of their members beyond convenient walking distance. This should constitute a warning to both the ministerial and lay leadership. It is difficult enough for one downtown church to survive, drawing members from a long distance; it is almost impossible for several of the same denomination to do so. These churches need to face the question of altering their program to minister to citizens living near by or of moving out of the area.

Membership analysis

There is no denying that the program of the church seems more attractive to women than to men, to older people than to those in middle years. Why is this? Is the Christian message itself more pertinent for one sex and for certain age groups than for others? The uniform answer of Christians is "No." The gospel is for all, and the church should minister to all. If this claim is correct, then it seems evident that the program of the church is not sufficiently developed to exert equal appeal, even though its message may have equal significance for all. To detect weaknesses in the program of local churches a graphic technique of membership analysis has been developed.

1. *The Population Pyramid.* In its demographic surveys the United States Bureau of the Census has employed the "population pyramid" to depict graphically the age and sex distribution of the people within a specific area. This same principle has been utilized for a number of years in the study of local churches in relation to their communities.

The pyramid consists of a series of bars extended from either side of a center line. Female population is represented by bars to the right, and male to the left. The lowest bar on the pyramid represents the number of children under five years of age; the next above, five- to nine-year-olds; and so on by five-year groupings through age twenty-four. From this point on ten-year age spans are used, through age sixty-four. Those sixty-five and above are included at the top of the pyramid. Age-sex data for every city in the United States are printed in the federal census volumes. Similar information is available by wards for cities of fifty thousand or more and by census tracts—much smaller than ward units—for sixty of the larger cities.

The total population of the area is counted as 100 per cent. The length of the bar representing each age-sex group is determined by the number of people in that group, taken as a percentage of the total population. A percentage scale is drawn at the base of the pyramid. It is important to bear in mind that the bars for the ten-year groups must be one half the length of the indicated percentage. For example, if 8 per cent of the population are females twenty-five to thirty-four years old, this is equivalent to 4 per cent in each of the two five-year intervals, twenty-five to twenty-nine and thirty to thirty-four. The percentages for the top bars—sixty-five and over —are divided by three, since at least three five-year spans are included.

2. *The Membership Analysis Chart.* The left-hand pyramid in Chart VI shows graphically the age-sex distribution of an Atlantic seaboard city. In a large city the population pyramid would ordinarily represent the population for the ward or census tracts immediately around the church. The two sexes are almost exactly balanced for all ages under sixty-five. The slight excess of women over men—5 per cent—in ages fifteen through twenty-four is accounted for by the large number of white-collar jobs and the presence of some light-manufacturing industries. There are also more women above age sixty-five. (This is true for practically all population groups.) In general the even balance of the sexes indicates that this is a city of families. The declining birth rate of the late 1920's and the 1930's accounts for the small number of younger children. The pyramid as a whole gives indication of a stable, well-adjusted community with a large proportion of youth and young married people.

The data [6] for this declining downtown church form the basis for a second pyramid showing the age and sex distribution of its members (the middle pyramid on Chart VI). If the church were serving a cross section of its city, the two pyramids would be about the same in outline. It is not expected that any one church will reach every person within its parish; but if its program is well rounded, it should attract persons of both sexes and all ages in approximately the same proportion as they are found in the community. It is apparent in this case that the two pyramids stand in decided contrast. This church evidently is far more effective in reaching women than men. More than twice as many females as males are in the membership, although in the population the sexes are evenly balanced. (Protestant

[6] See Appendix D for work sheet used in assembling data for the church membership analysis chart.

churches as a whole have a feminine membership of about 60 per cent.)
The contrast in the age distribution of the two pyramids is also marked.
The city is youthful, the church elderly. In the city 6.5 per cent of the people
are sixty-five or more years old; in the church almost 23 per cent of the
members are in this age range. The passage of another decade will mark the
loss of most of the people now over sixty-five. The bars representing the
young men are distressingly short. The larger number of young women is
accounted for by one club group, which is an appendage rather than an
integral part of the church life.

If a pyramid had been drawn twenty years ago, or even ten, this developing
weakness could have been foreseen and the inadequacies in the program
corrected. The church is now in a less favorable situation than twenty years
ago. For one reason or another it has not been winning a representative
spread of its community for two decades. An institution dominated by
middle-aged and elderly people, the majority of them women, is not
attractive to young couples or to men in their middle years. Unless new
ministerial leadership is imported or an unlikely revivification takes place
from within, the church, which is now paying its own way and is regarded
as successful, will become anemic and need mission aid.   ,

The right-hand pyramid in the chart shows the age-sex distribution of the
persons in the educational program, and includes not only those who attend
the church school on Sunday but also all others who belong to one of the
educational organizations holding weekly meetings, such as the young
people's society. If they meet less often, they are not counted. No person is
counted twice. The percentages determining the length of the bars in the
educational program are computed by using the total church membership as
100 per cent, thus keeping the two pyramids comparable. The same length
of bar will equal the same number of persons in each. If the total number
of persons in the education program is the same as the number of active
church members, the two pyramids will cover exactly the same amount of
area—though with a different outline. If there are fewer in the educational
program, as is generally the case with larger churches, the pyramid will
be smaller. If there are more, as often occurs in small churches and those in
rapidly developing areas, the right-hand pyramid will be larger.

On Chart VI two adult classes account for most of the people over
twenty-five years of age. Boys and girls under fifteen make up almost half of
the enrollment. A comparison of the second and third pyramids makes it
plain that many who are in the young people's organizations have not been
brought into church membership. The chart depicts a church suffering from
senescence. Fortunately this picture is not typical of urban churches, although
similar patterns will be found in many cities.

In gratifying contrast to the above church is the one which is analyzed in

Chart VII. This is in a growing, upper-income community toward the edge of a Midwest city. Long pastorates, skillful leadership, and considerable population growth have favored this institution. The left-hand pyramid shows the age-sex distribution of the population in the community. Few young married couples can afford to live here; therefore the bars representing them are short. While the sexes are almost evenly balanced, several discrepancies may be noted. There are more men than women forty-five to fifty-four, by about 25 per cent. Women predominate by 10 per cent in the thirty-five to forty-four age range and by almost 40 per cent between twenty-five and thirty-four. Probably the main reason for these differences is that men tend to marry women younger than themselves by two to four years. A number of the homes employ domestic servants, accounting for the large number of young women in the community. The bars from five to fourteen represent chiefly the children of the people in the longest adult bars, thirty-five to forty-four. All things considered, this is one of the most favorable types of community in which a Protestant church can be situated.

A glance at the active church membership (center pyramid) makes it clear that this institution has about as many men in its membership as women. The inner core, in solid black, represents the 241 members who had been in the church for more than five years when the study was made. The remaining portions of the bars stand for the 559 who have been added in the last five-year period. It is not surprising that the twenty-five to thirty-four year bars are shorter than those which are above them, because, as the left-hand pyramid shows, there are fewer people of this age in the community.

The educational pyramid, representing a total of 650 persons, shows strong primary, junior, and intermediate departments. The shorter bars for fifteen- to nineteen-year-olds are all too typical of Protestant churches. This particular institution is handicapped by lack of room—an excuse that it cannot long use, since it is engaged in a building project. The almost complete absence of older youth and young married couples from the educational program is also unfortunate. These are points where the program of the church can be strengthened. Nevertheless, although room for improvement is clearly indicated at several points, this church gives ample evidence of vigorous healthy growth.

A membership analysis chart not only shows the present composition of the membership, but reveals points of weakness and strength in past years and forecasts problem areas. If one minister was especially successful in reaching young married people, that fact will be recorded in the pyramid even ten years after he has left the community, for these people have formed their own fellowship in the church and are now growing older together. On the other hand, the effects of a "church fight" which occurred fifteen years ago between two cliques in the women's society, causing many to drop out of the membership, will be shown by a "scarred" or indented pyramid at the ages chiefly affected.

Recruitment of new members

No matter how healthy a church is, it cannot afford to be satisfied with its past achievement. To maintain its strength it must constantly be winning new members. People move from the community; some die; and others for one reason or another drop from the fellowship. Where there is a good educational program, and where parents train their children in the meaning of the church, there is a steady inflow of youth from the church school. Yet no institution can be content simply with the enlistment of its own youth. If it takes seriously its mission to win others to the faith, it ought not be satisfied to remain static.

1. *Discovering Prospects.* To discover new members requires time-consuming, patient effort. Every minister should maintain a live prospect list, placing on it the names of the nonmember parents of children who attend the church school; nonmembers who come to the pastor, for services such as weddings, baptisms, and funerals, or for counseling; visitors whose names have been secured by specially appointed ushers or who have signed the guest register at the entrance to the sanctuary; persons attending the women's society who are not members of the church. However, there is no adequate substitute for the door-to-door family canvass of the community, with a cordial invitation to join in the fellowship of "our church" and to send or bring the children to the church school. Calls of this nature are often best made by laymen. When a minister gives an invitation, many think he is simply performing his professional duty. When a layman voluntarily takes the trouble to seek out new members, he gives evidence that the church has meant much to him, and the invitation is more convincing. Of course the minister will make a follow-up call.

People who move to a strange community usually hope to gain friends and to become active in some organization. If they have been church-minded, they intend eventually to join a church. Usually, however, they are reluctant to take the initiative, so they wait for someone to issue an invitation. If none is forthcoming, they may go to the church of their denomination, but there is at least an even chance that they will find other ways of filling their "day of rest." Once they have lost the habit of church attendance, it is difficult to re-establish it.

Perhaps the most interesting experience I had during the religious canvass was at the home of an elderly woman. She came to the door in response to my ring and, with a foreign accent, asked what I wanted. When she heard the purpose of my call, tears filled her eyes, and she insisted that I come in. Over my protests she heated coffee and served it with little cakes. Never before in the twenty years she had lived there, she said, had anyone from a church called on her. She used to be a Lutheran in the old country and has occasionally attended since coming to America, but lately she has not gone out much. I had a hard time getting away.

It is not enough to say that this woman might have made a little effort herself. The Christian Church cannot evade its responsibility, which is to go out and reach people, strengthening the weak wills and encouraging good intentions.

The best time to call on a family is in the first month of its residence in the community. The sooner the call, the greater the likelihood of response. A family canvass made at regular intervals in the area around the church will ensure that no newcomers are overlooked. If no one is at home, a printed announcement of the call and an invitation to the church can be left under the door or, if properly cut, hung on the doorknob. In some cities the chamber of commerce or civic "welcoming committee" issues a list once a month of all new residents. This will furnish a prospect list for the local church, and a letter of invitation can be sent, or a call can be made on the new family. The point of importance is to reach the people in the community, to reach them soon, and to extend a friendly invitation.

2. *Welcoming Newcomers at the Church.* Experience has shown that people who do not intend to neglect the stranger often unwittingly freeze him out. The long-time members have so many topics to talk about among themselves that they gather into little conversational groups after the church service, and the stranger feels all the more unwanted because of the obvious satisfaction that the others are getting from their fellowship. Nor is a formal greeting and invitation to return enough to make the newcomer feel welcome. What he wants is to have someone seem actually interested in him, taking time to carry on a conversation, to find out where he comes from, what his interests are—in short, to treat him as a guest would be treated in a home. Only by such attention will his reserve and hesitancy be dissolved.

This is more of a problem in the large church than in the small one, where a stranger is easily spotted. In the former only an active leader would recognize by sight as many as half of the regular members. Visitors' cards in pew racks and a visitors' register near the front door are good devices, but few will sign unless urged to do so. It is desirable for the minister to call on those who leave addresses. But what is most needed is friendly, informal association initiated by the members of the church.

3. *Integration of New Members.* More is needed than to persuade strangers to attend the worship service. The church must go further and win them to participating membership. The reception of members into the church can be made an impressive, significant part of the worship service. Invite the

new members, even those who are being received by transfer, to repeat their vows audibly and in public. It is appropriate for the entire congregation to rise as new members are being received and orally renew their own vows. All should periodically be reminded of the import of belonging to the Christian fellowship. A cherished possession of many congregations is the record book in which every member of the church has entered his own name at the time of joining. If no such book has been kept, one can be started with appropriate ceremony and all of the church members be invited to sign. This is not a substitute for the official membership records, but has marked symbolic value.

The central church in one city, faced with the problem of incorporating new people in a rapidly growing congregation, developed an ingenious system of record keeping. When a new member is received into the church, he is invited to remain after the service and have his picture taken. A room has been arranged for this purpose, and one of the laymen, whose hobby is photography, is present to make the snapshot. Four prints are prepared. One copy is sent to the new member; another is attached to his church record card; the third is handed to the chairman of the area unit in which the person lives; and the fourth is retained by the pastor. He looks through these pictures repeatedly, associating the name and other characteristics of the person with the photograph. After a week he turns his copy over to the president of the women's society, the men's club, or the youth fellowship, as the case may be. By this procedure the leaders can quickly identify new members and avoid the remark so often heard in churches, "Sorry, I can't remember your name." This technique is an effective aid in personalizing the relationship among old and new members. It is important because the acquiring of a sense of belonging is the first step toward active and full participation in the work of the church.

CHAPTER SEVENTEEN

Leadership in the City Church

FEW except pastors and the members of nominating committees in local churches realize how serious is the shortage of Christian laymen who are able and willing to assume some leadership responsibility. In fact this is regarded by many urban ministers as one of the greatest handicaps in their church work. At the end of the year, when new officers and committee chairmen are to be elected, a panel of names is always presented in nomination, but not many in the church know how much telephoning, discussing, cajoling, and protesting have preceded the preparation of that list. The pastor and others on the nominating committee often find themselves in agreement with the ancient Italian adage, "He who can will not, and he who is willing cannot."

Many officers and committee chairmen are merely "headmen." Some accept the post willingly but have no clear conception of their committee responsibility; others acquiesce reluctantly and do not intend to trouble themselves over it. How many churches there are in which a membership committee, for example, is appointed but never acts, due in part to lethargy and in part to inadequate ministerial guidance. Indeed, there is a close relationship between effective ministry and skillful lay leadership.[1]

However, in spite of all the complaints of nominating committees, the fact remains that no other institution in America receives so generous an amount of unremunerated and intelligent leadership as does the Christian Church. An encouraging fact is that at one time these leaders too were inconspicuous, run-of-the-mill members. Here is the key to the solution of

---

[1] While ministerial leadership is not the primary concern of this chapter, it may be noted that there is a strong affinity between large, thriving congregations with rich leadership resources and experienced, able pastors. Is the church strong because of the pastoral leadership? Or does it draw an effective man because of the salary, prestige, and opportunity which it can offer? Certainly the small and weak organizations, which tend to be the churches with the fewest natural lay leaders, are often served by part-time, inexperienced, or unskillful pastors. If the small church does obtain an able young minister, the likelihood is that a larger church will soon be bidding for his services. Here is a problem which is rarely even discussed, let alone faced. It is a problem for the denomination as a whole, and specifically the responsibility of its administrative officers. Uncounted city churches would have developed into strong, self-supporting institutions had they had at the right time the guidance and inspiration of an astute, vigorous, and consecrated minister.

the problem of lay leadership in the local church: if some men and women have developed confidence in themselves, ability in problem solving, and a willingness to accept responsibilities within the church, so may others.

Who are the leaders?

A usable definition of a lay "leader" in a church is: a person elected or appointed by a recognized group or official of the church, for a period of at least six months, who has the duty of administration and/or supervision of the activities of others. This is not intended to include paid or professional leaders. It would embrace chairmen of *functioning* all-church committees, church-school superintendents and teachers, and the elected officers of the various organizations who formulate policies and program and/or direct activities—as the president and vice president, but not the secretary and treasurer unless they occupy a leadership role. A pianist, even though her service is important, would not be considered a leader unless she had the supervision of music for some group, but the chairman of ushers would be included. The chairman for a church supper or of a temporary committee, or the director of a pageant would not be counted a leader under this definition.

Some of these people may have little leadership ability, and others who are not leaders according to the definition may exert considerable influence in the church.[2] Nevertheless, members who are willing and have ability tend to move into one of the formal leadership positions, although they may not hold office continuously.

Perhaps it is not surprising, in a man-dominated society, that more men than women hold positions on the governing board of the church. In some denominations—for example, the Missouri Synod Lutheran—there are no women on the board. A recent study of officers in twenty representative urban Methodist churches[3] showed that, although only 41 per cent of all members were men or boys, 70 per cent of the members of the Quarterly Conference—the official governing body of the local church—were men. While men typically make up two thirds of officialdom in such churches, the leaders within the church school—officers and teachers—are dominantly women, frequently three times as many women as men.

Church leaders, particularly on the governing board, tend to be selected

[2] An interesting illustration of the latter is an invalided woman who is unable to leave her city apartment. The telephone is always by her side. With its help she makes calls on the sick, persuades a young man to take charge of a class of boys, solicits clothing for foreign relief. She is one of the most active and influential members of the church, although she never attends a service and holds no office.

[3] Frederick A. Shippey, *Religio-Socio-Economic Characteristics of Urban Church Officers* (unpublished thesis, Northwestern University, 1947).

from the upper age brackets. The older members have had more practical experience. When a leader is needed, it is easier to turn to a person who has previously held office than to take the time and effort to break in a novitiate. Further, many officers demonstrate a marked reluctance to give up the prestige of their position and the responsibility which they have carried for many years. Shippey discovered that although 22.1 per cent of the church members were fifty-five years of age or older, 38.2 per cent of the governing officials were in that age range. It is interesting to note in passing that of the total urban population only 15.3 per cent are fifty-five or over. Few church members under thirty-five years of age are intrusted with any leadership position, except in the young people's society or the church school.

Where the church membership includes various social and economic strata, the officials are likely to be selected from the more privileged groups. For example, there is greater probability that a school superintendent, doctor, or businessman will be given a leadership post than a man who earns his living by manual labor. The reasons are obvious, though perhaps not fully justifiable. Men with better education, who are able to express their ideas with clarity, and whose work constanly brings them into contact with people, have more confidence in themselves and less hesitancy to accept responsibility. Pehaps, too, the minister likes to be associated with persons whose status is similar to his own. The fact that they have higher incomes and tend to contribute a larger amount to the church and are looked on by most in the community with respect may also influence the nominating committee in asking their help.

An interesting interplay exists among the factors of (a) community type, (b) the economic status of leaders, and (c) the proximity of their residence to the church. In middle-class and upper-income areas most of the official leaders live within walking distance of the church. However, the lower the social standing of the community, the greater is the likelihood that many leaders will live one or more miles away. This is because the church tends to select the more "successful" people for its leaders, and the very traits which make them highly eligible for holding positions of importance also make it possible for them to reside in a superior neighborhood. Many of these men and women at no small inconvenience to themselves return to the old home church to direct the educational program and attend committee and board meetings. Often it is their financial and leadership assistance which keeps the church alive to carry on its traditional program.

Democracy or oligarchy in the church

A small minority of urban Protestant churches may be described as "one-man" institutions, with the program largely determined and the minister selected at the nod of some dominating layman. This person usually is sincerely interested in the Christian cause as he sees it, and gives generously to its support. He is a vigorous, aggressive personality, confident of the legitimacy of his authority and of the ability of the church board under his direction to solve any problems which may arise. As a rule he is a benevolent, gracious person, especially when his advice is followed. As time goes by, people find it easier to yield to his judgment than to oppose him. The few who are unreconciled to his leadership may drop out.

Far more common is the church in which a small group of from three to ten competent persons carry the responsibilities, see that the budget is met, and have final voice in the selection of the pastor and the nominations to subordinate positions. They may even play the role of "kingmaker": although occupying apparently unimportant posts themselves, they select and guide the presidents and chairman of organizations.

Neither dictatorship nor oligarchy is in accord with the democratic Protestant tradition. While in the short run they may result in greater efficiency and smoothness of operation, in time the costs heavily outweigh the advantages. The strong man or woman dies or moves away, and the organization totters because others are not ready to step into his place. Or, inflated with a sense of power, he becomes obnoxious in his leadership, and one by one members become inactive or drop out of the church. Or a young and vigorous clique arises to challenge his authority and may split the church into two factions.

This tendency of a few to accept power and then continue in it is one of the major reasons for the scarcity of leaders in Protestant churches. It is important that some of the youth and young adults be encouraged to assume positions of responsibility. In every year some new people who have skills and resources from which the church might properly benefit are moving into its parish. If, however, the leaders constitute an oligarchy within the church, youth and newcomers fail to develop their talents, and after a period of time the church becomes enfeebled. For this reason it is desirable to limit the tenure of church offices and to introduce new persons to leadership. Such a move to limit tenure will almost certainly be protested by some persons in power. When questioned about this subject, one lay leader in a large church replied:

No pastor has any business to object to a well-balanced and correctly functioning board, no matter how long any individual has been in control, as long as annual elections return the same officials to office in the church. After all, any officials so elected are the proper representatives of the congregation. . . . On our own board the baby member has served fourteen years, and the president is rounding out forty-four years of service. While none of the members are looking for these "jobs," they are nevertheless regularly returned by vote of the congregation.

CHART III

MEMBERSHIP ACCOUNTING 1931–1946

A SUBURBAN CHURCH

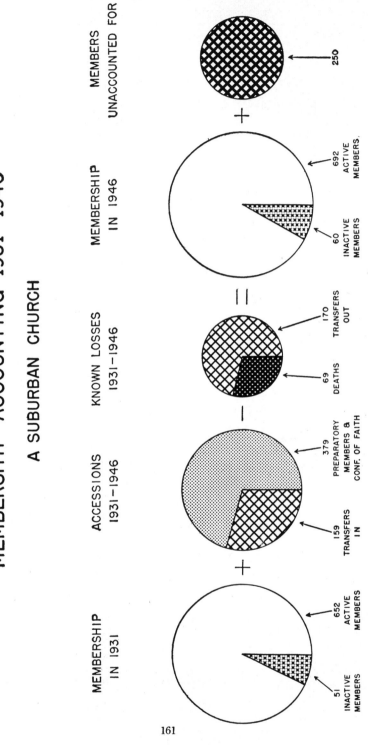

MEMBERSHIP IN 1931

652 ACTIVE MEMBERS

51 INACTIVE MEMBERS

ACCESSIONS 1931–1946

379 PREPARATORY MEMBERS & CONF. OF FAITH

159 TRANSFERS IN

KNOWN LOSSES 1931–1946

170 TRANSFERS OUT

69 DEATHS

MEMBERSHIP IN 1946

692 ACTIVE MEMBERS

60 INACTIVE MEMBERS

MEMBERS UNACCOUNTED FOR

250

CHART IV

MEMBERSHIP GAINS AND LOSSES 1940-1946
A CHURCH IN A RESIDENTIAL COMMUNITY

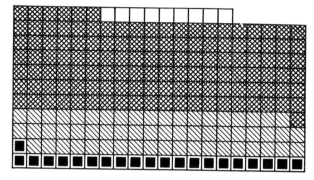

EACH SQUARE EQUALS ONE PERSON

GROSS ACCESSIONS 215   NET GAIN 9

LOSS BY DEATH 21   LOSS BY TRANSFER 58

LOSS UNACCOUNTED FOR 127

CHART V

PROXIMITY OF MEMBERS TO CHURCHES
FOUR DOWNTOWN CHURCHES

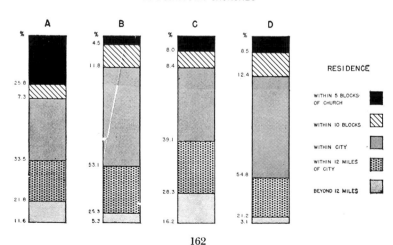

CHART VI

MEMBERSHIP ANALYSIS

A DOWNTOWN CHURCH IN DECLINE

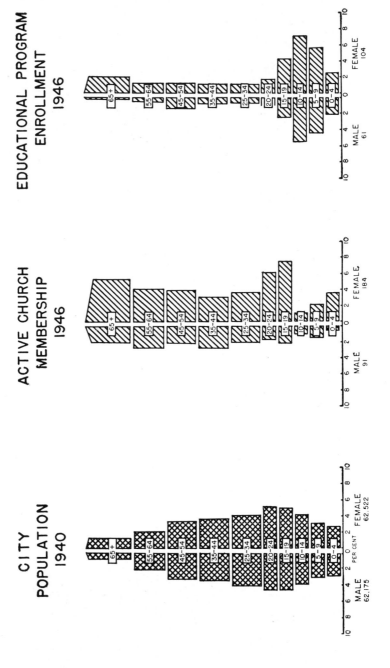

CITY
POPULATION
1940

ACTIVE CHURCH
MEMBERSHIP
1946

EDUCATIONAL PROGRAM
ENROLLMENT
1946

CHART VII

MEMBERSHIP ANALYSIS

A THRIVING RESIDENTIAL CHURCH

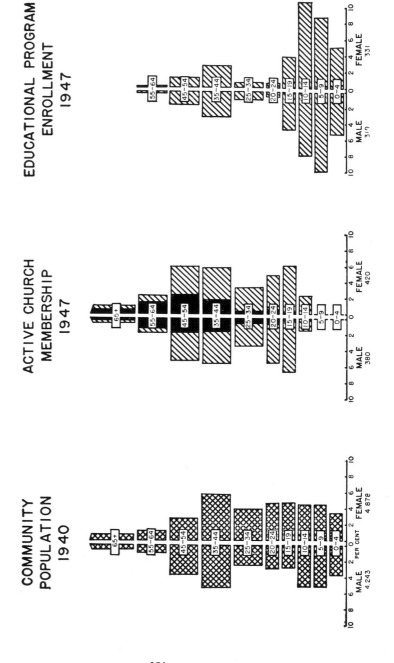

COMMUNITY
POPULATION
1940

ACTIVE CHURCH
MEMBERSHIP
1947

EDUCATIONAL PROGRAM
ENROLLMENT
1947

CHART VIII

CHURCH LEADERSHIP ANALYSIS

A CHURCH IN AN UPPER-INCOME RESIDENCE COMMUNITY

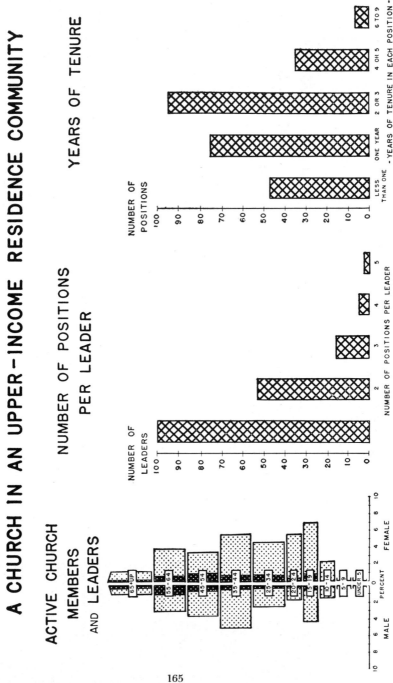

ACTIVE CHURCH
MEMBERS
AND LEADERS

NUMBER OF POSITIONS
PER LEADER

YEARS OF TENURE

165

CHART IX

ANALYSIS OF REGULAR GIVING

A CHURCH IN A MEDIUM—INCOME COMMUNITY

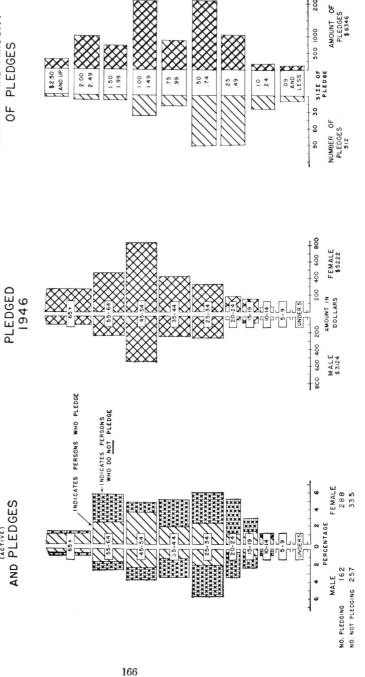

MEMBERSHIP
(ACTIVE)
AND PLEDGES

AMOUNT
PLEDGED
1946

NUMBER AND AMOUNT
OF PLEDGES

CHART X

FINANCIAL SUPPORT

BY LONG-TIME AND RECENT MEMBERS
CHURCH IN OLD RESIDENTIAL COMMUNITY

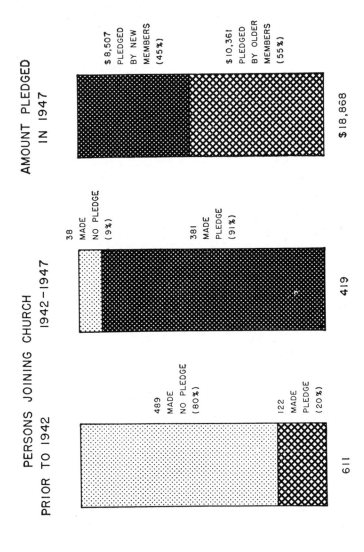

PERSONS JOINING CHURCH

PRIOR TO 1942

1942-1947

AMOUNT PLEDGED
IN 1947

489 MADE NO PLEDGE (80%)

122 MADE PLEDGE (20%)

611

38 MADE NO PLEDGE (9%)

381 MADE PLEDGE (91%)

419

$8,507 PLEDGED BY NEW MEMBERS (45%)

$10,361 PLEDGED BY OLDER MEMBERS (55%)

$18,868

CHART XI

AGE DISTRIBUTION

OF LONG-TIME AND RECENT MEMBERS

A DOWNTOWN CHURCH

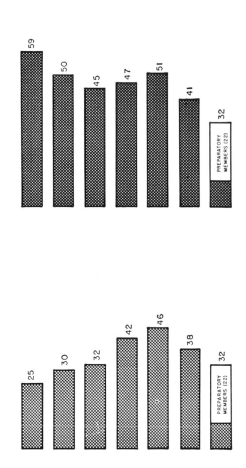

PRESENT MEMBERS
UNITING WITH CHURCH
PRIOR TO 1942

PRESENT MEMBERS
UNITING WITH CHURCH
1942-47

PRESENT TOTAL
MEMBERSHIP

65 & OVER

55 - 64

45 - 54

35 - 44

25 - 34

15 - 24

0 - 14

PREPARATORY MEMBERS (22)

80 PERSONS

245 PERSONS

325 PERSONS

What this layman fails to comprehend is that, although the organization may be functioning efficiently, it is not functioning well. A church is vital to the degree that all of its members are working together democratically toward the same great end. If this thought is kept uppermost, the difficulties of recruiting leadership will largely disappear. The city church, because of urban mobility, is particularly vulnerable to the loss of leadership and therefore should give special attention to training leaders and spreading responsibilities.

Criteria for effective lay leadership

Democracy can never be conferred but must grow from within. In fact, each generation in the nation and in the local church must achieve it for itself. While, therefore, no complete blueprint can be laid down for the democratic governance of a local church, a few guiding suggestions can be made.

1. *The leadership should, so far as possible, be indigenous.* That is, a church can come nearer the ideal of transforming the community in which it is located if most of its leaders come from the parish about the church. Imported leadership never quite belongs to the institution, and the rank-and-file members are likely to feel that it is superimposed and regards itself as superior.

2. *Leadership should be a cross section of the membership.* The program of the average church would receive more loyal support from younger members if they had larger representation on the governing board. Too often they have the feeling that the church is organized by and for older people, such as their parents. They themselves are recipients of religion rather than participants in it. In similar manner every economic class in the church membership should have some representation on the church board.

3. *Every officeholder should lead.* Unless a committee has a significant function to perform, it ought never be appointed. Therefore when a person is made the chairman of a committee, he and the others associated with him presumably have a job before them. Although he may need assistance in the form of ideas or perhaps a little prodding—part of the leadership training program—the chairman is expected to do the leading. There should be no offices—except those of the emeritus type—which are merely honorific.

4. *Tenure in office should be limited.* If a person holds a position for five or six years, he may assume he has a vested interest and therefore may have his feelings hurt if and when a change is proposed. Further, such long tenure often means that he is less receptive to new suggestions, and the program, in so far as he is concerned, becomes stereotyped. In addition other members of the congregation are prevented from gaining a broad leadership experience. Possibly an exception should be made in the case of

church-school teachers, but even here, if there are enough people available, change is desirable.

At first the difficulties involved in shifting from long-tenure to short-tenure leadership may seem almost insurmountable. However, the experience of a large church in Texas is illuminating. After prolonged discussion it was finally voted that no person should serve on the governing board for more than three years, although he might again be elected after an interval of a year. The members of the board drew lots to determine who should retire at the end of the current year, and who at the end of the second. When this was done, it was discovered that the chairman of every important committee was in the group which would retire at the end of the first year. The pastor, long an advocate of such rotation in office, was dismayed and wondered if after all the change in policy was a mistake. To his surprise and gratification, under the urgency of the situation other men who had not previously been counted among the leaders proved fully as capable as their predecessors in carrying forward the work of the church. In fact, intrigued with the new responsibility which was suddenly theirs, these men gave generously of their time, introduced a number of needed changes, were able to increase the benevolent and regular giving of the people, became active in lay evangelism, and in general brought new life to the organization.

5. *Newcomers to the community should not be kept waiting for five years or more "in order to prove themselves" before being given responsibility.* City churches will be faced with greater rather than less mobility on the part of their members and must learn the art of quick incorporation of newcomers into all aspects of the fellowship.

6. *Every church should consciously seek to discover and train people for leadership positions.* As a rule it is unwise to thrust heavy responsibilities upon an inexperienced person. Instead he can be encouraged to move up a "leadership ladder," from membership on a minor committee to membership on a major committee, to a chairmanship, and then to other more exacting duties. Each experience of participation increases his confidence and skill. Let it be part of the conscious program of the church to bring an ever-wider circle of the people into posts of responsibility, so that those who have developed leadership skills will find a satisfaction in stepping aside and assisting others to acquire similar abilities. This itself constitutes one of the highest types of leadership.

No one need fear that there will be too many leaders. Every year some move away. A few must drop out for reasons of health, because of a family situation, or other pressing duties. As leadership resources expand, the program will almost automatically be enlarged, more people be brought within the active fellowship of the church, and its influence extended throughout the community.

When members become aware of the leadership problem and set out deliberately to solve it, improvement can be made in a short time. For example, one church had been dominated for many years by a man who held seven important offices—chairman of the board of trustees, lay leader of the church, treasurer of the church, renting agent for the endowment property, and so forth. In the year 1945-46 out of the 283 active members there were only thirty-two leaders—using the broadest definition—occupying fifty-one positions. Two years later the pastor, with the help of a few determined laymen, had begun the revamping of the entire leadership pattern. Instead of thirty-two leaders there were sixty-five, and the number of positions had been increased to ninety-five. Forty-three of these had been filled within the past year. This is a demonstration of the way in which an inflow of new leadership is accompanied by an expansion of the program. It is not surprising that the church grew from 283 to 390 members in the two-year period.

Techniques for leadership analysis

If the leadership of a local church is concentrated in the hands of a few people, a change obviously is needed, but any frontal assault on the situation will only result in hurt feelings and perhaps a divided church. In such a case, and also in others where there may at first sight be no apparent need, an objective, impersonal study of the present spread of leadership will prove helpful.

Since leadership should be seen in relation to the age-sex distribution of the members, the study can best be made against the background of the membership analysis.[4] It is not difficult to gather the needed information:[5] the sex and approximate age of persons who hold office, the number of positions held by each, the length of their tenure, and perhaps the distance of their home from the church. A method for grapic presentation of these data is shown on Chart VIII. This portrays a vigorous church in a stable community, made up chiefly of single-family residences.

The left-hand diagram is the membership pyramid. The outline of it is identical with the middle pyramid on the membership analysis for the church. Here, however, a differentiation is made among the members. Shown on a percentage basis (black with white dots) are the persons who hold leadership positions. Of these, 73 are men, and 102 are women, out of a total church membership of 1,363. It will be noticed that all groups above age fourteen have some representation in this leadership core, but that most of the offices are held by persons from forty-five to sixty-four years of age. Although there are more persons thirty-five to forty-four in the membership,

---

[4] See pp. 150-54.

[5] See Appendix E for sample work sheet used in preparing data for a leadership analysis chart.

there are fewer in leadership positions among this group. The need for giving greater opportunity for leadership to younger people is evident.

The middle diagram shows the number of positions held by each of these leaders. An even hundred fill only one post apiece. Fifty-three hold two positions, and two hold five or more. Since it is desirable that leadership opportunities be spread widely, the more who hold one office only, the better. The third diagram shows the number of years each position has been held by the incumbent. In this part of the analysis the same person is recorded twice if he holds two different positions. He may have held one office for four years but be in the first year of the other. In this church 175 persons occupy 263 positions. Only 47 are in their first year of service. This is an exceedingly small turnover for so large a membership. It is clear that in each of the two preceding years more persons were inducted into new offices. The chart discloses the need for a conscious policy of leadership procurement and training.

Frequently small churches show undue and long-term concentration of authority in the hands of a few. It is not uncommon in a church of two hundred members to find two or three people who have held a given post for as long as twenty or thirty years. Is it possible that such lengthy tenure, and the lack of progressiveness which usually accompanies it, have discouraged youth and may in part be a cause of a church's failure to grow?

If a church is in an area of high mobility, the study should also take account of the place of residence of leaders. What proportion of the non-leaders live within a mile radius of the church? What percentage within two, three, or four miles? What percentage of the leaders live within each of these same concentric circles? One church of 350 members had an expected concentration of nonleaders—65 per cent—within the first mile. Yet only 10 per cent of the leaders came from this same area. Unless indigenous leadership is developed among the present nonleader members, the future of the church is insecure.

The genius of the Protestant church has been its democratic emphasis on lay participation and leadership in all aspects of its work. According to the Protestant concept, each member should feel that the church is in fact *his* church and he is in measure responsible for its well-being; through it his personality may grow and his life become significant. One implication of this is that each member, to the extent of his ability, should be assisted in becoming a leader, either actual or potential. With such a core of active and reserve trained leaders the future of the church will be guaranteed.

CHAPTER EIGHTEEN

Financing the City Church

THE church is not primarily a money-raising institution, even though people occasionally grumble that it is. Financing, like the maintenance of its sanctuary, is simply a means for achieving the church's objective—the salvation of men's souls and the building of a Christian society. But the church must have money to keep its property in repair, to pay for professional leadership, and to underwrite its varied enterprises throughout the world. Therefore the financial program, while secondary, is essential.

Relation of the community to finance

The problem of securing an adequate income is much more formidable for some congregations than for others. First Church in the average city has within its membership the successful businessmen, professional leaders, and a few devoted wealthy widows, all of whom have sizable incomes and can without much sacrifice give generously to the support of the church. The neighborhood church in a workingman's community may have few members who give more than a dollar a week. Here it requires the efforts of the women's society and often a year-end cleanup campaign to meet the budget. And the institutional church in a community where the number of active Protestants is small can be maintained only through the benevolent giving of the other churches in the city.

Yet, interestingly enough, there is usually a greater precentage of non-givers in the large church than in its small counterpart. In fact, if the entire membership is taken into account, the per capita giving may be no greater in First Church, in spite of its many wealthy people, than in Gray Mill Church, whose members earn their living in the near-by factories. This is in part because the size of the larger organization makes it easy for noncontributors to evade any financial responsibility.

The church in the better residential district or wealthy suburb has bene-fited as the more ambitious and financially successful people have moved out of lower-income areas, leaving their old church for others to support. High-income areas in effect skim the financial cream from the city, and oftentimes the churches in these areas, instead of accepting a commensurate respon-sibility for religious work in other communities, expend their increased funds for a larger staff and an elaborate and beautiful church sanctuary and educational building. An expanded program is altogther desirable if it is at the same time accompanied by a proportionate increase in missionary giving.

Utilizing resources

The chief financial resource of the church is the giving potential of its members. This potential is almost never fully developed. In periods of prosperity it is not uncommon to hear a pastor say, "Why bother with a study of church financing? We have no trouble in raising our budget." This is often true. But the finance committee of such a church should take account of its relatively favorable position, raise as much money as it can, and contribute more to denominational benevolences.

The finance committee is doing a favor to a member by making it hard for him to shirk his fair share of responsibility, even though the local budget can be met without his help. Indeed, once a person has in good spirit agreed to give regularly, he feels that it is really *his* church. The acceptance of obligation properly is associated with a sense of belonging, of being a participant in the enterprise. Beyond the warm glow of satisfaction for the individual and the benefit to the local church is the urgency of extending the Christian message throughout the world. If laymen and ministers would keep in proper perspective the awe-inspiring significance of this broader Christian program, most would give more generously than they do. Yet ordinarily more than half of the members, especially in the larger churches, make no regular contribution. The continuing welfare of the church requires that all members be trained in the art and satisfaction of regular giving. Often a conscientious analysis of the financial support of the church, when brought effectively to the attention of the people, will increase the giving by as much as 25 to 40 per cent.

While the sole resource of most churches is the contributions of the membership, institutional churches and others which carry forward a community program in underprivileged areas can legitimately request assistance from persons and agencies that are concerned with community betterment. Businessmen in the neighborhood who respect the work of the church with boys and girls are often willing to contribute toward the social and recreational, if not toward the religious, part of the program. In many cities trust funds have been established by persons of wealth for just such purposes. The community chest also is prepared to assist in covering a budgetary deficit, if high standards of group work and social service are maintained. The chest makes a payment only on condition that it approves the whole social work part of the program and that the institution is unable to secure enough money from other sources.

Basic standards

The minimum ingredients for an effective financial program may be listed briefly.

1. *An Annual Budget.* This should be based on the experience of the preceding years and especially on the budget and expenditures for the year past. It should be large enough to maintain the building in good condition, make appropriate payment on the debt if such exists, and cover the salaries, operating expenses, and program. A generous provision should also be made for benevolent activities outside the local community.

2. *The Underwriting of the Budget.* All organizations, including the Christian Church, need to know on what assets they can count. Random giving is notoriously unreliable. After the budget has been prepared and presented, a comprehensive effort should be made to secure promises of support from persons and organizations, to assure the meeting of the budget.

3. *Every Member a Contributor to the Church.* Each should contribute according to his ability, and even children who are members should contribute something, if only five cents a week. Giving should be regarded as a proper correlate of membership.

4. *Every Member a Contributor to the Benevolent Program.* This goal is secured automatically where there is a genuine unified budget, since part of each pledge will go for benevolences. In other cases each member should be encouraged to designate part of his total giving to the broader program of the Christian Church, in order that he himself may become a participant in the missionary and educational enterprises of his denomination.

5. *Carefully Kept Records.* Funds received for different purposes should be scrupulously recorded in the different accounts by the church treasurer, and every account should balance. Bills should be promptly paid.

6. *An Annual Audit of the Books.* For the sake of the church as well as the treasurer, an audit should be made of all accounts and bank balances. This may be done either by a certified public accountant or by a small committee of qualified persons within the church. The congregation is entitled to an annual printed or duplicated report on the receipts and expenditures at the close of the year.

Techniques for analyzing the finances of the Church

It is helpful to analyze the fiscal aspects of the program, including sources of support, and to present the facts graphically to members and constituents. This procedure often stimulates wider participation and more generous giving.

1. *The Budget Analysis.* The budget for next year should be prepared in ample time so that the financial campaign may be completed before the end of the current year. The first step in preparing the budget is an analysis of

income and expenditures for prior years, especially the one just closing. The finance committee with the help of the church treasurer should secure the most recent figures on income and expenditures, supplemented by estimates of receipts and expenditures for the balance of the year. Receipts should be reported according to their source, and distinction made between the different classes of expenditures. With this information before it, the committee is prepared to discuss the formation of the new budget: changes which should be made in the amounts proposed for the various current expense items, salaries, benevolences, and so forth, and in the funds to be raised.

This information should be prepared in tabular form, and may also be presented as a chart. A column chart would be most appropriate, showing in four columns the receipts, actual and expected, for the current year, the expenditures for this year, the proposed budget for next year, and the proposed expenditures, differentiating in each case as to source of income or type of disbursement. Such a column chart permits a comparison of actual income with the new budget and of the past with the contemplated program. It enables members and constituents to see as well as hear about the outreach of the church, and may serve as a stimulus to more generous giving. Similar comparison may be made over a five- or ten-year period to show expansion or decline in the program.

Another aspect of the budget analysis involves a critical appraisal of the methods of publicizing the budget and the work of the church which were employed last year. How can the committee do a better educational job? How can it reach nongivers effectively? Should more stress be placed on the giving of children and youth? An anslysis of the regular giving in comparison with the membership of the church will assist in answering these and other questions.

2. *Analysis of Regular Giving.* The largest and most dependable portion of the financial support in the average church comes from the regular, predictable giving of members. In most churches members are asked to make a pledge for the year. This may be paid off in a few installments or, utilizing the "envelope system," week by week. Some churches have objected to the idea of pledging. This is generally for one of two reasons. Either there is a fear that some members, for reasons beyond their control, could not keep their pledges and would therefore feel embarrassed, or the very idea of making advance commitments is obnoxious. The first objection is met by avoiding the word "pledge" and by making provision in the printed statement that a person can, on his written request, cancel his "statement of intention to give" at any time. The other objection can be dispelled only by wise education. People make commitments in other aspects of living and should not object to doing so in connection with the church, which must assume obligations and needs to know as accurately as possible how much support it can count

on. It may be necessary to initiate the "regular giving" procedure with the small number of members who are willing to participate, later extending it to a wider group. The chairman of the finance committee is often the key to the situation, and should be chosen with much care.

Since regular or pledged giving constitutes the major support for the average church, it is deserving of intensive study. By comparing the people of various ages who give regularly with those who do not it is possible to discover areas of strength and weakness in the financial program. For example, if a large portion of the support comes from persons under forty-five years of age, the future of the church is better assured than would be the case if it came from those over sixty.

A standard procedure for analyzing predictable giving has been evolved comparable to the membership and leadership analyses described in preceding chapters. An example is shown in Chart IX,[1] based on the records of a church in a community of skilled and white-collar workers with medium incomes. The left-hand pyramid on the chart is identical with the middle pyramid in the membership analysis for the same church. (The outline for it can be copied from the membership analysis if one has been made.) This church, like most, has a feminine membership of about 60 per cent (623 out of 1,042) . The center sections of the bars represent the number of members in each age-sex classification who pledged to the budget in 1946-47. The size of the pledge is not taken into account in this pyramid. If husband and wife are both members, pledge in the husband's name is counted as a pledge from both. Children in the family are not, however, counted as having made a pledge unless they do so individually. The outer (darker) portion of each bar indicates the number of members who are not giving regularly or predictably to the church. Less than half—472 out of 1,042—of the members are supporting this church in a dependable manner. The younger the members, the smaller the proportion of givers. For example, of those twenty to twenty-four years old, 15 per cent pledged; of those twenty-five to thirty-four, 34 per cent; while among the elders, sixty-five and over, 65 per cent pledged.

The future of a church inevitably rests with its younger members. Unless they can be sufficiently persuaded of the importance of its work to be willing to pledge some of their hard-earned money toward its support, the church will be faced with steadily mounting financial difficulties. Perhaps there is a relationship between the fact that few younger members have places of official leadership in the church and the fact that they contribute less to its support. The age distribution pattern of pledging members in this church is unfortunately typical or rural and urban, southern and northern churches. It may be contended that men and women will begin to give as they grow

[1] A suitable work sheet for gathering data for this type of chart is shown in Appendix F.

older, income rises, and their personal financial responsibilities are lightened. What is more probable is that people who do not establish the habit of church giving in their youth are not likely to find a place in their budget for it later. Only by skillful educational work can the potential threat to the future of the church be overcome. That it can be overcome, however, has been demonstrated in many of the churches where studies have been made.

The middle pyramid of Chart IX shows not the number of persons but the amount of money pledged in a given year by the age-sex groups.[2] In the main this pyramid supports the evidence of the first. In this church 14 per cent of the funds raised by pledging come from the oldest group of the church, which constitutes 7 per cent of the membership. The death of several of these persons could cause a financial crisis. (In some churches an ever greater imbalance is found, with as high as 30 per cent of the contributions coming from the oldest group.) If the number of pledges in the younger groups can be increased, the present financial structure and the future of the church will be more secure.

The right-hand diagram shows whether more dimes or dollars are given each Sunday. The figures in the center indicate the size of the pledge. The left-hand bar shows the number of pledges of a given size and the right-hand bar the amount of money derived from these pledges. On Chart IX the longest bars on the left represent the customary 25¢ and 50¢ pledges. But the ninety-five pledges from 50¢ to 74¢ a week yield only $2,176 in the course of the year, whereas forty pledges in the $1.00 to $1.49 range yield almost as much, $2,054. If members can be persuaded to "step up to the next rung" in their giving, it will mean a surprising increase in receipts.

This type of chart will make plain the importance of regular giving and show where the bulk of the present pledges falls. It also will give warning years in advance of impending financial crisis. If the finance committee takes the warning seriously, it can perform a service for the entire church, which will not only strengthen the program now, but assure its continuation in the future.

Participation of new members

The question often arises, particularly in churches located in large cities where there is a considerable population turnover. Can the church survive with so many old members leaving the area? Newcomers usually have smaller incomes, and the old-timers may feel that their institution is threatened. Such was the fear of many responsible members in a church located in a burgeoning south-central city. The pastor proceeded to analyze the number

[2] If the pledge is made in the husband's name, the amount is divided equally and half credited to the wife.

and size of pledges made by older and newer members. His findings are shown on Chart X.[3] In 1947 there were 1,030 active members. Of these 611 had joined the church prior to 1942, but only 122, or 20 per cent, were pledging in 1947. In contrast 381 out of 419—91 per cent—received into membership between 1942 and 1947 were contributing regularly. The old-timers had based their fear for the future of the church on the differences in income between the two groups. It is true that the old members who did pledge made larger per capita contributions. Nevertheless, the new members as a whole, including contributors and noncontributors, gave more per capita than did those who had joined the church earlier.

The lower income level of the new people in this community does not constitute a threat to the church. The real hazard is of many years standing: Four out of five of the older yet active members do not share in the support of the work. The 20 per cent who do pledge will leave a serious gap when they die. Of the money pledged 55 per cent is contributed by 122 people, many of them past sixty-five years of age. The first column gives evidence of poor leadership in the field of finance in the past. Just as certainly the middle column demonstrates able churchmanship by the present pastor, and a fine sense of loyalty on the part of the new members. When pastor or people think that they are confronted with a financial problem in their church, thoughtful study may reveal that their fears are groundless, or, on the other hand, it may uncover a genuine difficulty in some area other than the one at first suspected. In any case, periodic analysis of the finances of the church, of the groups contributing, and the amounts received, will disclose points at which improvements can be made and increased support secured.

It has been repeatedly demonstrated in studies of church financing that the average congregation operates at a lower efficiency than necessary because only a portion of its potential resources are being utilized. Like a twelve-cylinder car with three fouled spark plugs, it can be operated and, with effort, will even climb a steep grade. But a skillful checking of the engine can step up its power and increase the effectiveness of its operation.

[3] P. 167.

CHAPTER NINETEEN

The Program and the Community

BY definition every church has a program; that is, the organization of a religious society involves from the very start the assumption that people will participate together in certain common activities. The congregation may be small, but it does gather for a worship service and must occasionally convene for the conduct of some business, so it has a "program," although perhaps an inadequate one. The variables which determine the extent and effectiveness of a church's program are the location, attractiveness, and suitability of its structure, the population composition of the community, the personality and skill of the pastor and of the laymen who are associated with him in leadership, and the traditions of the denomination, which may limit the scope of the program by including some elements and rejecting others. Consequently among Protestant churches there is infinite variety in organization, scope, and significance of program.

Even institutions located within the same community behave very differently. A comparative study of Methodist and Presbyterian churches in several small eastern cities illustrates the point. In city A over a period of ten years the population and also the memberships of the churches of both denominations grew by approximately 25 per cent. In another rapidly growing city the Presbyterian church gained, but the Methodist church actually declined. City C registered slight growth, but the Methodist membership increased by 20 per cent, while the Presbyterian remained stationary. These differences can be accounted for only in terms of the inseparable factors of leadership and program.

In 1910 a few hundred homes were scattered over the southwest section of a western city. A large Protestant denomination with missionary alertness established two small bungalow churches and in 1912 added a third. These formed a triangle, each approximately a mile and a half from the other two. They grew slowly, in spite of the influx of easterners. In 1925 only one had attained a membership of more than a hundred.

At that time a Lutheran church was established almost in the center of the triangle. For a few years the older churches maintained their lead. Then the new congregation passed all of them in membership size and community outreach until in 1942 the Lutheran church, with a membership of 450, was twice the size of any of the others, whose memberships were 234, 195, and 60. In addition it had the names of 315 baptized children on its rolls, forecasting a further membership rise.

All four ministered to the same type of population—largely Protestant though in the main non-Lutheran. The pastor of the Lutheran church himself stated that most of his members were formerly Baptist, Methodist, or Presbyterian. Yet no one of the three older churches, in spite of its earlier start, had succeeded in spreading its roots so widely in the community.

Why the difference? The Lutheran minister who arrived in 1925 to establish the church was still there as pastor in 1942. In each of the three older churches until 1935 the average length of pastorate was about two years. Some of the pastors were capable; a few were not. But no men of talent and vigor remained to build a strong church. Perhaps even more important, the Lutheran church at once began a broad program of activities for children and youth. Within a year it had organized a parochial school. The other churches conducted for their first twenty-five years the conventional Sunday services, with an occasional supper put on by the women's society to raise money. The relation between leadership, program, and membership is vital.

Elements in the program

Every Christian church, by virtue of the gospel which it presents, has the obligation to perform certain functions for the people in its community. Several elements in the program designed to meet this responsibility are much the same, regardless of the size or type of community. However, the peculiarities of city life affect the response of the people and call for adaptations in the program.

1. *Worship.* Of primary importance in the minds of members and ministers alike is the worship service. Other functions may be duplicated by secular organizations, but the church alone conducts services for the corporate worship of God. The sanctuary is logically the one essential room in any church. It may be beautifully and expensively equipped with marble altar and stained-glass windows or simple and unadorned. But no church is complete until it has a worship room, where the principal services of the Christian Church are conducted.

City dwellers in particular need the elevating experience of worship. One who has not lived in the impersonal atmosphere of the city—where concrete replaces lawns and trees, where factories shut off the sunset, and where the noise of traffic substitutes for the song of birds and wind in the trees—cannot comprehend the dulling effect of all this on the spirit. For people who find little of beauty in the world about them there should be inspiration in a sanctuary so arranged and furnished as to be satisfying to the eye and quieting to the mind. Here in the worship service they can be lifted out of their cluttered, man-made environment, into the presence of the God who set the stars in their courses and laid the foundations of the world. Through participation in that worship members of the congregation may find meaning in life, strength and courage for ethical living, and Christian peace in the midst of a troubled society.

2. *Christian Education.* Any organization which hopes to survive must have a program for recruiting and incorporating new members. The Christian Church, with its rich heritage, must educate adults as well as children in its history and traditions, its distinctive purpose and program. For this task the most capable leaders should be chosen. If inept and unattractive persons are assigned the responsibility, many of the young people will be lost to the institution.

The city church is faced with two specific problems in Christian education. It draws people from varied cultural backgrounds and economic classes, in contrast to churches in rural areas and small towns, which tend to have a more homogeneous membership. Some may be well-to-do, conservative in politics and economics, but liberal in theology. Others perhaps have a low income, are attached to the political left wing, but are theological conservatives. Many come to the Protestant church from a Roman Catholic or a Jewish background. The majority are of native-born stock for several generations, but others still have a loyalty for the homeland of Sweden, Italy, or Japan. Preferences vary as to the elements in the worship service, and there may be disagreement as to whether a cross and candles should be on the altar. This heterogeneity is at once an indication that the Christian Church is bringing its ministry to diverse groups of people, as it should, and evidence of the important task of education which it must perform if out of this diversity a homogeneous congregation is to be developed. This means that it should have a well-rounded educational program for adults as well as children.

Another problem, especially in areas of great mobility, is discontinuity of leadership. This can be overcome to a degree by a continuous recruitment of new leaders to take the places of those who move away. However, recruitment must be supplemented by quick and effective training, or there will be lack of coherency in the program. The more mobile the population, the more important does stability in the pastorate become, in order that there may be a feeling of continuity within the church.

3. *Christian Fellowship.* The Protestant church should always be more than a congregation. It is not simply a group of people who come together to worship. Neither is it a club in which a person holds membership for social or economic advantage. Instead it is a body of men, women, and youth who, because of their Christian heritage and common quest, have a

sense of interdependence and brotherhood, as fellow travelers making the same pilgrimage.

It is an essential function of the church to develop this type of shared, significant fellowship, in which the arbitrary differences of financial status, learning, family prestige, race and nationality, often apparent in human society, will disappear, and all stand as sons of the same Father and therefore brothers. The city with its many lines of social cleavage is acutely in need of this unifying ministry. Because of the anonymity and the loneliness of the people in many communities, this may prove the one undergirding factor which supports them in times of crisis.

The emphasis on Christian fellowship properly extends beyond this life. There are many types of memorial which have been used by churches to recall and honor departed members, such as dedicated windows, church rooms and furniture, and bronze plaques like those naming the war dead. Memorial services may be held annually—on Memorial Day or All Saints' Day—with the names of all members who have died within the year printed in the bulletin. It would be appropriate and in many cases feasible for churches to maintain a columbarium back of or under the altar, in which the ashes of deceased members might be permanently stored. This would both reduce the present excessive cost of funerals and interment, and also constitute a significant tie between surviving members of the family and the church.

4. *Evangelism.* The Christian Church, unlike the Jewish synagogue, is "missionary" in its motivation. Implicit within the gospel is the demand that the good news be shared and others be brought within the fellowship of faith. Important as is the evangelistic emphasis in rural areas, it becomes even more mandatory in the city. Unless the church is increasingly effective in transforming the public and private lives of urban dwellers, the cities themselves will become far more "pagan" than were the rural districts of the Roman world when that word came to mean "non-Christian." And the cult of materialism will engulf not only the cities but, through their influence, the whole nation, since rural America increasingly reflects the attitudes and behavior of the city. The church is waging its crucial struggle today in the stable communities and the areas of underprivilege of American cities.

The church must take account of an obstacle relatively nonexistent in the small city or the rural community. City dwellers tend to cultivate a protective reserve or prickly crust which is difficult to penetrate. They have learned to be wary of strangers and are suspicious of any unrecognized caller. This is a particularly tough problem for the pastor who wishes to reach people in an apartment or rooming house. He must ring a bell and announce himself through a speaking tube before he has a chance to make a call on a new family. Many apartment-house people do not bother to answer the doorbell; and if they do, even a minister may be easily repulsed via the speaking tube. Yet once this barrier is hurdled, these same people usually display a deep appreciation of a pastor's call and a satisfaction in knowing that someone in the city has had enough concern to seek them out.

Pastors deal with the problem of making a first contact in a variety of ways. In general it is not wise to make calls at the rear door. Housewives will respond for the milkman's ring, but would be embarrassed if a minister should catch them at their household tasks. He may mail a brief card inviting the householder to attend the church and stating that on a certain afternoon or evening in the following week he will call. He may ask a member who lives in a block or in an apartment house to notify him of each new family that moves in and perhaps arrange for him to make a call. A third possibility, where the name of the family is known in advance, is to call by telephone and suggest a date for a later visit in person. Another procedure is to print on a small card, perhaps three by five inches, a picture of the church, its address, hours of worship, and other program activities, and on the reserve side an invitation to attend. The card may be so cut that it will fit easily over a doorknob or be attached to a mailbox. This does not take the place of a call but does afford a first contact. To make sure that no one is overlooked, a well-advertised, annual, house-to-house religious census should be conducted by the members of the church or group of churches.[1]

5. *Community Regeneration.* Christian churches usually are willing to admit, at least in theory, that their responsibility goes beyond the saving of individuals to the establishment of a more decent and just society. Often this is simply implicit and is not made explicit in the program. Yet most church members will rally to drive out taverns which corrupt the youth and to provide wholesome recreational programs for boys and girls. Many churches go further, campaigning for better housing, improved schools, and interracial understanding.

The more intimate contacts of the rural area facilitate the development of community concern. But in the city each family and person tends to be psychologically walled off from others. It is only by conscious educational work that the church and similar organizations can produce a sense of civic obligation and interest in the welfare of others. Once his imagination is stirred by the church, the city dweller is prepared to respond to its leadership in community and world-wide regeneration as is shown by the wholehearted response of church people in the city as well as the country to the postwar requests for overseas relief.

[1] See pp. 134-37, 154-55.

Criteria for judging the program

While church programs will vary in emphasis and detail, there are a number of basic tests of effectiveness which may be applied to any one of them. The responsible governing board, or a church council or "policy committee" made up of representatives from each of the organizations, should review the program periodically in the light of these criteria. Too often a conventional program continues from year to year without thoughtful review and objective analysis.

1. *Consistency.* The nature of the church puts certain restrictions on its program. Any activity which does not conform to Christian principles or which tears down standards of personal or community probity must be eliminated. For example, for a church to use bingo and other games of chance as a device for raising money, or for a church in its educational program to inculcate racial animosity, would be inconsistent with the ideals and teachings of the church.

2. *Coherency.* Frequently the various parts of the church's program have developed haphazardly and without reference to one another. In a well-integrated program the relationship of the parts to the whole and to one another is recognized. To the extent that the functions of the offices and of societies are clearly stated and understood it will be possible to have harmony and progress within the church. For example, the church council might prepare an annual calendar of activities to prevent overlapping and conflict. It might even foster a new organization if some group has been overlooked.

Coherency as a principle of organization extends even farther. Not only must its constituent parts be related intelligibly to the local church, but also the latter in turn should recognize its interdependence with the denomination to which it belongs, taking account of this tie in its own local program.

3. *Activities for All Ages and Both Sexes.* Every church should have an assortment of societies and clubs designed for different ages and both sexes, with such vital programs that a new member will be strongly attracted to one of them. Common to all churches are a church-school program, usually most successful in its kindergarten through intermediate departments, and a women's society with its committees and activities. Three groups, however, are frequently neglected.

a) Does the church hold its *youth?* Boys and girls after they reach the age of thirteen tend to drop out from the church school in large numbers, in part because of the lack of skilled leaders, especially men, on the teaching staff. A study of the church membership [2] will show points of strength and

---

[2] See Chap. XVI.

weakness and will indicate where the program needs constructive attention. Often the church fails to transfer the loyalty of its youth from the church-school class in the intermediate department to the church as a whole. Where teen-agers and older youth are carried over into active church membership, one may be sure there is a well-rounded, interesting program for them. Frequently the former church-school member feels that there is nothing of importance for him to do in the church. An alert youth fellowship will help him in making the transfer. If he has been a member of a youth choir, he can be advanced into the adult choir. He may serve as an usher on Sunday evening, teach a class of primary boys, or act as assistant treasurer in the church school. It is at this age that the training for church leadership should begin.

b) Does the program interest *men?* Although men furnish most of the official leadership for the church, they are as a group not strongly attracted by its program. For example, the average church has about 50 per cent more women than men in its membership. Men have more contacts and opportunities outside the home than do women. They are occupied during the day, and in the evening are fatigued and prefer to stay at home with their families. On Sundays there are household chores of repairing and gardening. The program of the church offers little opportunity for doing anything that seems important to most of them. The conventional men's club—a monthly dinner and lecture—soon palls for many. Too often it is established because "a church should have something for the men," and not because any vital interest is discovered which can best be met through such an organization.

First discover a job to be done (perhaps painting the church), a problem to be solved (maybe the increasing hoodlumism in the neighborhood), or some activity (such as athletics or hobbies) which permits the men to be participants instead of listeners. Visitation evangelism can become an intriguing project for some of the men, if they can go two by two in their calling and are not frightened by a heavy assignment at the start. Many will be attracted by a men's Bible class—which, however, should not be permitted to become a substitute church. The best approach to men is through their interest in their sons or in some concrete aspect of the church's work—improving the building and grounds, collecting goods for overseas relief, counseling in the Scout program, tackling local juvenile delinquency. A father-and-son council, with hiking, handicrafts, stunt nights, and occasional dinners, often calls forth large participation.

In some churches the conception of "men's work" is undergoing radical change. Particularly among younger people the idea of a "couple's club" is much more acceptable than separate organizations for the two sexes. Husbands and wives wish to share in the same social and intellectual activities. They meet as a group twice a month for forum discussions of various topics—political, religious, and cultural—and also for social fellowship. They work together on service projects which may involve actual physical labor or raising of money. While such an organization will not take the place of a men's club or a women's society, it is for a large number of adults a more logical and pleasant grouping. No one activity will appeal to all men. Therefore variety is necessary.

c) Do the *elderly members* of the community have any part in the program? The Federal Bureau of the Census predicts that by 1960 9 per cent of the United States population will be sixty-five years of age or older (in 1920 the figure was 4.7 per cent). The church, especially in residential communities, should make specific provision for these older people. Many of the women continue their activity in the women's society, but this organization usually meets only once or twice a month. For the men in later maturity the church frequently has nothing at all to offer. And time hangs heavily on the hands of people who no longer have many stated obligations. The church need not fear that they will forget their loyalty, but it is missing a chance to brighten their lives if it does not plan regular features for their enjoyment. "Borrowed Time Clubs" have proved eminently successful in many areas. A church might well arrange a "taxi service" conducted on a volunteer basis by younger members so that elderly people could always count on a ride to worship services and other programs simply by calling the church office.

4. *The Continual Recruitment of Members from the Parish.* The only city church which can have a widely scattered membership and survive is the downtown church which has an able preacher and a well-rounded program. Most congregations must continue to win new members to their fellowship from their immediate vicinity if they hope to endure. Therefore another test of the over-all effectiveness of a church's program is, Does it attract new members, on confession of faith as well as by transfer, from its own immediate parish? This is one of the most significant and also one of the most readily applied tests of vitality.

5. *Indigenous Leadership.* Some young people's societies and women's organizations subsist on talks by outsiders. They seem to lack either the ability or the courage to carry on a program with their own intellectual and spiritual leadership. This situation is found even in the most privileged communities where members have had unusual educational opportunities. A church in this plight is not producing mature and self-reliant Christians. It should, through its church council or other planning organization, develop a leadership ladder for the progressive training of young people and adults in the acceptance and fulfillment of increasingly difficult leadership responsibilities.

6. *Community Outreach*. Members assume that anyone in the community will know that he is welcome to attend the church and share in its program. Those on the outside feel different and view most churches as privately financed organizations maintained for the benefit of members. Many churches, however, have dispelled this conception and become a center for community life. The Scouts, Camp Fire Girls, interracial council, and Y.W.C.A. may all be using its facilities. At Christmas a well-advertised carolsing brings hundreds to its social hall or sanctuary. Lectures open to the public are offered on civic problems and world affairs. If there are many transients in the area, it maintains a reading room for their benefit. If it is in a "port of entry," social and recreational facilities are provided for young couples and children. If it is in a Florida resort town, where thousands of elderly folk spend their winter months, it furnishes a place for them to gather, visit, and enjoy entertainment programs—all with no thought of luring them away from loyalty to their home church. A church which recognizes this wider responsibility has an interest in playgrounds for children, city zoning, and the improvement of housing. One that does not see beyond its membership is to that extent deficient in its program.

7. *Use of Community Resources*. Every community has a number of resources on which the church can draw. The pastor is frequently faced with some problem which is beyond his scope to solve. It may be that one of his members is an admitted alcoholic; an elderly woman comes to him with a question involving her property; or a young mother seeks counsel concerning behavior problems of her child. The minister cannot help them adequately unless he has previously become acquainted with persons and agencies in the community specializing in these areas of human relationships. These latter will welcome him as a fellow public servant, knowing that he often can assist them in his own special field of religious living. The principal of the public school, the head of the visiting nurse association, the superintendent of the hospital or the doctor in charge of the clinic, the local leader of Alcoholics Anonymous, the judge of the municipal court and the police officer in charge of juvenile offenders—all will be pleased to have the minister show an interest in their work and problems. They are concerned with community welfare and will gladly cooperate in solving the problems of his parishioners. Seldom are ministers aware of these rich community resources which can be utilized to improve the service of the church to people.

8. *Flexibility*. The final and perfect program has not yet been fabricated. Nor will it be. What is an adequate, well-balanced program in one community will not suffice in another. What meets the needs of a young growing church may be quite inappropriate years later. Therefore, good policy

calls for periodic review of the program and, if conditions require it, a willingness to revise.

Techniques for program analysis

The program of a church reflects all other aspects of its organization and life. Therefore analyses of church membership, leadership, and finance —the series of pyramid charts described in preceding chapters—will be helpful in studying the effectiveness of the program. If the church through its activities is reaching and winning people of different ages and both sexes, the membership pyramid will be relatively balanced and similar in outline to that for the community. Where bars are short as compared with the community pyramid, it means that people are not participating in proper number and the program for that age-sex group needs to be improved. Admittedly a large bar does not necessarily mean that all in that age-sex group are active in the church. Sometimes the membership list is not well kept, and names of young people are left on it out of deference to their parents, even though the youth no longer live in the community. The financial analysis will furnish a check at this point, indicating the loyalty of various age-sex groups as measured by their willingness to contribute regularly. Best results will be obtained where these charts and the one on leadership are studied together.

Many churches, especially those of the institutional type, would benefit by a use-of-plant study to determine whether they are making the most of their space resources. The sanctuary of the church, which by its nature has restricted usage, will naturally be costly per hour of occupancy. However, the more intensively the rest of the church plant is utilized, the lower the per-hour cost of maintenance and operation. The use-of-plant charts will quickly show inefficiently employed facilities.

A conscientious review of the present organizational setup of the church and the work done by its societies may be conducted in a round-table discussion by the church council or policy committee, on which all organizations should be represented. A good procedure is to bring in an outside minister-counselor who, with the innocency of the stranger, can ask questions which the local pastor might hesitate to raise. Concerning each of the established organizations he may inquire: What is the function of this society? For whom is it designed? Are these people responding, or do only a few of the eligible turn out for the meetings? Is it reaching new members, and is it training new leaders? Is it operated by a clique? How can present limitations or inadequacies be overcome? Are there tensions among organizations? How can these be resolved?

Is the community aware of the church? Let the visiting counselor do some informal interviewing in the neighborhood. He will soon find to what extent the church is known and will discover points of weakness and strength which may surprise the members. Does the program meet the third criterion: suitable activities for all ages and both sexes? Are there unreached groups in the community? The other criteria should also be applied by the church council in its discussion.

Courage and effort will be needed if the church is to undergo this process of self-examination. But Christians who take their profession of faith seriously should be willing to face such frank analysis in order that they and their church may bring the Christian message more effectively to people. If this review process is well conducted, the members of the church will be psychologically and spiritually prepared to tackle their problems with renewed faith and energy, and to go out seeking others who will join the fellowship.

The revival of an almost defunct downtown church in a large industrial city illustrates the results of enlightened programming. In 1940, after many discouragements and a series of short pastorates, the membership had declined to 187. Their age spread is shown on the left-hand diagram of Chart XI.[3] They were the loyal and elderly remnants of a once-strong congregation. As the society was heavily in debt, most of them were resigned to the closing of their church. It was then that an alert, undiscourageable young pastor was appointed. He came with a proposal that instead of dying, the church could renew its life. The surprised but pleased remnant rallied to give him complete support. A thoughtful study of the program resulted in many changes. With the introduction of varied activities appealing to younger groups new leaders were recruited, and old ones found new hope. In seven years 332 persons were received into membership, and 22 were added to the preparatory roll.

Had it not been for this inflow of new members, the church would by now be closed. Of the 187 members in 1940 only 80 were active in the organization by 1947; 13 because of age were listed in the home department; 19 had moved out of town; 37 had died; and others had transferred away. Of the 332 who were received from 1940 to 1947, 235 were active at the end of that time. Most of these are in the younger age groups, as will be observed in the right-hand diagram. A new church membership is being built, gradually replacing the old.

No church should be closed, if there are reachable people in its community, until a conscientious study of its program has been carried out and a sincere effort made to match the program to the life and needs of the community. *Where there are people, leadership and a program can build a church.*

[3] P. 168.

Part IV

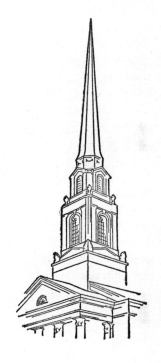

CITY,

REGIONAL,

AND CHURCH PLANNING

CHAPTER TWENTY

Regional Planning
a Foundation for Church Planning

SINCE the opening of the present century the city planning movement has expanded rapidly until now the large majority of cities have planning boards. These are consciously seeking to direct the development of the industrial areas and residential communities in order to provide a physically healthful and socially wholesome environment for man. This movement has far-reaching consequences for the church.

City planning is not disruptive or revolutionary. As Charles Robinson remarked over thirty years ago, it is "merely deciding what you would like to have done when you get the chance, so that when the chance does come, little by little you may make the city plan conform to your ideals." There always has been planning of a sort. Whenever a subdivision is staked out, a street laid, or a park or school site selected, informal planning is taking place. But the effort in recent years has been to replace retail, uncorrelated, and individualistic planning with wholesale, far-sighted, socially beneficial planning. The church dare not be ignorant or unmindful of the long-range master plans now being carefully prepared in American cities.

Objectives in planning

Good planning is for people and not primarily for the sake of buildings or roads. The aim is to increase the beauty and comfort of living. Zoning is a relatively simple and widely used device for achieving this goal.[1] Modern city plans reach far beyond zoning laws. They involve long-range studies to determine where new communities are to be founded and what transportation facilities must be provided to accommodate the future population. It is too expensive to wait until a community is settled and then condemn enough property for a six-lane highway. It is too late to set aside parks and forest preserves when these areas have already been occupied. Planning aims to prevision the development in order to control it in the interests of the citizens. It seeks not only to safeguard residential areas, but also to provide

[1] See p. 133.

for commercial and industrial development. Unless jobs are available, the citizens cannot be economically secure; the more diversified the industrial life of the city, the better the protection against the hazards of depression. A satisfying, efficient organization of the physical life for the whole city and the surrounding region is the goal.

Many devices have been worked out to make residential districts more attractive in appearance and more stable in population. Within the neighborhood curved streets and cul-de-sacs (dead-end streets) are becoming more popular. These diminish and also slow down local traffic. Through traffic is routed on broad, protected highways around residential sections. Planners recommend that more space be provided for gardens, play areas, and parks. They seek to prevent the entrance of deteriorating factors such as cheap construction and basement stores. Instead of following the older, conventional zoning plan of having only single-family residences in one tract and apartment houses in another, it is now proposed that both be included within the same community. Most of the land may be used for single-family residences. Near the center, where the necessary shops and institutions such as the school and churches are located, will be a few three-story apartments and a considerable number of two-story structures. Young married people without children and older couples whose families have been reared may prefer one of these less expensive and more convenient homes. The theory is that people can then reside in the same community through their whole life if they wish.

Regional planning is now generally supplementing city planning. One of the most conspicuous trends in urban life is industrial and population decentralization. The territory around the urban center is so closely related to it that the entire region must be viewed as a unit. The airport and many of the recreational facilities for urban dwellers are often located beyond the city boundary. Highways do not stop at city boundaries; neither does the subdivision of real estate. Therefore planning must extend into the area where industry and people are moving, and, as a matter of fact, it is in the undeveloped territory that the planners can have the freest hand.

However, planning also has a contribution to make in the rehabilitation of blighted and deteriorating areas, which are characterized by the greatest tax delinquency and highest social cost. If for no other reason than to protect the solvency of the city these sections must be made more suitable for human habitation. The majority of publicly financed housing projects are located here. Recent legislation in many states is designed to increase the power of planning commissions to acquire, by condemnation proceedings if necessary, several acres which can be developed as a unit. Only heroic measures of this type will be adequate to deal with the problem of slum clearance.

Supported by increased grants of money and broader legal backing, city planning bids fair to remake large sections of our cities, replacing outmoded, unsanitary, crowded housing with pleasant, well-constructed, efficient dwelling units. And at the same time regional planning aims to control the use of undeveloped territory on the fringes and beyond the city, to prevent a repetition of the mistakes which created blight in other years.

Limitations on planning

City and regional planning faces certain limitations. In the first place, it is no better than the ideals and intelligence of the planners. Increased knowledge may point to a far-sighted program for transportation development and land utilization. But the desire for near-term profits on the part of real-estate promoters—selling narrow, shallow residential lots or too much "business" property—may result in an inadequate or inefficient plan.

Planning is subject to the difficulties involved in all types of prediction: While it is possible to study past developments and to predict the general course of future trends, there are always some unforeseeable contingencies, as a business depression or a war. Further, it is impossible to forecast with certainty the action of a legislature in granting funds for a superhighway system or slum clearance project.

Planners are handicapped by the fact that their work must usually be corrective rather than creative. The land has been occupied and the mistakes have been made. The large investments and conflicting interests of industries, railroads, and other corporations are formidable barriers to any wholesale change. Frequently legal complications and foreclosure delays interfere with the plan's execution. Citizens are not well informed concerning the importance of planning and may be actively opposed to granting necessary powers and funds for rehabilitating a section of the slums. A planning commission cannot carry out its proposals by decree, but must slowly and laboriously develop a supporting public opinion, persuading hundreds of property owners that it will be to their advantage to co-operate. The most effective planning can be done in the small city, before problems become too complicated to handle. Unfortunately humans have a tendency to avoid critical analysis and planning until driven to it. Yet in spite of the lethargy of citizens, the reluctance of property owners to accede to public regulation, and the hazards of forecasting, planning will continue. In fact, so great is the complexity of urban life and so serious the financial plight of many cities that there is no alternative to increased planning.

Relation of church planning to regional planning

Local churches, and even denominational missionary societies, have rarely given a thought to industrial development or population trends in their cities. Their attention has generally been institution-centered, and changes in the community are not noticed until they impinge painfully on the local church. An extreme illustration: A pastor came in distress to discuss where his church could relocate. He had discovered, only two months before condemnation proceedings were to begin, that a major superhighway was to be built through his community which would cut off the rear half of his church. This highway project had been in the planning stage for six years. Had either he or others of his denomination been aware of what was taking place, the church could have had several years in which to lay plans for relocation. Large commercial and industrial corporations have long since learned the economic necessity of keeping abreast of regional developments. Telephone and public-service companies have maintained sizable research staffs which co-operate with the city or regional planning commission.

Just as the city must plan for the future and acquire a regional point of view, so must the church. While it is not expected that every pastor can be informed of all impending urban changes, this certainly is a function of denominational officials who are responsible for the opening of new parishes and the conservation of older ones. The difficulties of forecasting community growth and of locating churches are so great that they cannot rely on their own "hunches" or the advice of a realtor. The planning board will gladly put its information at the disposal of reliable persons. Many of the insights which it can furnish will prove invaluable to the church officer.

The church can also render a service to planning officials. They often know little about the needs of organized religion, and yet in their plans they must take into account the church as a community institution. The planning board of one large city was working on the details for a development which would house fifteen thousand people. The area was to be zoned in such a manner that churches could be located in only one small section. When asked about the matter, the planner said, "Why, I thought that the churches would all like to be clustered within a block or two, just the way the stores are." Planning officials need and will welcome the counsel of churchmen. If such co-operation is forthcoming, new legislation—such as a zoning law—can be helpful rather than restrictive to the work of the church. The church will not be represented in planning councils unless it takes the initiative and maintains the contact. Once established, this contact is appreciated and conserved by the planning board. The latter recognizes that the success of its work depends on a favorable public opinion and knows the importance of maintaining cordial relations with agencies such as the church which influence that opinion.

CHAPTER TWENTY-ONE

Protestant Strategy for the Expanding City

THE churches of a city are more closely related than they usually recognize. They proclaim the same gospel and teach essentially the same doctrine. They have a similar point of view concerning public morals, reforming the school system, and aiding the impoverished. Whether they are Baptist, Congregational, or Presbyterian, they behave surprisingly alike when in the same community. Founded about the same time, they tend to develop and, in certain urban areas, to decline together. If one suffers from an adverse population movement, the others do also.

The development of interdenominational co-operation

In spite of their similarities, co-operation among Protestant churches has existed more in name than in fact. The minister of a local church is kept busy with the details of his parish and the preparation and conduct of religious services. He and his people make a point of sharing occasionally in enterprises of their own communion, attending a conference or youth institute and supporting some missionary endeavors. But the average layman is unaware of other denominations, except as they are represented by buildings down the street. He knows they exist, but it has not occurred to him that any interdenominational organization is either necessary or desirable.

Usually interchurch co-operation, especially in smaller cities, is quite casual. A ministerial association, to which the pastors of most evangelical churches belong, meets each Monday or once a month. Its purpose is the edification of the members, who may read papers which they have prepared or hear a guest speaker on some theological or social issue. Several of the churches may conduct a union Thanksgiving service and join again for special observances during Holy Week. This type of co-operation laymen expect and approve. Occasionally in addition the churches jointly sponsor a religious canvass of the community, with some members from each congregation participating. Such projects, while thoroughly desirable, leave untouched the basic problem of developing a Protestant strategy for the entire city.

The council of churches

Important as denominational programs are to ministers and church administrators, there has been a growing conviction that Protestants must work together on behalf of the ideals which all cherish. In a few cases denominations have actually united. More common has been the establishment of organizations such as the National Council of the Churches of Christ, and state, county, and city councils of churches, in which each denomination preserves its identity and freedom of action but participates in a common program for making the total work of Protestantism more effective. There are about 2,700 such organizations. Approximately 160, serving cities of 10,000 or larger, have paid professional staffs. Volunteers do the work in the large majority of the councils.

1. *Origin and Organization*. Most of these have been established since 1920 in response to the conviction that leadership and financial resources could be better utilized through joint action. They have had their most extensive development in the larger cities, where evangelical Protestant denominations are well represented. Among the churches which have played a significant part are the Northern Baptist, Congregational Christian, Disciples of Christ, Evangelical United Brethren, Evangelical and Reformed, Methodist, Presbyterian, and United Presbyterian. In some cities the major Negro denominations are also included. The policy of Episcopal and Lutheran bodies varies from city to city.

The council may be staffed by a part-time executive and a secretary, or, where its program is more extensive, it may employ ten or more people, with a budget of $100,000. It is usually incorporated under the state law and is managed by a board of trustees and an executive committee representing all participating denominations.

2. *Program*. Since its early beginnings the program of the typical council has broadened to include many phases of religious endeavor. Each phase is assigned to a committee or department, whose work is conducted under the guidance of a paid executive, in larger councils, or a group of volunteers appointed by the denominations. The usual program includes the following:

a) Christian education. This department or commission is responsible for the organization of vacation church schools, weekday religious schools conducted on released time, and teacher training classes.

b) Evangelism. This commission plans and conducts union Holy Week services and evangelistic meetings. It may sponsor a comprehensive visitation evangelism campaign.

c) Social service. This section is concerned with general social welfare, care of the Protestant needy, counseling of youth who have been involved in court difficulties. It may maintain a chaplain to work in the city jail or the county hospital.

d) Christian citizenship. Many issues arise in every city which have moral implications for the Christian: racial tension, labor-management conflicts, political corruption, legislation on housing, provision for the mentally ill, and so forth. The committee investigates these issues from the standpoint of the Christian ethic and presents its findings, perhaps with suggestions for action, to ministers and local churches.

e) Comity and church location. This commission supervises the placing of Protestant churches so that every area in the city and environs is served but none is overchurched.[1]

f) Finance. Funds are solicited from co-operating denominations, their local churches, endowed foundations, and other sources.

g) Additional departments or commissions are often included: women's work, youth activities, and publicity and public relations.

h) A union ministers' meeting, generally held once a month except during the summer, is also a customary part of the program.

3. *Problems.* The continuing problem for the council of churches is the development and maintenance of an active interest on the part of pastors and laymen. They tend to be devoted to the work of their own church and have little enthusiasm for an interdenominational project. Even if their interest is roused, they can give only a small margin of time to the work of the council. The same financial problems which confront their churches also plague the council, with the added difficulty that the sources of income tend to be organizations rather than individuals, and it is often harder to persuade an organization than a person to give.

4. *Contributions.* The church federation performs several unduplicated tasks. It generates interdenominational understanding and fraternal good will. Through it Protestantism can speak with a united voice and exert a powerful influence for righteousness in the city. Such federation is the one means by which it can achieve a parity with Roman Catholicism in the urban North and East. Recently in one metropolis the bold leadership furnished by a federation committee on citizenship rallied other like-minded groups to force the retirement of a politically corrupt board of education. Only through the organization of its comity commission is any united strategy for churching the city possible. Each participating society has some distinctive contribution to make because of its own experience or personnel, and all can benefit thereby.

The comity commission

At first the term "comity" meaning "courtesy, civility, kindly and considerate behavior toward others," seems a peculiar title for a commission of

---

[1] See below.

the federation. Yet the connection is most appropriate, for the comity commission has as its task the settlement of denominational differences in the churching of local communities.

1. *Function.* New suburban developments are ideal places to start a church, since their inhabitants are family people who expect to live there permanently. If there is no agreement, or comity, among church administrators, any denomination with funds and the impulse will feel free to establish a society of its own in the area. In many instances two or three denominations have purchased land and organized congregations, unaware of the fact that others were doing likewise. The community which might support one or two strong churches is overwhelmed with three or four.

In the earlier days a comity agreement was simply an arrangement between executives by which each would inform the others as soon as plans were laid for purchasing a site or establishing a church. This frequently prevented overchurching, but the fact that one church was already in the area did not keep others from moving in also. Gradually and with much debate procedure has been standardized, and the comity commission has become an important agency in the council of churches. Now in many cities the co-operating denominations pledge themselves not to buy lots for a new church or open a Sunday school without first securing permission from the comity commission. This agreement is not enforceable in law but, once arrived at, is adhered to with grace and courtesy if not always with satisfaction. Of course, non-co-operating churches are bound by no agreement and may organize congregations wherever they choose.

2. *Procedure.* A denomination wishing to start a church submits in writing a request for permission to organize a Sunday school or perhaps to purchase lots in a given neighborhood. The commission takes the request under advisement and notifies all interested parties, including the pastors of the nearest Protestant churches. In some instances only those affiliated with the council are notified. A "hearing" is then held, where the request is discussed and objections are heard. If there are no serious protests, and sometimes even if there are, permission may be granted, and the denomination proceeds. In other cases the request may be refused because it is contended that near-by established churches can serve the new section or that the petitioning communion already has a church in adjoining territory and some other denomination should organize the new society. In this situation nothing but the "comity" agreement stands in the way of the petitioning denomination's doing as it desires, but among Christians this is usually enough.

Where research experts in church planning are associated with the comity commission, either on a voluntary or compensated basis, the procedure may be more elaborate. A church administrator asks that a survey be made of a new territory in order to determine whether there is a sufficient congenial population to warrant a request for an "allocation" by his church extension society. Permission for the study is usually granted by the comity commission, since this does not involve a commitment to agree to any subsequent request. When the survey has been made and reported to the commission, the denomination may ask leave to establish a church school in a private home or to organize a congregation. Until this request has been granted, it is deemed an unethical procedure for any church to canvass the neighborhood soliciting members.

An allocation—permission to initiate a program and perhaps also to buy a lot—entails a reciprocal responsibility. A clear field is granted by all other denominations in the comity agreement, and in turn it is expected that the petitioner will start a church to which all evangelical Christians will be welcome. If the privilege has not been utilized within a given period of time—one or two years—the assignment is canceled, and some other denomination may apply for the territory.

It is easier to reach equitable decisions in such matters if a regular procedure exists for handling cases and if reliable data are secured on the background and religious preferences of the population and the future prospects of the community. Helpful materials include: (a) A map showing the relation of the area to adjoining sections of the city, on which are plotted the location of all churches, not only inside the area but also within a half mile or, better, one mile of its borders. (b) Data showing the present size and trends of population in the territory, based on the federal census, public-school enrollment figures, and planning commission estimates. (In a depression period the school enrollment may rise sharply, not because of a population increase, but because Roman Catholics, to save tuition money, transfer their children from parochial to public school.) The issuance of building permits is another gauge of community growth. (c) Present religious complexion of the community, secured by means of a house-to-house canvass. Of significance in this connection are the number of people who are maintaining active contact with a church in the city, the number with only nominal membership, and the number of unchurched; the denominational attachments of people in the first two categories, and the denominational background of those in the third. (d) Spot maps showing the location of the members of churches in or within walking distance of the community, to indicate whether the territory is now adequately covered.

3. *Reaching a Decision.* Weighing these data, the comity commission should be able to answer the following questions: Is the community at present sufficiently well served by existing churches? (Because a church is near an area does not prove that it is serving the people in it; and if it is not

reaching them, it has no right to object to another church's entering.) Will the near-term expected growth provide an adequate population for a new church? If so, to what denomination can the responsibility best be entrusted? Simply because a denomination asks the privilege of starting a new church does not mean that it is best suited for the task. For example, if a Baptist church is already located within an area, and there is a large enough population to justify a second church, the latter should not be a Disciples of Christ, which resembles the Baptist in doctrinal beliefs, but rather a Congregational, Methodist, or Presbyterian. If there is room for several churches, it is better that they present variety in doctrine and tradition. If there is only one, the comity principle assumes that its services will be open to all evangelical Protestants. It is recognized that no one specific church will at present serve the needs of all Protestant groups. Practicing Episcopalians do not feel at home in a Congregational church; Presbyterians do not join a Church of God; and Lutherans in the Missouri Synod are not content with membership in a Methodist society. However, within the past two decades Protestants of all types are showing increasing readiness to cross denominational lines, making possible a more effective program under a comity commission.

It is not always the denomination which initiates the proposal for an allocation. The commission, especially if it has research assistance, may discover an area without adequate churching and suggest that some extension society accept the task of placing a church there. During the war, especially in industrial housing projects, the comity commissions of a number of cities took such initiative.

No scientific formula has been devised to determine how many churches can be supported in a given section. However, the following suggestions will serve as a rough rule of thumb for growing residential communities: Determine the number in the adult population—persons eighteen years of age and over. Deduct the number who report themselves to be attending Jewish synagogues or Roman Catholic churches. Next deduct the number of people who now have and expect to maintain active membership in an established Protestant church within or outside the area. Account must also be taken of the number who belong to small sectarian groups or to one of the exclusive or doctrinally rigid denominations. Approximately half of the remainder can be expected to respond more or less actively to a new church, providing it is congenial to their background and presents a good program. After all such allowances are made and if the territory is not more than 25 per cent built up, there ought to be a remaining nucleus of at least 150 adults or 60 families to whom the church might make its appeal. Not all of these will respond, but additional families will be moving into the neighborhood, and a church under capable leadership should have a good chance for growth.[2]

4. *Problems*. In spite of all the rules that have yet been devised for comity procedure, the chief strains that develop within the council of churches occur in connection with allocations for new work. The dictionary definition of comity *is* appropriate. Only by courtesy and tact can the goals which are sought be achieved. Any organization sufficiently irritated by an adverse decision may threaten to withdraw from the agreement. The fact that the threat is scarcely ever carried out is not sufficient to prevent tension and the feeling on the part of some that unfair pressures are applied. A comity commission which has proceeded amicably for ten years during a long depression may, with the return of prosperity, suddenly find itself burdened with a basketful of problems. The rapid outthrust of population and the increased funds in the treasuries of the extension societies make all of the denominations eager to expand at the same time, and there is competition for new locations.

Another source of irritation has been the desire of a few denominations to divest themselves of their struggling institutions in areas of underprivilege which must be heavily subsidized. The funds saved can be used for expansion in territory where a modest original investment will in two or three years mean a new, self-sustaining church. In the meantime the other communions continue their costly institutional church programs for low-income groups who cannot finance their own projects. The question is, How can all denominations be persuaded to carry their fair share of responsibility in the deteriorating communities?

An unsolved problem is the relation of the small to the large denominations in comity. The larger organizations feel that the new church should be established by the denomination with the most adherents in the local community. Smaller church bodies contend that assignments should be made among the denominations somewhat in rotation, since they themselves would never have opportunity to found a new congregation if they had to wait until a plurality of the people preferred their particular communion. According to the first proposal the Baptist, Methodist, or Presbyterian church would usually have first chance. According to the latter a community with many Baptists, Methodists, and Presbyterians might find an Evangelical United Brethren or a United Presbyterian church assigned to it. Neither of these alternatives is thoroughly satisfactory. Although a compromise between the two is sought, it is not easily achieved or maintained.

A final threat to comity is the independence of action possessed by

[2] See also p. 140.

churches that are organized on a congregational basis—Baptist, Congregational, and Presbyterian. The church extension society of such a denomination may co-operate in good faith with the commission. But in the crucial
test it cannot compel acquiescence by a constituent church to an unfavorable
decision. The local church may not feel bound by the comity agreement; and
if it acts in opposition to the vote of the comity commission, little can be
done to prevent it. To save face the whole denomination that is involved
might conceivably withdraw, which no one on the commission would
desire. Or the local congregation could be dropped from its denominational
association, an alternative understandably dreaded by that organization,
which may have difficulty in preserving the fellowship within its communion.
Of course it is possible for the comity commission and the missionary society
to reprimand the recalcitrant congregation, but that in itself rarely helps
the situation.

The comity commission should be more than a "trouble shooter," ad-
judicating issues as they arise. It should seek to develop an over-all
Protestant strategy for city and hinterland. If it can secure a professional or
amateur research staff, it may discover so many fields for new churching that
the denominational executives will have all the opportunities they can
finance. Real as are the handicaps for any general Protestant strategy, comity
commissions can and do function with considerable effectiveness and Christian tolerance. Short of actual unification of the denominations, an unlikely
prospect in the immediate future, comity is probably the best solution to
this important phase of urban church life. Conviction as well as necessity
underwrites its continuance.

The council of churches is the co-ordinating agency and voice for
Protestantism in the city. This is true in the field of Christian education,
where the public-school authorities are not able to deal with each denomination as a separate unit. It is likewise valid in the field of citizenship and
social reform. Without a church federation and its comity commission there
would be no Protestant agency to which the builders of New City [3] could go
for advice as to the number of churches to plan for and the best selection of
sites. The over-all effectiveness of the council in last analysis rests on the
willingness of the denominational leaders, lay and ministerial, to support
its projects, help in the development of its policy, and underwrite its finances.
Equally important is the subordination of denominational interests at
certain points to the welfare of the larger whole. However, excellent as its
program may be, the council of churches can never perform the functions
of the local congregation. Neither can it be a substitute for the denomination.

[3] See p. 118.

CHAPTER TWENTY-TWO

Denominational Strategy
for City and Suburbs

IMPORTANT as is the work of the comity commission as clearinghouse, correlator, and in some instances arbiter of disputes, the actual placement and support of new churches must be the responsibility of the denominations. Too often denominational leaders have thought solely in terms of individual churches and have not seen the interrelations among them or between them and urban social forces. Or again, they have delayed constructive action until a problem in churching became insistent instead of attacking it in its early stages. The task of working out a long-range plan of both church extension in new areas and conservation in the older communities is imperative in our rapidly changing cities. Such a program is the best guarantee that new churches will be started when the opportunity is ripe and older ones will receive the guidance and perhaps material aid which can keep them flourishing.

To be comprehensive and reliable a plan must be based on adequate preliminary study and dependable research. Churches established on the basis of superficial "planning" often close within five years of their opening; others continue through a long life but always in a feeble condition. For example, in a large metropolitan city one major denomination opened twenty-seven churches between 1920 and 1945; of these fifteen were closed by 1945. This represents an immense waste of church resources. Time and effort spent in preliminary research could have prevented most of these mistakes. In another city the same denomination after careful study established fourteen churches between 1942 and 1947. Of these ten were self-supporting by the latter year.

The planning and supervisory function of the denomination

If any city-wide strategy is to be worked out, there must be an over-all planning agency, for each local church is primarily interested in its own immediate program and membership. Sometimes, indeed, a church is even antagonistic to any proposal from its denomination to establish a new congregation.[1] Persistent and skillful educational work may be needed to persuade the churches of their larger responsibilities. The logical agency for this purpose is some type of city missionary society.

1. *The Denominational Missionary and Church Extension Society.* The task of developing a strategy for the city and its environs can be carried forward successfully only provided the churches, large and small, prosperous and mission-aided, recognize their relation to and participate in the process. Therefore it is necessary to create a representative organization which can marshal the resources of the church. For quick effective action—such as is needed in the purchase of a church site before rumor of the plan doubles the price on the property—responsibility must be vested in a relatively small executive committee of this missionary society.

The membership of the society generally consists of the pastor and at least one layman from each church. A common policy is to have one lay representative from each church for every five hundred members or major fraction thereof, provided each church has at least one delegate. These delegates are elected annually by the official governing body of the church and are expected to report back to the congregation on the activity of the society. Other classes of nonvoting members, such as contributing and life members, are sometimes included for educational and money-raising purposes.

The society has the usual panel of officers, a board of trustees, and a board of managers. The constitutions of some societies limit the length of tenure for the officers. The board of trustees is the official custodian of the real estate and trust funds. The board of managers or executive committee is responsible for administering the general program. Whereas the society meets once or twice a year, the board of managers convenes monthly or bimonthly. It is made up of the officers of the society, members of the board of trustees, the chairmen of the standing committees, and, ex officio, the administrative officers of the denomination in the city and area, such as superintendent, bishop, or moderator. An important duty of the board of managers is to define in detail the functions of the society itself, of its several committees, and of the executive secretary or director, who is responsible to it.

The society conducts a wide range of interchurch activities dealing with Christian education, evangelism, social welfare, and citizenship. It usually sponsors a large annual meeting and banquet to which the members of all the churches are invited. In most societies, however, the major function is to correlate the work of the denomination, give oversight to problem churches, and develop plans for ministering to new areas. Because of the

[1] See pp. 73-74.

technical problems involved in property acquisition and sale, and the personalities that may be discussed in selecting leaders for mission projects, the responsibility for this phase of the program is usually left to a subcommittee of the board of managers. This "missions committee" or "planning board" is made up of carefully selected individuals who work with the executive secretary.

2. *The Planning Board of the Society.* The planning or strategy board includes the local administrative officers of the denomination, the executive secretary of the missionary society, and five or ten of the ablest, most far-sighted lay members of the church. Among these may be a realtor who has a wide acquaintance with land values, but who in all cases involving the church will be financially disinterested; a lawyer well versed in the legal aspects of property matters; a city or utility planning expert who has professional knowledge of population trends; and perhaps a banker.

This board convenes regularly, at least once a month, to receive reports and act on matters of church planning and property acquisition. It cannot be expected to do preliminary research and "foot work," but is in a position and has the authority to act on the proposals which are brought to it. Because of the broad experience of its members it can weigh the evidence and recommendations and may in some cases ask that further studies be made before a decision is reached.

3. *The Director or Executive Secretary of the Society.* The executive secretary—elected by the board of managers or appointed by the bishop—has chief responsibility for promoting the work of the society and in a large city will devote his full time to it. In a smaller city, where demands are less heavy, a pastor or layman may perform these functions in addition to his regular work. The executive is not an officer of the society but is responsible to the board of managers. One of his duties, perhaps with the aid of a research assistant, is to develop specific proposals concerning the missionary and extension work of the denomination for presentation to the planning board. After the board has formulated its policy, it is the further responsibility of the director to put it into effect and report back on progress made. His major task will be the supervision of mission-aided churches in his city and the extension of the church program into newer areas. These are the two fields of missionary endeavor: the inner city, chiefly in areas of underprivilege, and the outer city, the areas of new growth. The function in the former is conservation or renewal; in the latter, development.

One of the duties of the executive secretary or director is—or should be—to make public each year, preferably in advance of the annual meeting of the society, a description of the achievements of the year, problems faced and solved, and those remaining, and also a detailed, audited report of income and expenditures. Carrying as he must large program and fiscal responsibilities, he is under obligation to keep the society and the churches which it represents fully informed.

To fulfill the varied requirements of such a position, the executive will need, in addition to a sincere devotion and unquestioned integrity, several other attributes: patience coupled with ability to act firmly and decisively; an understanding of the processes of urban growth and change, as well as of church problems; practical administrative skills and some experience with church building and financing; ability to establish rapport with people of all walks of life; willingness to dedicate himself for at least a decade to an arduous task which is essential for the building of the church. Simply because he occupies such a position as this, the executive tends to be earmarked for many miscellaneous time-consuming assignments which will take him away from his primary task unless he is protected by both the supervising board of managers and his own conscience. In even a medium-sized city his is a full-time job.

Background materials for planning

Once the denomination has established a suitable organization and selected a director for its missionary and extension program, the next step is to assemble data so that the work of the churches and denomination can be seen in historical perspective. Information on land use, transportation, and population distribution is available [2] and can be presented in a series of maps to be used repeatedly and for years to come as a background or frame of reference against which the problems of local churches can be studied. Population trends, zoning, plans for new transportation facilities and regional development are likewise pertinent.

Information should also be assembled on the churches. It is helpful to have in convenient form the life history and the membership and financial analyses for each of the congregations in the denomination. But in addition the executive secretary needs to secure an over-all picture of the denomination. One helpful device for this purpose is a rate-of-growth chart, which presents a comparison of the population growth in the city—and perhaps also the county—with membership and church-school increase. This permits one to see whether the denomination is holding its own, gaining, or losing in proportion to the population, and constitutes a check on the success of the church in reaching new people who are entering the city.[3]

---

[2] See pp. 132-33 and Appendix A.

[3] The rate-of-growth chart is prepared on a semilogarithmic base, in order to show comparative rates of growth rather than actual numerical changes. This type of chart can be worked out with the assistance of a high-school teacher in mathematics, a civil engineer, or anyone who has a general acquaintance with mathematical techniques.

It is also desirable to prepare a historical sequence of maps which will show the location and size of the various churches at different periods in the city's history. The years selected for the series of maps will be influenced by the age of the city and the periods in which it developed most rapidly. A good average sequence would be 1900, 1920, 1940, and the current year. A study of these four maps will reveal the areas in which the church is growing, those from which it is moving out, and perhaps others which have always been neglected. By use of several colors gains and losses can be shown more graphically.[4]

In interpreting these maps one should bear in mind that not only community but also personnel factors affect the growth or decline of churches. A congregation which dwindles under one pastor may grow rapidly under another. Two churches which appear to remain the same size may actually be very different in their impact on the community, for in one instance most of the members may have left the area while in the other a new local constituency is being steadily recruited.

This series of maps will have continuing value for the executive and the planning board. Detailed comparison will show the gradual drift of churches out of some areas and into others. Because there are few or weak churches in an area, it does not necessarily follow that these could not be strong institutions. What is needed in this case is a detailed study of the community and of any church in the denomination that is located there. In the city of M—— two large adjoining communities with a population of 25,000 held 1,230 persons who considered themselves more or less attached to a particular denomination, yet that communion did not have a single church in the area. Consequently only 270 of the entire number made any claim to be church attendants. Practically any city has inadequately churched areas, and these maps will furnish a cue as to where further studies ought to be made.

Current studies and planning

Historical studies have value only as they are pertinent to an understanding and solution of current problems. Every city has an ample supply of the latter. In one area there are three weak churches of different denominations with a long history of small membership and continuing

[4] Each church is represented by a circle whose center is at the location of the church on the map. The size of the circle is drawn to the radial scale shown in Appendix C, so that the areas of the circles are proportionate to the number in the actual membership. If a new church has been established since the preceding map, it will be shown in a different color—such as green—from the continuing churches. If one has disappeared, it may be shown in red on the next map after its closing. Changes of location are also shown by means of an arrow. Churches which have opened *and* closed since the preceding map may be shown by a symbol such as a black square.

struggle. Should the one for which the society is responsible withdraw? Should it merge with another? Should additional funds be provided to enlarge the program? Elsewhere is a church which has been growing so rapidly that it cannot house its church-school classes or the Sunday morning congregation. Should it move a few blocks away to obtain a better site, or rebuild on its present crowded property? The downtown church, for many decades an institution of great strength, has had two short pastorates and lost many of its lay leaders. An insurance company offers a good price for the corner it occupies. Should it sell out and relocate, or ought the ministry be strengthened and the program undergirded?

In every city the denomination is faced with an array of problems, in the light of which the missionary and church extension society must make decisions. Some of the issues are less pressing than others. The planning board with the counsel of the executive secretary can begin by selecting the more urgent for immediate attention. The first step is the clear definition of the problem. What specifically is the issue? All available pertinent data should be marshaled. In the light of these data each possible line of action should be carefully explored and the advantages and disadvantages—from the standpoint of the members of the church, the needs of the local community, and denominational strategy—noted and weighed. With the evidence and relevant interpretations in hand, the planning board is in a position to formulate a policy.

No matter how wise the decision of the board in particular cases, it cannot be effective unless the whole denomination knows about and has a sense of participation in the program. That is, a significant part of the work of the planning board and its executive officer is the education of ministers and laymen concerning the interdependence of all of the churches and their responsibility for unserved areas. The city is one, and the problems of the various local churches are interwoven into one major query: How can we bring the spirit of Christ into city and into community? There is no room for complacency because we have met our own budget and have a beautiful sanctuary and an efficient parish house. We must create in our local churches a fellowship of faith and a mutual concern for the successes and failures of every other church and mission.

The work of the church in the city is full of drama and when presented with conviction and missionary zeal is certain to win a response from earnest Christian men and women.

L—— is a southern city of over 200,000 which has been growing rapidly for almost a decade. When the Reverend Henry H—— was appointed as superintendent of the district within which this city was located, he discovered that his denomination

[Methodist] had been "treading water" for many years and had given no thought to the newer sections of the city.

As soon as possible he organized a district missionary and church extension society. Preliminary studies indicated that not fewer than three new congregations could be established. He then went from church to church, describing the opportunity and inviting any who wished to do so to join the "Methodist Associates," a group of persons each of whom promised that he would pay five dollars toward the building cost of any new church which was begun in the district within the next three years. With little effort he secured over a thousand associates. Before the end of the three years three new churches had been established, and the Associates paid more than $5,000 toward each enterprise. The most rewarding aspect of this undertaking was not the money which was secured, but the heightened interest on the part of laymen in the progress of the new congregations and in other phases of the church extension program.

It is not easy to establish a new church and assure its future success. Too frequently inadequate planning and financing result in a weak congregation housed in an unchurchly structure. Such a start may constitute an almost insurmountable handicap for the future development of the church. Because of rising building costs, some financial aid as well as know-how should be available from a strong denomination, to insure that the new edifice will be not only beautiful and suitable to the community, but also usable. Many good architects know little about the needs of churches.

Church planning begins with careful, objective studies. It proceeds by the educational process to enlist the interest and support of ministers and laymen. If the planning is wise and the work of education is well done, it always ends in action. And each action, whether it be the strengthening of a mission program for homeless men or the building of a sanctuary in Evergreen Gardens, is seen as a part of the total strategy by which the Christian message can be brought to people of every social stratum and in every community.

CHAPTER TWENTY-THREE

The Future of City and Church

AMERICAN cities are the creation of the industrial age. Manufacturing, transportation, and commerce have united to pile up population by the hundreds of thousands in metropolitan areas. The whole of the nation's economic, political, and cultural life has been increasingly dominated by these cities. Now there is evidence that the pattern of population concentration is changing. What the future is for the great cities and their smaller sisters no man can now say with certainty. But several significant trends may be detected.

Trends in city growth and population movement

For more than a century, prior to 1930, the large American cities grew at a faster pace than rural communities or small municipalities. With the decade of the 1930's the pattern changed, and for the first time in the nation's history the major cities grew more slowly than the nation as a whole. The increase which these cities did show came chiefly in their outlying sections. In contrast the most rapid expansion occurred in cities of 10,000 to 50,000. The war, which put a premium on decentralization of industry, confirmed this newer pattern.

Four general predictions can be made on the basis of trends now discernible in the movement of urban population. (1) The great metropolitan cities, particularly in the North and East, have passed the period of most rapid growth. A few which continue to expand—New York and Los Angeles—have such far-reaching city boundaries that they include within their corporate limits vast stretches of semirural territory. (2) Suburban towns and small cities on the fringes of the metropolis will continue to enjoy rapid growth. (3) Because of various economic and political pressures large sections of the deteriorated or slum districts in major cities will be rehabilitated, and some population will move back into them. (4) The principal urban growth will be registered in smaller and medium-sized independent cities under 100,000 population.

Apparently a city of 10,000 to 100,000 has greater appeal for people, just as it does for industries, than one which is larger. In it there is more likelihood that they can own their home and attain a sense of economic and social security. There they can have the educational and cultural advantages procurable in urban centers without the attendant heavy monetary and social costs of the metropolis. Some are also aware of the fact that in the event of another war the great concentrations of population will probably be attacked by air.

A fifth important trend affecting churching is the southward and westward shift of population. The rapid development of southwest and west coast cities is a war and postwar phenomenon of first magnitude. This westward trek gives every evidence of continuing.

Trends and challenges in church strategy

Until the opening of the twentieth century Protestant denominations conducted their religious work in cities and rural areas without much consideration of the geographic setting of churches or the particular needs of local communities. The report of the Roosevelt Commission on Country Life in 1909 awakened the churches and the rest of the nation to the importance of the rural community in the national life. Denominations developed rural life commissions and appointed secretaries for town and country work. A decade passed before churchmen began to recognize that urban living also had distinctive implications for the church.

Increasingly denominational leaders are becoming aware of the importance of the city in American culture and are asserting that the church must adapt its program to meet distinctive urban needs. It clearly would be inappropriate and unwise to diminish the attention now given to the rural ministry of the church. But the fact that the standards of living and morals for the whole nation are being re-formed by American cities makes it essential that the church strengthen its witness in urban centers.

The Protestant church has been none too successful in certain types of urban communities. It has flourished among the middle- and upper-income groups, which could pay for an increasingly elaborate program, and has tended to follow them as they moved into new suburban communities. Too often it has withdrawn from or presented a weak program in areas of underprivilege. Here is a major challenge to the church: to develop a comprehensive and, because of its cost, perhaps interdenominational program making possible the effective presentation of the Christian message in the areas of greatest human need, where the birth rate is high and where political and social issues are frequently determined.

The newer population movement to cities is more favorable to Protestantism. First in small numbers and then, after 1940, in a mighty tide, rural Protestants moved into low- and middle-income areas of the cities, northern as well as southern. Earlier immigration (1890-1915), especially in northern cities, had been largely from non-Protestant countries of central and southern Europe. This change in the cultural background of new-comers to cities represents an opportunity and is another significant challenge for Protestant churches. Many of these rural people, partly because of their conservative background, do not feel at home in the city or its churches. Urban churchmen must plan for and welcome them. By making suitable adaptations in the worship services and program—as stressing Bible-centered, evangelical preaching—the church will not only render a spiritual ministry but also ensure its own continuance.

There is an increasing interest, which perhaps amounts almost to a trend, in urban religious research and church planning. This development—more a challenge for the future than an achievement of the past—has come in part because of the example set by city and regional planners, and in part because of the rapid expansion of urban residential communities. Research and planning cost money but are an economy in the long run. Far-sighted denominational executives are placing increasing emphasis on urban church planning, even though money is hard to secure, so as to make strategic use of missionary and extension funds.

It is being driven in on urban ministers more and more that the church has a responsibility to re-create the sense of community and develop the values which formerly were found in the dependable relationships of the small town. These tend to be lost in the increasingly mobile and impersonal city, with its disorganization and insecurity. The sense of community is a logical by-product of the Christian fellowship, but it will not emerge unless people are brought into more intimate association than is possible in a formal service of worship. The church must constitute a stable core in which its members will find strength. Its aim must also be to help them become mature and adequate to make their own contribution toward stabilizing the urban community round about.

The changes which are taking place in American cities demand that churchmen, with their broader understanding of the significance of urban life, must by hard thinking and careful planning fit the Christian message to the very real and somewhat distinctive spiritual needs of city man. The future of the city, like the future of everything else which is material, rests uncertainly in the balances in a world of atomic power and willful or stupid men. But the church, symbol of a power which transcends even that of the split atom, has and will continue to have a mission to perform until the cities crumble and the mountains are brought low.

Appendixes

A. *Criteria for Classifying Communities*

Communities may be distinguished from each other on the basis of their physical and social traits. It is important that churchmen seeking to strengthen the program of the churches of the city and to establish new congregations be aware of the relation of community traits to their work. Avowedly the church is eager to reach and serve people wherever they may be found. Yet the income of the people and the economic status of an area—as reflected in rents, condition of housing, occupation, and so forth—will influence the size and type of church structure which should be erected, the amount of debt which can be carried safely, and the amount of mission funds which ought to be appropriated.

From ten to twenty traits—characteristics of the population or the area, such as average rent, physical condition of the housing, percentage of nonwhite population, and extent of delinquency—which have significance for the church may be discovered by consulting the proper sources. Many of these traits, listed below, are closely related to one another and may be combined to form an index. The advantage of an index, as compared with the use of a single trait, is that it presents in a summary figure a more complete picture and avoids the bias which may be inherent in any one set of statistics.

An *index* is formed by assembling statistics on a community-by-community basis for each of several related traits. The prevalence of each trait must be recorded for each community. The communities are then arranged in order on the basis of the trait, from best to poorest. Number 1 is assigned to the community with the highest rank, 2 to the next, and so on. For example, crowding is an undesirable trait. Therefore the community with least crowding would be numbered 1, and, if there are twenty communities or neighborhoods in the city, the one with the highest percentage of crowded dwelling units would be numbered 20. In the rent analysis the area with the *highest* rent would be numbered 1, but in the delinquency analysis the area with the *lowest* delinquency rate would be numbered 1. The areas are classified in this manner for each of the traits.

The *index rating* of each community is secured by averaging its score on all of the traits which are included in the composite—adding the numerical ratings on each of, say, four traits and dividing by four. By this method a single figure is obtained for each community, showing in simple but summary fashion its position with relation to all other communities of the city.

The major factors which are commonly used in differentiating communities, and the source for the information, may be listed briefly. Data on traits marked * are available in supplemental housing bulletins published decennially by the

United States Bureau of the Census (1940) for all cities which had a population of fifty thousand or more in the preceding census (191 cities in 1940). This information is on a block-by-block basis. Data on traits marked † are available by wards for cities of fifty-thousand and over in 1940, and also by census tracts for 60 of the larger cities, in special bulletins published by the Bureau of the Census. Information on traits marked ‡ must be secured from the social welfare and other agencies within the city.

Traits

* *Rent Rates.* The average or median rent for all dwelling units within the block, census tract, or community.

**Age of Housing.* Percentage of dwelling units erected prior to 1900.

*† *Condition of Housing.* Percentage of dwelling units which need major repairs; percentage of dwelling units having no private bath. These two factors can be treated separately or in combination. Information is also available on the percentage of homes which lack private toilets and which have no running water.

*† *Crowding.* Percentage of dwelling units having more than 1.5 persons per room. For example, 7 persons living in four rooms.

*† *Home Ownership.* Percentage of all dwelling units occupied by the owner.

†*Foreign-born Population.* In some cities it may be desirable to assemble data on the percentage of population born in the dominantly Roman Catholic countries, which will reveal possible limitations on the growth of the Protestant church. It should be borne in mind, however, that a large proportion of Czechs and Italians are only nominally Catholic.

†*Nonwhite Population.* Percentage of persons in each area who are listed as nonwhite. In most cities this is practically equivalent to the Negro population.

†*Age Distribution.* The proportion of young people in the population and of those in the childbearing period, especially between twenty and thirty-four years of age. These groups are particularly significant in church planning.

†*Occupation.* Percentage of gainfully employed persons who are engaged in the main occupational classifications. Usually it is sufficient to show the percentage distribution of unskilled and semiskilled workers—laborers, domestic service workers, and operatives—indicating the lower-income groups, and also the distribution of professional workers, executives, and proprietors, indicating high-income groups.

†*Education.* Years of schooling completed for all persons twenty-five years of age and over.

‡*Mobility.* Change of residence as indicated by records of public-service company connections and disconnections of gas and electricity, or by a study of transfers in and out of the elementary public schools. Neither of these is applicable to the areas of greatest movement—rooming-house districts and the apartment hotels—for many who live there do not have private utilities connections and generally are childless. Information on mobility may be secured as a by-product of a house-to-house canvass.

‡ *Dependency.* Percentage of families in the area on the rolls of the family welfare agency or receiving public relief.

‡ *Juvenile Delinquency.* The percentage of boys between the ages of ten and eighteen who have been arrested during a recent one- or two-year period.

‡ *Family Disorganization.* The ratio of families in which there has been divorce

or desertion in a given period of time. Certain areas in the city may be marked by high desertion, a few by high divorce rates, others by neither.

Indexes

The most useful composite ratings or indexes based on the above traits are:

Index of Economic Status. Factors which have bearing on economic status may be combined. The average rent per dwelling unit is always included and sometimes, because of its importance, is weighted (counted twice) in the preparation of the composite index. Other factors frequently used are: occupation, crowding, age of housing, and physical condition of housing, perhaps including both percentage of dwellings needing major repair and the percentage lacking private toilet facilities.

Index of Social Disorganization. The significant factors are those which indicate personal tension and social conflict, such as family disorganization, delinquency, dependency, and any related situation such as overcrowding of dwellings.

Index of Mobility. Frequent change of residence is a symptom and a cause of personal insecurity and low community cohesiveness. On the other hand, a high rate of home ownership is associated with community stability. The extent to which residential areas differ from one another in mobility may be determined from an index based on such factors as transfer rates in the public-school system and the percentage of home ownership.

A general composite index, combining all the major factors, is frequently employed by city and regional planners and other students of community life. A sample index may be made up as follows: (1) median monthly rental, (2) median number of school years completed by adults, (3) the percentage of dwelling units erected prior to 1900, (4) owner occupancy of dwelling units, (5) dwelling units needing major repairs, and (6) dwelling units with 1.5 or more persons per room. The percentage of (a) foreign-born whites and (b) nonwhites is sometimes correlated with such an index.

The use of these criteria will show that no city is homogeneous, and that marked contrasts in the physical as well as the social composition of communities exist. It will also be evident that communities which have similar ranking in the composite index tend to adjoin one another and to be part of a belt of similar communities around the city. Just as the areas of new growth are generally found toward the periphery, so the areas of physical deterioration and social disorganization tend to be grouped near the central business district and industrial areas.

B. *Instructions for Religious Census Takers* [1]

Purpose of the religious census

A religious census or house-to-house canvass is undertaken from time to time in order to gather information concerning the religious interests and affiliations of the people in an area. It should perform two functions: (a) discover persons in the community whom the churches are not reaching but should be, and (b) assemble information on various related subjects, such as movement of population, which

[1] These instructions are prepared for use with the religious census card shown on p. 135.

have important bearing on understanding community conditions and the development of the church program.

For the census to fulfill these functions,

1. The information you secure must be *accurate.*
2. What you write on the card must be *readable.*
3. The census cards must be *completely filled out.*

General procedure

The community is divided into tracts or areas, each of which is numbered
and each of which includes several blocks, also numbered.

You will receive a bundle of survey cards. On the top card is a map showing
the number of the tract, the blocks where you are to call, and the number of
each block.

Be sure, before you start, that you know exactly where you are to call. Time
is wasted and embarrassment may be caused if you call at the wrong addresses.

Take at least two sharpened pencils with you. Use a No. 2 black pencil and write
plainly or print.

When you arrive "on the field," check your assignment to be sure you are
starting on the right block. Check the map on your bundle of cards with street signs
or inquire at the first call.

Begin at one corner and call at every home around the block before crossing
the street to start the next block in your assignment. Keep the cards banded together
for each block.

Use one card for every dwelling unit unless there are two families living in the
same house or apartment, in which case use two cards.

If no one answers the bell, enter the date of call in the proper place and the
time of day: "A.M.," "aft" (afternoon), or "eve" (evening). A return call should
be made at some other hour.

If information is refused, indicate by noting the date in the proper place.

If, after the interview, you think a pastoral call should be made in the near
future, put an X in the lower left corner and write the details on the back of the
card. Make a copy of that card when you finish your calling for the day, and see that
it gets to the appropriate person as soon as possible.

Before turning in your cards, scan them carefully to see that all possible spaces
are filled in legibly and that your initials are in the lower right corner.

Procedure in filling out the census card

1. Before ringing the doorbell write down on the card
   a) tract and block numbers (see your map)
   b) address of the home (street and number)
   c) the family name if it is on the mailbox
2. When your knock or ring is answered, introduce yourself and explain the
purpose of your call: "I am representing the churches of . . ., which are conducting a
religious census. We would like your help in filling out the census card." Proceed
at once with the first question. Be brief: your time and that of others is valuable.
Be businesslike. Do not be sidetracked by unnecessary or unprofitable discussion. If
the party puts a query to you, answer directly, briefly, and then proceed with
the interview.
3. A good sequence to follow is: Where do you attend church? What is the
address of the church? How many Sundays—or Sabbaths in the case of a Jew

or Seventh-Day Adventist—in the last year did you go? Are you a church member? Where? What is your religious background? Then secure comparable information for husband (wife), other adults, and so forth. However, there is no rigid order which must be followed. Ask questions in the sequence which seems most natural, but be sure to get *all the data* called for on the card.

4. You need not inquire as to first names of persons, although this information may advantageously be written on the card if it is offered by the person interviewed.

5. Information to be secured, in addition to that already recorded before the bell is rung:

a) *What church do you attend? Where is it located?* Secure name, denomination, and location, such as: Vermont Ave. Methodist, Vermont and 42nd St.; First Baptist, Albion, Mich. If none, write "none." If the information is the same for other adults, write "same."

b) *Approximately how many Sundays did you attend church in the past year?* Exact number is not needed, as the data will be tabulated in the following groupings: none, 1-5 times, 6-26, 27 or more.

c) *Are you a member of a church? If so, what is the name and location of it?* Get specific information as under church attended. If it is where the person attends, write "same." If none, indicate "none."

d) *Religious background.* Denomination in which the person was brought up or went to Sunday school, as "Baptist."

e) *Other adult.* Secure information on above items for any other adults eighteen years of age and over. Write in the person's surname. State relationship, such as "daughter," "wife's mother," or "housekeeper." Be sure that the "other adult" lives at this address. If more than two "other adults," use back of card and mark lower left corner.

f) *Children under eighteen living at home.* "M" means male and "F" means female. Indicate the age and sex of each child. Example:

M———8

F———5

If first name is given, write that in also.

g) *Receives religious instruction, where?* Give specific school attended, such as "Judson Baptist," "St. Pius (parochial)." If none, write "none." If children are members of a church, indicate this fact in proper column.

*h) *Years lived in this community?*

*i) *Former address.* Give the name of town and state.

*j) *Own present home?* Indicate "Yes" or "No."

6. Check over the card. Are all blanks properly filled in? Is the family name recorded?

7. After leaving, mark in proper places the date and your initials.

Courtesy, tact, and accuracy are the characteristics of the effective Christian visitor.

*NOTE: Since there is sometimes objection to answering these three questions, it is best to leave them till last. The director may decide to omit them.

C. *Tools and Techniques for Chart Making*

Equipment

The essential equipment for chart making includes: A set of pen nibs which will make lines of different widths. The "B" series of nibs is suitable for making round dots on a spot map. Ruler, compass and protractor, the latter two used in making larger circles, as on a historical sequence map. Colored India inks and poster paint or tempera. Brushes for use on large surfaces, with either ink or paint. A lettering guide may be helpful. More elaborate equipment, such as a tilt-top drawing table and a glass-top copying table, is desirable if one is doing considerable work, but is not necessary.

Chart layout

A convenient size for charts which are to be used before a small audience is 2 by 3 feet. Most printers carry in stock "book paper" (25 by 38 inches), which is quite suitable and which will carry ink or poster paint. The first step in preparing a chart, after data are in hand, is to work out a small pattern, determining the relative size of columns, titles, and so forth. Then space the material on the large sheet. Each chart should present one type of information clearly and forcefully. Too much information on one chart will prove confusing. Each chart should have a clearly stated title, preferably printed in plain block letters. Use only capitals.

Colors may be used to show contrast or sequence. If they are to show sequence —as percentage of population increase in different wards—use colors from one side of the spectrum, as yellow, orange, red, violet, black; other intermediate colors can be introduced if necessary; do not introduce a blue or green.

Membership spot maps

Three devices are used for spotting members: colored pins which can be moved; ink or pencil dots; and gummed stickers, which are least satisfactory because they peel off easily.

If pins are used, the map is mounted on some type of wallboard and may be hung on a wall. It can be kept up to date, showing current addresses of members. If one color of pin is used for a member and another for a prospect, the former can be substituted for the latter when a person is received into membership. The disadvantages are that the map does not give a permanent record of membership spread at any particular date. Pins sometimes fall out, and, if the map has been used for a time, it is almost impossible to discover from which hole the pin fell. A "member" is lost, in so far as the map is concerned.

The ink spot map is a permanent record and shows the location of all members or church-school attendants at a given time. Valuable first as a map showing current conditions, it is of equal worth years later for studying changes which have taken place in the meantime. A map of this type is simple to make and can be rolled up and stored away, as a pin map cannot.

As a general rule it is better to use a dot for each member rather than one for each family. Otherwise a family with only one church member is as prominent on the map as a family which has five. If it is desired to show the family relationship, the five dots in the latter case can be placed at the proper location touching one another. If there are two unrelated members at the same address, a slight space can be left between the dots. In some studies where problems of lay leadership are involved (see Chapter XVII) a distinction is made between the dots which represent the officers and leaders of the church and those for rank-and-file members. This can be done by using red ink for leaders and black for the others. If desired, church members and church-school attendants can be shown on the same map by using different colored pins or inks. If the church is in an area of high mobility, members received in the past three or five years may be differentiated from older members by use of two colors. This permits one to ascertain the impact of the church in recent years in the immediate vicinity, a fact which may have important bearing on its future.

Circle area scale

The following table lists the appropriate length of radii for circles representing the indicated numbers. While the radius may be measured in either inches or centimeters, the latter is recommended as being more accurate and easier to compute. This scale may be multiplied by 2, or divided by 2, 5, or 10, if larger or smaller circles are desired. Determine the scale on the basis of the size of the chart and the membership of the largest church to be shown. Where intermediate numbers are involved, proportional adjustment can be made in selecting the correct radius length.

Unit of Area	Length of Radius	Unit of Area	Length of Radius
50.	1.0	1000.	4.4
100.	1.4	1200.	4.9
200.	2.0	1400.	5.3
300.	2.4	1600.	5.7
400.	2.8	1800.	6.0
500.	3.1	2000.	6.3
600.	3.4	2500.	7.0
700.	3.7	3000.	7.7
800.	4.0	4000.	8.9
900.	4.2	5000.	10.0

D. *Active Church Membership Analysis: Work Sheet* [1]

This is a form for the recording of data on the age and sex distribution of the active and preparatory membership of the church and also of those enrolled in the educational program, furnishing the basis for a valuable analysis of the total church program.

It will be necessary to do some estimating of ages, but it is possible to guess fairly accurately whether a person is in one ten-year span or another. If the pastor is not thoroughly acquainted with the membership, he may ask two of the older members to check over the rolls confidentially with him. Record each person

---

[1] This work sheet is prepared for use in gathering data for Charts VI and VII, pp. 163 and 164.

Age Classi-fication	Active and Preparatory Church Members				Educational Program (church-school enrollment **plus**)			
	Male		Female		Male		Female	
	No.	%	No.	%	No.	%	No.	%
65 and over								
55-64								
45-54								
35-44								
25-34								
20-24								
15-19								
10-14								
5-9								
0-4								

with a tally mark in the proper sex column and opposite the estimated age. Record preparatory members with a red or blue pencil. Under "Educational Program" include not only those enrolled in the church school but also those who participate regularly, on a weekly basis, in any other established educational program—for example, the youth fellowship. However, do not include any one person twice under the educational program.

Percentages for subgroups are computed by dividing the total number—males and females—into the number of persons recorded in each age-sex group. The total of the percentages computed should be 100 per cent.

E. *Church Leadership Analysis: Work Sheet* [1]

This is a form for recording basic information used in analyzing objectively the leadership in a local church in comparison with the rank and file of the membership. For definition of "leader" see page 158.

Prepare on a sheet of paper a list of all leadership offices. After each office note the name of the person holding it, his approximate age, sex (M or F), and the number of years that particular office has been held by this person.

[1] This work sheet is prepared for use in gathering data for Chart VIII, p. 165.

Example: Pres. of Men's Club........Fred Anderson........48   M..........3 yrs.
         V. Pres. of Men's Club...George Foster........39   M..........2 yrs.

List other positions below this, similarly. The same person may be listed opposite two or more offices. The age will be the same, but the tenure may be different. Use additional sheets of paper as needed.

On the basis of this list of offices and persons, fill in using tally marks the following tables, which will be used in preparing the Leadership Analysis Chart.

1. *Age and sex distribution* of the leaders. Here one person is counted only once. This will be matched against the age-sex distribution of the total membership as shown in the Membership Analysis.

AGE:	10-14	15-19	20-24	25-34	35-44	45-54	55-64	65+
Female								
Male								

2. *The number of positions held by each leader.* One leader may hold two or three offices or only one.

1 position	2	3	4	5 or more

3. *Years of tenure in each position.* The same person will be represented by three tally marks if he holds three positions. These marks may all be in one space or spread over three.

Less than 1 year	1 year but less than 2	2 years	3 years	4 or 5 years	6-9 years	10 years and over

F. *Church Financial Analysis: Work Sheet* [1]

Church Budget 194_____ -194_____, including funds raised and expended by all church societies:

   Total current expenses $_____   Total benevolences $_____
   Total raised by pledges to the church budget $_____
   This analysis is concerned with the *regular, predictable giving of church members.* It may be based on the actual giving of the past year or on the pledges—that is,

[1] This work sheet is prepared for use in gathering data for Chart IX, p. 166.

anticipated reliable giving—for the current year. It does *not* take into account special gifts, loose collection, or giving of nonmembers.

Procedure: Secure the list of members who give regularly to the support of the church. Follow each person and pledge through the three sections of the work sheet before taking up the next name. Under Section I place a tally mark in the appropriate space, indicating whether the person is male or female and also his approximate age. If a pledge has been made by husband and wife, each will be counted as pledging, even though the pledge may be only in the husband's name.

Under Section II note the amount in dollars of this person's pledge in the same age level and under the same sex column. If a pledge is from husband and wife, half of the amount will be counted as coming from the husband and half from the wife. In this section distinction may or may not be made between giving for benevolences and for current expenses.

Age Classes	SECTION I Church Members Who Pledge (Do not include nonmembers)				SECTION II Amount Pledged	
	Male		Female		Male	Female
	No.	%	No.	%		
65 & over						
55-64						
45-54						
35-44						
25-34						
20-24						
15-19						
10-14						
5-9						
0-4						

Total Ms_____   Total Fs_____   Total $_____ $_____

Section III is not based on age and sex, but on the *size of contributions*. Age and sex of members are not involved. Use either the weekly or the annual scale. Under

"No. of Pledges" place a tally mark opposite the amount of the pledge. In this section a pledge by husband and wife is not divided, as in Section II, but is treated as *one pledge*. Under "Amount" list, at the same level, the number of dollars pledged. The "Total" column is to be filled in after all pledges are recorded.

Children are not given credit for pledges made by parents.

SECTION III

Amount of Individual Pledge or Subscription		No. of Pledges	Amount of Each Pledge	Total Amount
(Week)	(Year)			
$3.01 and over	$156.01 and over			
2.01- 3.00	104.01- 156.00			
1.51- 2.00	78.01- 104.00			
1.01- 1.50	52.01- 78.00			
.76- 1.00	39.01- 52.00			
.51- .75	26.01- 39.00			
.26- .50	13.01- 26.00			
.11- .25	5.21- 13.00			
.06- .10	2.61- 5.20			
.05 or less	2 60 or less			

A Selected Reading List

Building the Future City. Annals, American Academy of Political and Social Science, Nov., 1945.

The City Church. Department of Urban Church, National Council of Churches of Christ in U.S.A. (Issued bimonthly except July and August.)

Douglass, H. Paul, and Brunner, Edmund de S. *The Protestant Church as a Social Institution*. New York: Harper & Bros., 1935.

Drake, St. Clair, and Cayton, Horace R. *Black Metropolis*. New York: Harcourt, Brace & Co., 1945.

Fichter, Joseph H. *Social Relations in the Urban Parish*. Chicago: University of Chicago Press, 1954.

Gist, Noel P., and Halbert, L. A. *Urban Society*. 3rd ed. New York: Thomas Y. Crowell Co., 1948.

King, Clarence. *Organizing for Community Action*. New York: Harper & Bros., 1948.

Koos, Earl L. *Families in Trouble*. New York: King's Crown Press, 1946.

Leiffer, Murray H. *City and Church in Transition*. Chicago: Willett, Clark & Co., 1938.

———, ed. *The Church in Urban Life, a Fact Book*. New York: Board of Missions, The Methodist Church, 1954.

———, et al. *Crowded Ways*. New York: Board of Missions, The Methodist Church, 1954.

McKibben, Robert A. *Methodism Looks at the City*. New York: Board of Missions, The Methodist Church, 1954.

Mays, Benjamin E., and Nicholson, Joseph W. *The Negro's Church*. New York: Institute of Social and Religious Research, 1933.

Miller, Kenneth D. *Man and God in the City*. New York: Friendship Press, 1954.

Mumford, Lewis. *The Culture of Cities*. New York: Harcourt, Brace & Co., 1938.

Queen, Stuart, A., and Carpenter, David B. *The American City*. New York: McGraw-Hill Co., 1953.

Sanderson, Ross W. *The Church Serves the Changing City*. New York: Harper & Bros., 1955.

Shippey, Frederick A. *Church Work in the City*. New York and Nashville: Abingdon Press, 1952.

Warner, W. Lloyd, and Lunt, Paul S. *The Social Life of a Modern Community*. New Haven: Yale University Press, 1941.

Whyte, William F. *Street Corner Society*. Chicago: University of Chicago Press, 1943.

Index